IMPRISONED BY FEAR

KATHY LANGE

First Edition

Fulton Books, Inc.
Meadville, PA

Published by Fulton Books 2020

This is a work of fact with references noted within the document and as listed. Some names have been purposefully omitted at author's discretion, but incidents that occurred are true to the author and names mentioned herein are of public record. Some events that bear any resemblance to other actual persons, living or dead, or events is purely coincidental.

ISBN 978-1-64654-315-1 (paperback)
ISBN 978-1-64654-316-8 (digital)

Printed in the United States of America

ENDORSEMENTS

Beneath the fabric of these extraordinary events, the thoughtful reader will ponder the deeper meaning of the right to defend one's life and property, and the tragedy emerging from two teens trapped between drug abuse and risking their lives without fear of consequences. Kathy tells a very personal, authentic narrative showcasing the ripple effects of drug abuse and how Byron Smith, an honored Vietnam vet, felt alone in constant fear of home invasions bursting out of control. —J. Chandler, Research Professor, Krasnow Institute for Advanced Study

As a Navy Veteran I feel that Byron Smith was a victim of young people taking advantage of his generosity and his interest in being a mentor for them. How would you react to the fear of someone invading the privacy of your home time and time again. Even worse,your feeling of being abandoned by the very system of why we served our country. We have always been told to "Defend our Castle!" —Bill Osberg, Little Falls, MN

My family knew Byron from spending Thanksgivings together. He is a friendly, quiet person. My sister tells this story with all her sincerity and heartfelt sadness in a tragic outcome for everyone. —Cheryl, sister to Kathy Lange.

Once I started reading, I couldn't put this book down. My emotions were so strong, because it was not only my sister's family dealing with all this, but because Byron never got a break with the justice system. So very frustrating! —Diane, sister to Kathy Lange

DEDICATIONS

To my Mom and my sisters, Cheryl, Lynne, Diane, Kari, Staci and brothers, Gary and Dan. You are the best family a girl could have!

To my children, Greg, Laura, love you to the moon and back!

To John who never stopped defending his friend even through all the challenges.

To Beth, your strong will and advice has created a new and lasting friendship. I can't thank you enough.

To my son, Dilan, your kindness and caring for others is like no other, but most of all words cannot describe your selfless decision to invite our neighbor into our home without a second's hesitation. You set the best example for true humanity.

To my dearest friend, Claudia, for giving me courage, strength and empowerment. I will be forever grateful.

And to Byron, you have more community support than you know. Never lose hope.

When we are at our best…when we guide each other toward redemption, that is the best of humanity. —Joaquin Phoenix, accepting his Oscar for Best Actor on February 9, 2020.

A true, tragic story of teens, drugs, burglaries, and a homeowner's fear of death by his own guns.

CONTENTS

Paragraphs in italics throughout the book are from author's journal entries in 2012-2014.

Byron Smith is a retired State Department employee and Vietnam veteran who came back to his hometown of Little Falls, Minnesota, for an early retirement and to take care of his elderly mother. After his mother passed, he wanted to remain in the home his father built, enjoying the solitude of his thirteen acres along the banks of the Mississippi River. For two years, he led a comfortable, quiet life, taking occasional trips out of state to mentor with various Boy Scout troops. On November 22, 2012, Thanksgiving Day, two teens broke into his home by shattering his bedroom window with a metal pipe. It was the sixth time in five months that his home had been burglarized. He shot and killed both teens as they descended his basement stairs. Even though they were in the commission of a felony and guns had been stolen from previous burglaries, he was arrested the next day and charged with second-degree murder. As evidence was gathered, one of the teens involved in previous break-ins was a kid that Byron Smith had wanted to help by teaching and offering him yard work and the opportunity to take him deer hunting. The Morrison County prosecutor's office labeled his actions as cold-blooded and the local sheriff called him an executioner. Byron Smith, who served his country in the Air Force and continued to work for the United States for another sixteen years, went unsupported by the United States State Department, his own county government, including judge and jury and the sheriff's department. Was the fear of exposing a multitude of criminal activities from high school students the decision that led the judge to not allow any testimony at trial from them? Was Sheriff Wetzel's fear of publicly exposing no investigation into Smith's burglaries the decision that turned Byron Smith into a murderer instead of the victim? After all, was it Byron's responsibility to "save" the kids instead of himself? Minnesota statute 609.065 states that the taking of a life is justified if that person is in the commission of a felony in one's abode. Certainly the two intruders on Thanksgiving were there to steal before they attended dinner with their families. Were they stealing for the mere thrill of it or to buy drugs? After all, prescription pill bottles from a previous home invasion were found in Nick Brady's car. As a nation, the opioid epidemic causes a new set of problems not only medically, but drug-related crimes increase across many communities. How do communities keep everyone safe—the decent, law-abiding homeowner minding his own business and then those addicted and committing crimes? In this case, why was Statute 609.065 completely ignored by the jury?

This story is a personal look at the real Byron Smith, a man without so much as a parking ticket, who stands convicted of murder. This is the other side of the story that the media never wrote or spoke about. It is a story of consequential fear. The fear that led Byron Smith to feel unsafe in his own home for months as he was terrorized by misguided teenage thieves. He had spent great time, energy, and expense on dead bolts and replacing previously damaged locks and security cameras. On Thanksgiving Day, he had locked all windows and doors to deter entry. If he had wanted them to enter, as was the prosecutor's trap theory, it doesn't make sense that he wouldn't have left the doors unlocked to make sure they came in. This is also about community fear. The community's fear of exposing drug traffic in nice, quiet neighborhoods with little resources or lack of leadership to stop it. It is all these fears—the school, the judge, the sheriff, the community, but most of all, the misunderstood, underexposed fear of Byron Smith. Was Byron Smith's fear less significant than all the others' fear? His was a fear that none of us could ever imagine being subject to. How many of us have come into our home finding every drawer and room ransacked, cherished items gone, wondering if and when the invaders will return? They have also stolen your guns. How many of us have felt that we may be killed by our own stolen gun? That fear would be incomprehensible for any of us and certainly not the average juror. Byron's fear was dismissed, discarded. The deepest fear none of us should ever experience.

CHAPTER 1
THE NEIGHBORHOOD

It was the Saturday after Thanksgiving in 2012, and my fifteen-year-old son, Dilan, was already asking about putting up the Christmas tree. At his age, I was a little surprised at how excited he was for the Christmas season as it seemed a tradition that only little ones got really excited about. It was eight thirty in the morning as I started the decorating process. We had enjoyed a lovely Thanksgiving dinner with my two older children, Laura and Greg, and my mother-in-law, Colleen. Laura and Greg both live only thirty minutes away but have weekend jobs that keep us from seeing one another as often as we like. I had taken my thirty-minute walk that day as soon as I had the turkey in the oven as the temperature outside was going to take a dramatic drop later in the afternoon. On the way back from my walk around noon, I had noticed an older little red sports car and had wondered who was visiting today. As it was parked on the avenue, not in front of anyone's home, I wondered which neighbor the car belonged due to its odd parking spot. This car would come to change the lives of myself, my family, and our neighbor forever.

One person in particular was missing for our Thanksgiving celebration. My husband, John, had invited our neighbor, Byron Smith, for the last few years. He had retired from his national security position with the State Department when he moved back to his family home to take care of his elderly mother. I first met Byron in 2009, after his mother passed, when he and my husband visited about restoring a classic car. He seemed quiet, somewhat reserved, but a very interesting conversationalist as he had lived all over the world. His job with the State Department had afforded him opportunities to live in Beijing, Cairo, Moscow, Tokyo, cities in Germany, West Africa, and many more. Each job assignment lasted three years, and then he would move on to the next embassy to install a new security system. This was not a career conducive to having a wife and children and might be part of the reason he never married. Byron was not a tall or muscular man, but spoke gently and owned a thick head of hair for a sixty-four-year-old man. I admired his intelligence, but aside from being gifted intellectually, his gentleness spoke through his wanting to care for his mother, who had passed away a few months after his retirement. He came from a family of four children. Byron was the second son. His two younger sisters were not close to him or their parents in their adult life, although one lived only thirty miles from the family home, which was now his with the passing of both parents. Byron inherited the home, and he and his older brother split the family assets. Their father had purchased stock from working at Minnesota Power, and that stock had doubled in the 1980s. Both parents lived very frugal lives, I was told, as I had never met them. When we moved to the Riverwood neighborhood in 1997, I knew of an elderly woman down the street but never had the opportunity to meet her. Their home was somewhat secluded from the rest in the neighborhood. You could see the detached garage, which Byron used as a shop to work on small projects. His father, Ted, short for Edwin, was a maintenance supervisor for the local electrical plant, a caring father, and husband to his wife, Ida. The children grew up in the fifties and sixties, going on family vacations and spending quality time together. Ted was a teacher to his children, and they did what was expected of them and were taught good behavior. Byron talked very lovingly about his mother. He once told me that his mother had called the mother of a girl he wanted to date so she could get to know the family first, as mothers would do sometimes, and he didn't much care for that. I said that I had to side with his mom, because I would do the same thing. All the family photos showed them as a very close and active family. The only bad thing I had ever heard him say about his mom was that she was too lenient with the youngest daughter. She always made excuses for her tardiness or lack of ambition. Ida was also in the armed forces, along with Ted, so military life was embedded within the family. After Ida died and Byron was no longer a caregiver, he and my husband began to talk back and forth in the neighborhood and build a friendship. That Thanksgiving Day in 2012, Byron had declined our invitation and stated that he had not been feeling well. We later learned how very true that was. John had said that he had been acting differently for the past several weeks as several offers to go to bologna days, where one ate all the bologna your stomach could hold on a given weekday, were refused. Byron would regularly stop over to chat, but it had been at least ten days since he had walked over. Soon we would learn why.

As I started decorating the Christmas tree, I was surprised to see several police cars headed down Elm Street toward Byron's home. His home is at the dead-end of Elm Street with a straight view from our living room window. After several cars, came several more, and soon it was a frenzy of law enforcement vehicles in the neighborhood heading down Elm Street. Then it came, a large van with the lettering BCSU—Bemidji Crime Scene Unit. As my thoughts collected in a panic, I went to find John and told him that he needed to call Byron right away. Something terrible had happened to him. John tried his home phone. There was no answer. He called his cell number. No answer. It was a stream of law enforcement vehicles headed down Elm Street. As we watched for several hours as more came and some left, a large white suburban drove into our driveway, and two police officials knocked on our door asking questions about what we had seen in the neighborhood on Thanksgiving. I told them right away that we were friends of Byron and I did not have a bad word to say about him. By this time, through social media, we had learned that two teens were shot in a basement as they broke into someone's home. The deputy and investigator flashed their badges, then sat down, turned on a recorder, and informed me that they wanted to record my statement. I had seen the strange red car parked on the avenue around noon on Thanksgiving and just explained that it was parked in an odd spot. These officials seemed interested in what time I noticed that car parked and when I had first seen it. They recorded my answers and went out to talk with John, who was with some of the other neighbors gathered outside. They talked with John for several minutes, asked questions, and then left. They gave no further indication of what actually had happened at Byron's home. As we wondered about our friend, Facebook was a source of information about the two teenagers that had been shot and killed burglarizing a home on Thanksgiving. My heart sank as I discovered that the red car was the car of the teens and our friend was now in jail for shooting them as they broke into his home.

Nick Brady and Haile Kifer were teens unknown to me even though I had a son who went to Little Falls High School and knew who they were. Their Facebook pages appeared to show that they were very troubled teens, obviously as they were breaking into someone's home on a holiday. Rumors from schoolmates spread that Haile had recently been in rehab for chemical dependency. Another rumor insisted that she had moved away from her parents and had been living with a boyfriend right after she turned eighteen. Nick had the reputation of being a bully. He had been attending school in Pillager, a town thirty miles from Little Falls, and had been living with his grandparents. His Facebook page showed him holding a gun, and it wasn't a hunting picture. His best friend, Cody Kasper, was said to have gone on this burglarizing mission along with the other two, but an invitation from a friend, Logan, to go snowboarding trumped the burglary. Little did he realize then that decision saved his life that day. Cody had been hired by Byron to do yard work during the summer of 2011. John said that Byron had been talking about what a great kid he was and how he wanted to teach him to deer hunt with a bow and arrow and what a hard worker he was. Cody happened to be at our home one day, and when my son got home from school, he asked what that kid was doing in our yard. John had hired him to stack some wood, along with another young man, Colt, who was a classmate of Dilan's at the time. Dilan was very upset with his dad for hiring Cody. He stated that Cody had a bad reputation and seemed to always find trouble. Dilan was so adamant about Cody John immediately told Cody he was done working.

On October 27, 2012, Byron had gone to St. Cloud, a thirty-mile trip, and was gone for about six hours. When he arrived home, he noticed the door to the basement had been kicked in and as he entered, every drawer had been overturned, and every room upstairs had been turned upside down. He called the police right away. A deputy, Jamie Luberts, arrived thirty minutes later. After the deputy reviewed the scene and left, Byron later discovered a shoe print from the door panel that had been knocked out. It was the print of a skateboard-type shoe, so it was determined by Byron himself that the burglars were likely younger in age, not adults. He actually took the shoe print from the door to the sheriff's office on the following Monday as the deputy had missed this piece of evidence. He spent about one and a half hours at the sheriff's department waiting to show the deputy this piece of evidence. During that time, he talked with another deputy about the hopelessness, the despair, and the fear he had felt in the last several months due to missing guns and cash. The deputy stated that "if they want to get in, they'll find a way." This was not the first break-in to Byron's home. The first known burglary started in July that summer with about three thousand dollars in cash stolen. He had recently decided to pay for things with more cash and less credit cards. He had not reported the theft because he knew there would be nothing that could be done about it, and a small part of him thought maybe he had misplaced it. Someone had gained entry without force, saw the envelope of cash, and helped themselves. Many times as he did yard work on his acreage, he would leave the house unlocked, as many of us do in our seemingly safe, quiet neighborhood. But in September, he also noticed that a new chainsaw had gone missing from his garage, among other small tools. Again, he thought maybe he misplaced the items. Then he realized, around the beginning of October, a couple of guns his father had purchased long ago in the upstairs closet were not there. He was unsettled and didn't know what to think. He kept wondering if he had misplaced the items, so he never reported anything at that time. During this time, he had also been frightened by the ringing of his doorbell at strange times during the night. When he got up to answer and turned the light on, there was no one at the door. Then came October 27. Not only was thirty-two thousand dollars' worth of gold coins and cash taken, but also his father's 1962 Rolex watch given to him by the French government for being a POW, a camera he purchased overseas with a one-of-a-kind lens attached that was worth about six thousand dollars, and a video camera. He believed that thieves who steal guns use guns. His panic turned to sheer fear as he went to Walmart and Iron Hills Pawn to replace the stolen rifle and shotgun. Byron gave the deputy a list of all the neighbors to question that might have seen something that day. None of the neighbors even knew about this break-in at the time as that deputy assigned to investigate never contacted any of the close neighbors or notified any of us to be on our guard for possible burglars in the neighborhood. Byron was in constant fear of his own life as not only did they take sentimental valuables but these thieves also had his guns and ammunition. The garage of his other property adjacent to his family home had also been broken into on the same day in October, the door kicked in and tools taken, just as the door had been kicked in at his other home. It was obvious that a pattern was emerging, and it was not if they would come back but when. He dared not leave his home for fear of it being burglarized again. And he was fearful of staying there, as he knew the burglars were getting more violent and they now had his weapons. Every break-in had occurred when he was not at home, seemingly in broad daylight. Who was watching to know when he left his home so burglars could come in and take whatever they wanted? He started sleeping with a pistol and carried it all times while on his property. Since he didn't have a permit, he left it at the end of his driveway when he went to the grocery store. He started taking sleeping pills for the first time in his life. He could only sleep about three hours each night even with the sleep aids. Was there someone in the neighborhood watching him leave? Since his home was at the dead-end of Elm Street, only a few neighbors could see his comings and his goings. Pine trees sheltered the house, so it was hidden from street view. No one would ever see suspicious activity. During the past several months, unusual doorbell ringing was concerning. This had happened so many times that he reversed the tone, so that instead of *ding dong*, it rang *dong ding*. He did this because he thought he was dreaming and this would convince him otherwise. He was correct. He knew by early October that when the doorbell rang, it went *dong ding* and he was not dreaming this. He knew someone was wondering if he was home or not. If he wasn't home at night, burglars would be then free to do another home invasion. Several of the other neighbors had stated they heard their doorbell ring in the middle of the night too. On the Monday before Thanksgiving, Byron cleaned out a space in his garage to store his 1969 Nova. John had told him about the recent vandalism in Swanville, a nearby town in Morrison County, in which car windshields had been broken to steal contents in cars on the main street. He feared that the same people committing those crimes were possibly breaking into his home. On the Tuesday before Thanksgiving, he cleaned out another stall to store his SUV. On the Wednesday before Thanksgiving, he continued to secure two motorcycles into the same garage to protect against vandalism or theft. As he was cleaning, moving, and storing, Byron noticed a flicker of light near his home. He sped off at once, running toward his house for fear it was being robbed again. When he discovered no one at his home, he continued to move more items in the garage.

Nick Brady and Haile Kifer had entered his home on Thanksgiving Day by breaking a bedroom window. Nick was the first to enter. Byron had installed surveillance cameras after the October burglaries upon the recommendation of the deputy. The cameras showed Nick Brady casing the house, trying to get in through doors, and then noticing the camera and trying to turn it away from him. Byron had locked and dead bolted all doors and windows in order to deter anyone from entering. This was an everyday habit. Since October 27, he set up an audio recorder every day to record any sound of a burglary. With his extensive background installing security systems, his ultimate fear was that he might die a violent death one day and wanted a recording so police had some clues to the crime. He had become a prisoner in his own home. It was likely that someone watching, possibly in the neighborhood, had to have notified Nick and Haile as they saw Byron leave in his silver pickup, undoubtedly, they thought for a Thanksgiving dinner with friends. Byron had to pass over twenty homes with his truck that morning. Was there someone watching him leave? He left his yard to move his pickup that day to continue his moving and storing and also to prevent that vehicle from the dangers of vandalism. The garage he was moving things for storage was about a quarter mile from his home, so at times his property would not be visible to him. As he left his yard around 11:30 a.m., he stopped to chat with a neighbor, Bill, for a few minutes and then proceeded to park his vehicle a few blocks away from his home. The camera showed Byron walking back into his home at 11:45 a.m. Nick Brady was first seen on the camera at 12:35 p.m. During this time, Nick had parked his red car on the avenue, and both had to walk down along the edge of the pine trees that bordered Byron's properties. Their walk would take about five minutes, but they would go unnoticed by any neighbors due to the thickness of the pine trees. Before proceeding to more cleaning and storing, he decided to sit down and read for a while. His reading area was downstairs, in which he had a comfy wingback chair between bookshelves. There were many windows facing the river side of his home, so the sunlight during the middle of the day was perfect for reading. He had been sitting for about thirty minutes when suddenly he heard a doorknob rattle. He heard footsteps on his wooden deck and saw the shadow of a person peering through the large picture window of where he sat. He heard another doorknob rattle. All doors and windows were locked. All doors were dead bolted, so there was no way they could get in. His thoughts were, *Please, go away, just go away*. The monitors to the video cameras were in another room, but he dared not get up from his chair to risk being seen. Then he heard the shattering sound of glass breaking and footsteps above him. He thought to himself, *This is going to be bad*. His cell phone was out of minutes and had been for a month. He had been too afraid to drive to St. Cloud to buy minutes for it. He then heard footsteps that started down the stairs toward him. They hadn't stopped in any of the rooms upstairs. The footsteps did not pause and were coming directly down to him. As he sat frozen, he reached for his replacement rifle. As the figure further descended the stairs, he shot. Afraid they had his own guns, he took a shot in the hip of this person coming to him. A young male dropped and fell to the bottom of the stairs. He could now see his face and didn't recognize him, but thought he looked about twenty-six years old. What he did recognize were the shoes that had fallen off when he fell. They looked like the same footprint as the door from the break-in in October. They were a skateboard-style shoe, and Byron was familiar with them as he wore this style while hiking. Nick Brady started getting up after the first shot and coming toward Byron. He shot again, this time at his chest, but it didn't seem to affect him as he still came toward Byron with a mad, mean look on his face, and then he held up both hands at Byron with both middle fingers pointing straight up at him! The threat continued. Byron shot at his hands and head, and it was over. Nick Brady was no longer a threat. He sat down to catch his breath. He was frozen, and blood was pumping rapidly and heavily into his ears. The adrenalin was out of control. Blood was starting to flow on the carpet, so he got a tarp from his shop area that he used for logs for his wood burner and placed the body on the tarp. He sat back down to catch his breath for several minutes. When almost ready to call for assistance, the sound of more footsteps was heard above him. Was another intruder entering his home? The window was already broken. They could crawl in without making a sound. With the sound of gunshots still ringing in his ears, he saw another figure descending down the stairs. Byron took another shot at a black-hooded figure coming downstairs. He shot in the head so there would be little chance of another physical encounter. This time a second figure dropped to the foot of the stairs. This person looked thin, dressed in black pants and a black hoodie with the drawstring tied so tight around the face that only the eyes and nose were showing. The black sweatshirt had a Hard Candy logo in pink letters. He noticed black leather gloves. She had obviously put some thought into her day's activities with her large pink tote bag, yet empty, except for her glass pipe. (Byron did not look in the bag. This pipe was noted in law enforcement reports.) She was gasping, "Oh my god, oh my god." He placed the gun to her head, and it seemed to him that she laughed because at that moment, the gun jammed. The only other weapon that remained close to him was a small .22 rifle, so he shot her again in the head, and she was still gasping. His thoughts turned to more people coming down the stairs. He moved her body next to the other. He didn't want to look at these intruders, but as he moved the girl's body, he noticed she was still gasping. Because he didn't want her to suffer, he shot her again. His thoughts now were that more intruders must be coming. He thought the girl was a neighbor that he had suspected of stealing from him previously over the years. But now Byron started to wonder if there were additional burglars. He thought maybe the girl's dad would be coming after her or maybe he was in on all the burglaries that had been happening this summer. He was frozen and wondering who was coming next. He felt abandoned by law enforcement because they had done little to no follow-up on these attacks on this home. The one follow-up visit that was done was a short conversation with Deputy Luberts, who fiddled with this radio after a few minutes, said he had to leave, got in his car, turned on the lights, and left in a sudden hurry. Byron noticed that by the time he went passed onto Highway 10 alongside his house, the lights on his car had already been turned off. Byron had suggested to Luberts that there might be some drug traffic on his street, which was when the deputy suddenly had to leave. He had shown Luberts the installed cameras on his property because there was "nothing else they could do." Now he had shot two people who entered his home to steal once again and was now wondering what window had been broken. Who else was coming through the broken window? Was there anyone else coming in the house? His thoughts were now that there might be more coming. He sat there in the corner of another room in his basement waiting in fear, doing nothing, but waiting for more to come. He stayed hidden for the next twenty-four hours when he finally felt safe enough to go upstairs. His cell phone had no minutes due to his reluctance to leave his home for fear of another break-in. His landline phone was in the kitchen upstairs, so he crouched to the kitchen counter in case anyone was watching yet and reached for the phone. He called his neighbor, Bill, and asked him to contact a lawyer and asked if he wanted to come over. He told him that the burglaries were finally solved. Byron wasn't sure at this time if other intruders were still on his property, so he didn't want to alert other burglars to law enforcement, so he asked for no sirens. Law enforcement arrived about an hour after the call was made to the sheriff's office. Byron came out with his hands up to show he had no weapon and invited them into his home. After showing the two deputies the bodies, Byron was placed in a sheriff's car within sixteen minutes.

The thieves had broken in through a west bedroom window, which would be undetectable to any neighbor as it faced the Mississippi River. It was Byron's bedroom window, where he had a huge shelf of record albums, hundreds of them. One of his passions was music, and this was one of his extensive collections. Byron was proud of his well-built family home. Byron was close to older brother, Bruce. Bruce was semiretired now and had once lived on a ChrisCraft boat in a California marina for several years. He now had residence in California, but he also spent much of his time with his daughter in Pennsylvania. Bruce is six feet, four inches, thin, with a very deep voice, a contrast to his soft-spoken, much shorter younger brother. Bruce commanded a presence with not only his height but his graying hair and a gray moustache. He could remind some of the Monopoly man, professional and smart. Bruce had been married but was now divorced and had two children that he raised as a single father. He was a grandfather to four grandchildren. His daughter's husband had died suddenly at a young age while she was pregnant with their second child. Bruce was a proud grandfather and was enjoying the Thanksgiving holiday with them when Byron called to summon him to Little Falls as something bad had happened and come as quickly as possible. Bruce was on a plane the next day without even knowing that his younger brother had shot two burglars that day in their family home.

After Bruce's arrival, the Lange home was constantly filled with the drama of the shootings. Byron had been sitting in jail now for two days. They had arrested him because the sheriff thought he had gone "above and beyond defending his home." The prosecutor's office referred to the incident as a cold-blooded killing. They had taken him into custody on that Friday afternoon. Bruce was there to help his brother sort out this mess and get him out of jail at some point. For now, he was safer there. The community was stunned. They were upset that these "innocent-looking" kids had been killed. Their angelic-like faces were splashed all over every news media outlet. Even from the *Sacramento Daily* newspaper to one in the corner of Florida. They were splashed on every TV newscast in the state, plus some nationally as well. Byron's mug shot was shown alongside, looking, of course, like a space alien, but of course he hadn't slept for thirty hours. The media was literally camped on our street in front of our house. They were everywhere. Bruce finally put a locked gate at the foot of the driveway so all the lookers would not come directly up to the house. As Bruce took up residence in the family home, John and I walked over to Byron's house to discuss the events with Bruce and bring him up to date. It felt uncomfortable being in that presence with all the drama that was surrounding the home. We sat in the kitchen. It looked like it always had, everything neat and tidy. As I sat there, I kept thinking that two people had just died here. It seemed eerie to be present there after what had just occurred a few days before. Bruce was amazingly comfortable in his family home. But he said that the incident didn't happen to him and he didn't know all the details yet. My cell phone rang while we were talking with Bruce. It was my son, Dilan. "Mom, Channel 5 is here. Can we talk to them?" I told him to wait and I would be right there. I knew five of his good friends were spending time at our house. They were all stunned that this had happened and were trying to figure it all out and talk with one another. Most of his friends knew Byron and understood his fear. They had no time or much compassion for the two who were killed. Dilan's friends knew them to be the kids that were in trouble in school. The Channel 5 news guy wanted to interview the kids and get their reaction, of course, to this tragic event. As they saw me driving from Byron's home, they were determined to get pictures of the house where it had happened. The news reporter asked about what had happened and what I knew, but I didn't really know anything at that point. I was still stunned myself about what had happened in our neighborhood. I agreed to an interview at the time because I didn't want Dilan's friends on TV at that point. I stated that Byron was not the type of person to hurt anyone. He wanted to help kids, not harm. My son's band had practice sessions there all last summer in 2011. He volunteered his garage for this. This was a tragedy for everyone involved. A couple of the other kids said a few things about how Nick was always in trouble and was considered a bully on the school bus he rode. The news reporter didn't leave from there. He was insistent upon driving down to the house. I told him to leave Byron's family alone, but he didn't listen. He drove right down there, and five minutes later he was back. Bruce had told him to leave at once, along with a few other choice words. He wasn't tolerating any of the drama.

John happened to be downtown when he heard people talking about Byron and how crazy he was and that these kids had crashed into his garage and he shot them outside. The rumors were running rampant, like they do in a small town. John was upset that all these bad things were being said about his friend. As he got home and there were more news media camped in the street, he invited Channel 11 (KARE-TV) in our home to talk about the real Byron, the Byron that he knew as his good friend. They set up a camera right in our kitchen and threw questions at him for about thirty minutes. John wanted the public to know that Byron was a nice guy. Mission accomplished, except they put his name in the clip when it aired and our home phone lit up like a Christmas tree. Every newspaper and TV station wanted an interview with him and also Byron's brother. There were the crazed people that called, too. A few calls were very threatening, as we were supporting "the killer". The callers would curse at us through our phone for supporting him. Every night as I got home from work, the media watched us and called our phone for more information. It was like having the paparazzi all the time for the next ten days. We finally disconnected our home number to stop the threatening calls. As I went to work at the local hospital, I knew people were talking about how my husband was supporting our neighbor. Some were supportive, though, but the wounds were still fresh. We later learned that Nick Brady often wore a bulletproof vest to school, almost every day. He was proud of it and called it his friend. The public wanted to know why Byron waited so long to call someone for help. Why didn't he just wound them? Not many knew that he had been burglarized many times before and had lost faith in law enforcement all together. He had been offered little help from the Morrison County sheriff's office other than install cameras so next time they came, they would have clues.

As days went by, the media was still present in the neighborhood. Bruce had agreed to let one newspaper reporter from the *Star Tribune* photograph the outside of the home and the window that they had broken to gain entry. Our home was a gathering of our neighborhood to try to determine how this happened and who did what. The kids in school were talking too. It was evident that these teens had been in Byron's home before. Nick and Haile had broken into a home on the south end of town the night before. This home was in the same neighborhood of Haile Kifer's parents. It was the home of a retired teacher who had been out of the country and came home to a broken glass door with house in disarray. They had stolen his prescription medications, among other various items and collectibles. The hugest piece of the puzzle was trying to figure out how those kids knew he had left his house, thinking he was going to be gone all day. Someone in our neighborhood must have been watching. He suspected a neighbor girl whose parents lived next to Byron's property. He believed she had come to his property before. When she was about thirteen or fourteen years old, she had left evidence of a smoked joint in one of his cars outside his garage. It was rumored that she had taken some clothing and had worn to school a military jacket with the name Smith embroidered right on it. Byron had seen a trail of clothing leading from his house back to her house and had realized his jacket was missing. He didn't call the police due to the evidence of marijuana in that car on his property. He worried about getting charged with possession of an illegal drug. I actually had fired this same girl from babysitting as jewelry and makeup had been missing from our home during the time she was babysitting. She had denied this, of course, but I planted some makeup in my bathroom one day, just to see if she would take it. Well, she took the bait, and I confronted her, which she denied, but never asked her to babysit again. John also found about fifty cigarettes butts in our garage behind the grill that were also left by her. No one else in our home smoked. She had the opportunity to watch Byron's entering and leaving every time he left his property.

Meanwhile at work, I tried to stay focused even though this tragedy was all over the news. My husband's public support of Byron was all over the news. Our community was in judgment. And it seemed most were horrified with Byron shooting two teenagers. I had been to church the Sunday after all this happened. When the pastor prayed for the two teens and not for Byron, I could hardly stand to be there. I thought about getting up and walking out. I didn't want to draw attention to myself. I could barely sit there any longer. I was deciding, "Should I just leave or listen to more prayers about criminals?" I happened to notice the President of our hospital and his wife in the back. I was still in shock when I spoke with them after the service. He and his wife had been out of town until last night and had not heard any news. The next morning, he came into my office to ask if I was okay. I know when I spoke with them on that Sunday, I was in shock and overcome with sadness that this had happened. Our hospital offered many services to their employees, such as counseling. I thanked him but was partly embarrassed about my open and honest talk with him in church. But the feelings and emotions were raw and real. It was hard to focus at work, but it was a refuge away from the people in my home every day trying to figure out this mess. I would come home to strange people discussing the shooting and guns. This Thanksgiving tragedy was in my home constantly. I couldn't get away from it.

Bruce had been working with the local sheriff's department to protect the property from further vandals. He stayed overnight there even though I offered him our home. I admired his strength for doing that. But after all, that was his family home too. He was protecting it from all the cars who went sightseeing down Elm Street. There were hundreds every day that just went to the driveway and had to turn around because it was a dead-end street. This lasted for weeks. It was a parade of constant traffic down Elm Street. My husband and I did not visit Byron in jail, but Bruce said he was doing as well as could be expected. The first night he was there, Bruce said that he thanked the jailer because he finally felt safe somewhere, because he hadn't felt safe in his own home for months. After a few weeks, though, and as the news media somewhat dissipated, Byron felt safe to be out. I had written a letter to him in jail as we had no other communication during this time. I wanted him to know that he was our friend and both John and I supported him. My letter stated that there were people that understood his reaction to the burglary and that Dilan's friends were also concerned about him. I told him about all the rumors that had been exaggerated about him and John came to his defense without hesitation. John was steadfast in his support of his friend. The letter to him was encouraging but didn't bring forth what we had learned about the two who had broken into his home. I ended the letter with offering him support and help in whatever he needed. Bruce had hired Steve Meshbesher, a notable defense attorney from Minneapolis. Mesbesher had represented some of the Vikings football team players in a sexual assault case in this area and had a reputation for winning. His father, Ron, had been the defense attorney for Marjorie Caldwell, the Duluth heiress who had been accused of conspiracy to kill her mother, Elisabeth Congdon, at the Glensheen Mansion in Duluth in 1977. Ron had won an acquittal in that case, and Steve had worked on that case with his father as a young attorney. Meshbesher had requested a bail hearing on December 18, and Judge Doug Anderson agreed to release him for fifty thousand dollars cash as long as he would relinquish his passport and stay in the state of Minnesota. Bruce set things in motion to get bail money. He called me in my office at the end of that day and was having trouble getting a check cashed to get fifty thousand dollars in cash. No bank would cash a Morgan Stanley check until it had cleared the bank it was written on, which would take about ten days. He had called me to ask if my bank would take this check if I cashed it. I doubted this because you would have to be a credit union member, but I would inquire for him. It was almost 4:00 p.m., so I went downstairs to ask the president of the credit union if she could help. I had worked with Margurite before. She purchased my homemade candles from me, a business I started about ten years ago. As I entered her office, I closed both of her doors so no one would hear my request. "The things I get myself into," I first said. I told her that Byron Smith's brother had a check to cash for his bail and was having trouble cashing it right away. He wanted to get Byron out of jail for Christmas. I told her he needed fifty thousand dollars in cash.

"Do you even have fifty thousand dollars cash in this bank?" I asked. She smiled and said, "Of course I can help you, but you have him sign the check over to you because you are the member. You are assured that it is good, right?"

"Yes, it's good, that's not a problem." I told her that I would bring Bruce with me tomorrow morning to do the transaction. When I called Bruce and told him that my bank was good with this, he was elated and thankful. "I'll be right over," he said. He wanted discuss the details of the transaction.

Tuesdays were my days that I worked at the Albany Hospital. It was a thirty-five-mile drive that I enjoyed every Tuesday and Thursday. I told Bruce that we could go to the bank at 8:30 a.m. He would pick me up so we could get this cash, and then he could bring me back home so I could leave for work and then he could get Byron out of jail. We drove past the jail to see if any media were still camped out from the night before. News reports revealed they were all camped out waiting, finally, for a new picture of the famous Byron Smith. None of the news media actually knew what he really looked like beyond an awful mug shot. As we drove to the back of the jail, there didn't seem to be any sign of news media. Bruce had a plan, though, to get his big parka and sunglasses and make a fast dash for the car. As we arrived at the bank, I knocked on her door as Margurite was finishing a phone call. She was usually not in this early as she worked later than most bankers. I felt a little uneasy as the other employees were staring at Bruce, the extremely tall, gray-haired man in his long, black wool coat. He definitely looked like a high-priced lawyer or some professional corporate executive, someone really important that was not usually seen around Little Falls. The cash was placed in a regular-size money bag, and I was somewhat astonished at how small a space fifty thousand dollars in cash actually took. After all, how often do you see that much cash? We sat in her office, and Bruce signed the Morgan Stanley check, and then I put my signature on the back as well. She asked me if I wanted to count the cash back. She had it in bundles of ten thousand dollars each. Five bundles fit snug into the zippered bag. I thanked Margurite for helping. Byron would have had to wait until after Christmas to be out of jail, and Bruce didn't want him spending the Christmas holiday there, nor did Byron want to stay any longer. Margurite was asking Bruce questions about him. She said it wasn't for her to judge him, or for anyone that matter to judge when you don't know the whole story. My respect for her grew that day. If only everyone else thought that. She had asked where Byron would be staying then, and as she looked at me for an answer, I told my first white lie of many that I would tell people about where he would be living. I don't know if it was fear of random people knowing or my own fear of what might happen if people found out his location. Most of my fear generated from the Little Falls High School where Dilan attended daily and how the kids, who were burglars, seemed to be memorialized. I told Margurite that I didn't know and that Bruce and his attorney were talking about living arrangements. Steve Meshbesher was a very prominent name in the field of law and he didn't come cheap—one hundred thousand dollars retainer to start. Meshbesher explicitly stated that he didn't want Byron back in his home. Bruce and I had this discussion the night before about where Byron would stay. He couldn't, of course, go back home. The scene was not cleaned, and investigators (from his defense team) still needed to view it. We left the bank, and as quickly as I wanted to get out of there without being seen, only one employee noticed me with the tall, black-coated, strange man. Hopefully she would ask no questions. Bruce drove me back home so I could begin my work day.

When I got home from work that afternoon, I walked into the back door to be greeted with a big hug from Byron. It was a tight hug from someone who was very thankful to be free. He had been in jail since November 23, and it was now December 18. All were gathered in my kitchen discussing the events and telling Byron what had been discovered about the teens that he had shot and that they were part of a small gang of kids who dabbled in drugs that had been robbing him over and over and over. He couldn't believe that he had been betrayed by Cody Kasper, someone that he had wanted to teach him to deer hunt, and hired to do yard work. He was astonished beyond belief as we told him who the attackers on his home had been. *Attackers* was Byron's word for the teens. It was how he felt about who they were. He had sat in jail knowing virtually nothing about the two intruders. His first words, as he contemplated all the information, were, "How can we teach kids ethical behavior?" His purpose in life was still the mission he had always lived by, teaching kids to be successful and proud of their accomplishments. How ironic that these teens would pick his home to burglarize and how ironic it was that his occupation had been international protection when he personally needed protection when he moved back to his hometown. He had always felt safe all over the world, but he had to come back to his hometown to feel unsafe.

History of Events Leading Up to November 22, 2012

1. In early June of 2012, Cody Kasper, along with Nick Brady, drove Brady's red car up to the Smith property looking for work. They had previously made other visits but didn't find Smith at home. Byron turned them away as he was going to do all his yard work himself that year.
2. Shortly after that, Byron was hearing his doorbell ring between midnight and 2:00 a.m. about once a week. When he got up to answer, no one could be seen. This continued through September and increased to two times each week. He could see no one when he turned on the lights to check the door.
3. During the first week of July, $3,200 in cash was stolen from his home. Byron thought he might have misplaced it so didn't report it, plus it would be impossible to recover. (Later he noted that when he was doing yard work, he left his home unlocked and would not have noted persons entering his home if he was working down by the river.)
4. During late summer of 2012, he noticed many misplaced/missing items, later to be found stolen. He went to an annual Boy Scout weekend, where friends noticed him nervous and withdrawn but said nothing. These friends were from

Avon, Elk River, and a professor of Environmental Science at SCSU. In mid-September, he missed a regional scout meeting for the first time due to the fear he was being burglarized. Around September 10, he noticed two missing guns. The paranoia really set in, and Byron was afraid to leave his house, afraid to leave tools on his work bench. He began installing dead bolts, locking vehicles inside the garage, and hiding valuables and went to Walmart to purchase the missing rifle and Iron Hills Pawn to replace the shotgun.

5. In early October, he reversed the doorbell tone to verify that he was not dreaming when the doorbell rang. When it rang in reverse for the first time, he knew he was not dreaming and the doorbell ringing was intentional, but he still could not see anyone. He finally knew that someone was wanting to know if he was home or not.
6. The weekend of October 14, 2012, he had to go out of town. Upon his return, he noticed a new Stihl chainsaw was missing along with some copper wire. He still wondered if he had put the chainsaw in another location as he had been moving things around. Cody Kasper admitted in court that they had been to his property that weekend and there was too much to carry, so they hid some things in the pine trees, only to come back later. This rash of misplaced items had become an epidemic, and desperate frustration set in. By compulsively locking everything, Byron felt somewhat safe. That changed on October 27, 2012, with a violent break-in. A dead-bolted door to the basement was kicked in to gain entry. Stolen were $32,000 worth of gold coins and jewelry, a $6,000 special-order Nikon camera and lens he had recently purchased, war medals, and his father's Rolex watch gifted to him by the French government.
7. On Monday, October 29, 2012, Byron spent one and a half hours in the ready room at the sheriff's office in Morrison County. He waited for Jamie Luberts, who was the assigned investigator. Byron brought in the door panel as additional

evidence that the deputy had left behind when he observed the scene. While waiting, Byron discussed at length the break-ins, being afraid and hopeless with the receptionist and other deputy there at the time. That deputy stated, "If they really want to get you, they will always find some way in." After almost two hours, it appeared that Luberts was not coming in, so Byron left.

8. The Monday before Thanksgiving, Byron cleaned out a space in the three-car garage to store his 1969 Nova, working on only four hours of sleep each night and carrying a pistol for protection. On Tuesday, he made room in another stall to store his SUV. On Wednesday, he asked a neighbor to assist him in pushing his two motorcycles into the same garage. (Motorcycles were being rebuilt, so not running at the time.) John had mentioned to Byron that the town of Swanville had had about $100,000 damage to cars in which windshields were broken to gain entry to steal items in cars. This detail made him more nervous about his own vehicles along with his own break-in.
9. On Thanksgiving, Byron planned to continue cleaning and put away various items in the two-car garage. Since he needed room to work, his silver truck had to be moved outside. Feeling serious threats of vandalism, he felt it risky to leave anything outside his home. He moved the truck in front of a highway patrol's home about two blocks away, where he thought it would be the safest outside.
10. On the Saturday after Thanksgiving, Byron told his neighbor, Bill, to retrieve the twenty-pound turkey he had thawing in a large pail of ice water in his shop and take it to the Lange's. He had declined their standard Thanksgiving dinner invitation that year. When Bill entered the shop, he found the large pail of pinkish water right where Byron said it was, but no turkey in it. There had been no one on the property in those two days except for law enforcement and an assistant county attorney. Where did the turkey go?

11. Byron was bewildered by unusual questioning when he showed Deputy Luberts the bodies of the home invaders. He had been asked by Deputy Luberts repeatedly if he had seen "something on the boy's waist." This was immediately after law enforcement arrived to his home on that Friday after Thanksgiving. The deputy also asked if he had noticed anything on the girl's boot. That same deputy left the room to make a phone call in a hushed voice. Both Nick and Haile were labeled as unarmed when they entered the Smith home. However, friends of Nick Brady claim that he had stolen a bulletproof vest and had worn it to school, bragging to many about it, and also never left home without it. Why would the deputy ask these questions to Byron if there wasn't something there in the first place?

CHAPTER 2
SETTLING IN

The days that followed Byron's release from jail resulted in all of us adjusting to having a guest in the house. We had been the third home asked to have Byron live with us and the only one with a child attending the high school. His close neighbor on Elm Street was reluctant because they had grandkids over all the time. That was their reasoning anyway. Another one of Byron's friends said his wife thought it was okay to have Byron stay in their shop out back, but there were no living quarters. Bruce then asked John, but he needed to discuss with me before he agreed. When I was asked by Bruce to have Byron live with us, my main concern was solely for Dilan. If the kids at school who were grieving about these two classmates found out he was in his home, he might be the target for some type of retaliation or bullying. Drug use also heightened the level of concern. I needed to discuss this with Dilan as he was the one this would affect the most. He always had many friends that came over. He preferred having them here instead of staying elsewhere. I explained to him that he would be very limited to having friends over if Byron lived with us. I explained that this would change his lifestyle for a while, but after thinking only for a second, he told me that he wanted to help Byron in any way he could. This didn't surprise me. My son has always wanted to help those in need. He is very kindhearted and Byron was someone he looked up to. We knew this would be an adjustment for all of us, including Byron. He was used to working in his huge park of a backyard and living as a single guy. He also was sensitive to smell because when he came into our home on previous occasions, he commented if it had a strong smell of candles I had been making, especially during the Christmas season. I would no longer be able to burn or manufacture candles every day, which was the least of my worries right now.

The first order of business was a neighborhood watch system with the parade of cars that continued to go down Elm Street. Being an expert at video surveillance, he set up a system to have every vehicle that went down Elm Street documented. There seemed to be extra traffic at the end of Elm Street, and there were still suspicions of possible drug activity in that house. Byron was certain that drugs played a part in his burglaries. The next order of business was to retrieve some of his personal belongings from his home. With Bruce still here, but with plans to leave soon, Byron gave him a list each day of the things he would need while living with us. The list included suits and other clothing, personal toiletries, wine (he belonged to a monthly wine club), and his favorite movies. I put a shopping list pad on our refrigerator so Byron could let me know what he wanted for groceries, etc. He wouldn't be going out himself in public, at least for a while anyway. So Bruce brought over some things from his house. Some were his favorite movies, which included the whole series of *Lord of the Rings*, *Spider-Man*, TV episodes of *Babylon 5*, and *Max Headroom*, along with many foreign movies with subtitles and Academy Award-winning titles. One night, Byron and I watched *Lawrence of Arabia*, a winner of many academy awards in 1962. It is a four-hour-long movie. I was not a person to ever sit and watch a four-hour movie. John would run away at the thought of a movie that did not contain car crashes or elements of continuous action. Byron had brought over his huge, forty-eight-inch flat-screen TV, and we installed it in our family room downstairs. The TV has surround sound, and it was just like you were in a movie theater. The day he set it up, we all sat down in amazement at the huge screen. We were all ready to watch something right away on this big screen. Byron had his first real laugh in days because all three of us were eagerly sitting on the sofa waiting for him to put a movie in. He said we would have movie night tomorrow, so we had to wait until all his Blu-ray movies were brought over. As his movie collection was slightly different from ours, Dilan was willing to watch a few of these with some interest. I wanted him to feel welcome and safe so was willing to watch some of these old movies he enjoyed. The four-hour-long ones were a bit much for me, though.

Byron wanted to get his cell phone activated, and he didn't want to go out yet, even to St. Cloud, so Dilan and I drove to the T-Mobile store at Crossroads Mall in St. Cloud. I wasn't prepared for all the questions because all I wanted was a little SIM card with a new number to activate his phone. It was an old phone, which he had for a long time, sufficient enough to receive and make calls. A young man asked to help us, and I told him what I needed. He then proceeded to ask for the city we lived in so he could assign the number. By this time, Byron had been in every newspaper from here to Florida. When I said Little Falls, the guy looked at me and said, "Oh my, how are things up there?" inferring to the recent shootings. I played along and said, "Fine." Then he asked for a name. I thought for a second if I should use my own name or Byron's. In my thoughts, if I would say his name, they wouldn't recognize it because Smith was a common name. I was wrong. When I said Byron Smith, he gave me a look of "Oh my gosh, it's him!" I quickly stated that he was a friend of ours and we were running errands for him. I thanked him for giving him privacy and confidentiality as I was afraid his number might be given out if someone overheard us. I know the T-Mobile guy was in utter shock that he had helped activate Byron Smith's phone. Dilan looked at me in disbelief that we couldn't get by with getting a new number for him without someone recognizing his name. As we drove home, Dilan and I decided that we would not tell Byron about the T-Mobile experience. It might worry him for nothing, so we kept it to ourselves. Similar things happened when I stopped at the local coffee shop. His face was plastered on the front page of all the newspapers—the *St. Cloud Times*, the *Brainerd Dispatch*, and the *Minneapolis Tribune*. People were talking about it as I stood in line to get coffee. I heard varied opinions about why he did it and a few opinions that the kids deserved it too. I was standing there silently listening to all the words and thinking if they only knew the whole story. If they only knew he was my neighbor, a person just minding his own business, and that he was living right in my home now. It was all so surreal.

A few days later Byron's attorney assigned an investigator to his case. Ross drove a black Cadillac and wore bold gold jewelry and black leather cowboy boots. He reminded me of those TV investigators, all calm and cool, dressing really slick. He had interviewed John and I, along with Dilan, and now wanted to concentrate on the burglars. We actually had one of their classmates living in our home for several weeks by the name of Colt. Colt had also helped Byron do some yard work one day last summer. He was a teen with a strained relationship with his single mom. He and Dilan had been friends a couple of years ago but had drifted in different directions. At the beginning of October, a city policeman called me to ask permission to have Colt stay in our home for the night. Colt had an altercation with his mother, and rather than fill out foster home papers, the officer told me that Colt had named our home as a place he wanted to stay. Instead of one night, he ended up staying in our home for six weeks. I had called the officer twice during this time. My phone calls went unreturned. After several weeks, I finally went to his mother and said that she needed to work on a good relationship with her son. The tensions were growing between my son and Colt. He had overstayed his welcome with Dilan. Otherwise, I think he would have lived with us forever. Since Colt was living with us during the October robbery at Byron's home, and because of his connections to some of the teens involved in the robberies, Byron thought that maybe he could be the one watching his home while he was living at our home. But I would have known if he would have had money or any kind of take from a robbery of that magnitude. The day Byron's home was burglarized, Colt had been working away from our house with my husband, so he would have had no opportunity to be watching. While Colt was living with us, we went shopping for new clothes, and as Colt was with, I bought both Dilan and Colt new clothes for school. Colt stated that he had never experienced that before. It felt good to do something for someone who appreciated being treated kindly. After Colt had moved back in with his mother, he caught me in the local Walgreens shortly after the shootings and was troubled about the fact these classmates were dead. He had asked me if Byron really killed those kids and what I knew about it. Colt mentioned a couple of other teens that were involved, so Ross, the investigator, was contacted. Ross needed to talk to Colt to find out more information. He asked if I would help. I knew Colt would freeze up and not talk if an investigator was asking about them, so I agreed to call Colt to see if he would come over and hopefully, Colt would tell Ross all that he knew. I texted Colt that Friday night and asked for his help loading music into my computer. He agreed right away and stated that he wanted to pay me back in some way for the clothes I had bought for him. Three hours later, he texted saying that if my wanting him to come over had anything to do with Byron, he was not coming. I wasn't sure how to handle that, so I waited until the next morning and told him that it didn't. I felt bad lying to him, but we had to find out the truth. I knew he was protective of his classmates, but the truth needed to be brought forward. So when I picked him up at his home, I explained that I had seen the investigator's car in the neighborhood and that this investigator had accused Dilan's band of robbing Byron, which, of course, was not true. Colt agreed that in no way did that happen. We briefly talked about how well he knew the two teens, and then Ross appeared shortly, and after some conversation, he began to tell Ross everything he knew. Colt had seen Cody Kasper and Nick Brady at the mall with a fistful of cash. They were buying new clothes, snowboards, and snowboarding outer wear. He stated that they had a lot of money in their possession and that he had seen it. Ross continued to question him for another half hour. Ross gave a thumbs-up when he left as he had good information to help Byron's case.

On Christmas Eve, our tradition was to head to Crosby to John's mom's home. We celebrate with her and the rest of the Lange family. Bruce was still in town, so he and Byron would spend Christmas Eve together at our home. Before we headed to Crosby, I had some gifts I had bought for both Byron and Bruce. I had bought Byron a new gray-and-white flannel shirt and also found a book he wanted to read called *The Purpose Driven Life.* He said one of the inmates in the county jail had a copy and he started to read but never finished. I had found it in a second-hand shop for two dollars. Since Byron was such a frugal person anyway, he would appreciate that fact. I gave each of them their Christmas gifts, and we left for Crosby.

The next morning, we started out early to celebrate with my side of the family in South Dakota. It was about a two-and-a-half-hour drive, but the time there was always full of love, laughter, and noise. There were about forty of us when we all got together. We had a nice dinner, played a dice game to exchange gifts, and then headed for home about five o'clock. My family had asked about the shootings, of course. It had been in their local paper too. John had told them the whole story so far—what we knew anyway. He did not tell anyone that he was living with us. My brother, Dan, seemed the most concerned for our safety, but he, like many others, had only heard what the news media reported. John and I had agreed that we would not tell anyone that he was living with us. When we got back home, Byron and Bruce had spent Christmas afternoon together and were in the middle of cooking a dinner for all of us. Byron had watched the parade of cars that were still going down Elm Street. He was amazed that twenty-seven cars spent the Christmas holiday observing a crime scene. We all had a glass of wine and toasted Christmas as best we could.

Bruce left several days later. He wanted to get back to celebrate Christmas at his daughter's home, where he had to abruptly leave over Thanksgiving when Byron summoned him to Little Falls. On February 5, 2013, Cody Kasper appeared in court charged with two counts aiding and abetting burglary. Byron received the letter last week, and his attorney said he would appear on his behalf. Cody Kasper's guilty plea was entered on April 26, 2013. He confessed to being the lookout on three different occasions. During the summer of 2012, he and Nick Brady went to Byron's and stole cash and a Nikon camera. He told the court that Nick went in and he hid in the pine trees so he could see if anyone was approaching the home. They again went to the Smith residence between the eleventh and seventeenth of October. He again acted as a lookout, and Nick entered the garage to steal a chainsaw, copper wire, and a gas siphoning kit. He also stated that they left some things in the trees because they couldn't carry everything, but they would come back at a later date to pick up. When asked if he assisted in carrying items to the car, he said, "No." They each had cell phones with the lines of communication open in case anyone approached the residence. He was sentenced to ninety days of electronic home monitoring and probation. If he committed any further crimes before he was age twenty-five, his juvenile criminal record would remain with him forever.

That day while in my office, a writer, Terry Lehrke, from the Morrison County Record asked if I could let her know when things were happening with Byron's case. Her husband had met Byron a few months back in his work at the Minnesota DNR. Terry had been very supportive of Byron and had also agreed not to print our names if we told her any information. She was very respectful of the fact that this was a stressful time, and she commented that "I have to live in this town too," so writing carefully was important to her. I had not even thought of alerting her to this new event. Of course, the fact that these teens had been burglarizing Byron for many months should give the public more understanding of his reaction. I tried to convince Byron that he needed to submit a nice picture of himself for this article. This was his chance for the public to see him as a good guy instead of through an awful mug shot. Byron kept refusing, telling me that he was planning to go to a professional photographer and didn't want to have a picture that would not be as nice because it would be permanently used. I tried to explain that there was no time for that. This was already Wednesday, and the paper would get printed on Friday. I even asked if he would do me this favor and just let me scan his driver's license picture, but no deal.

I met Steve Meshbesher for the first time on February 7, 2013. He wanted to spend the day in Little Falls to see how our family lived, where Byron was staying for now, and reenact the shootings with Byron. By this time, Byron had been living in our home since December 18. We all went over to Byron's home as Steve wanted to inspect the window that was broken and go over the details of that Thanksgiving Day. Steve seemed very polished and confident, as an experienced lawyer would be. He was standing outside Byron's home when we drove up. He looked at me and then looked at John, whom he had met before, and asked if I was really his wife. "How long have you been with him?" he asked me in a surprising tone. My husband and I are polar opposites. John is very outspoken and bold. He says whatever is on his mind, with no filter, and I try to balance all that with calm and quiet. As Steve talked with Byron, he came face-to-face in Byron's personal space, telling him that the prosecutor would be hard on him, would anger him, and would prove that he shot the kids out of anger instead of fear. He pulled on Byron's zippered-down overcoat as if to anger him right there. He was in Byron's face while he was explaining how hard it would be to prove him innocent of the charges. He explained to Byron that he should be thankful to have such good friends and then turned to John and then pointed at me and told Byron to "listen to her." I am not quite sure what he actually even meant by that, but I was quite surprised by such firmness with his client. After they headed down the basement to reenact the crime scene, I left. I didn't care to go downstairs, and I got the impression that Byron was uncomfortable with us hearing the audio for the first time. Byron had been so frightened of being killed by his own guns he made an audio so someone would find it in case he was killed by burglars. He wanted to ensure there was some evidence in case that occurred. Security was his career, thus the recording. Unfortunately, this recording became the focal point of his trial. People's emotional response was immediate. Any reenactment of death is ugly. The recording revealed a desperate man in anguish, who, alone, was forced to deal with a situation that would be incomprehensible to anyone.

For several days, I had been contemplating about telling my boss that Byron Smith was living in our home. I was always on alert, afraid someone would find out. And even worse, my fear was if students in the high school knew he was living in our home, Dilan's school life would be negatively impacted. Would they bully him or make it impossible for him to attend school? The teachers in the high school, Dilan stated, for the most part, seemed very sympathetic toward the teens even though they were killed committing a crime. Dilan had come home one day and was feeling upset because they were selling bracelets in memory of Nick and Haile. He was asked to buy one and refused. I told him we would not be spending any money on bracelets and he was right to refuse such a purchase.

One day I received a call from a friend of mine later that morning. She was upset with me because I had told the investigator something she had mentioned while we had lunch one day. It was about Nick Brady and what a bully he was on the bus. He basically controlled the bus atmosphere by instilling threats and fear on the other riders. When I mentioned this to Ross, the investigator working with Meshbesher, he thought it important information. When he called my friend, she was livid about being called about it. She was so upset that she stated we couldn't be friends anymore. Furthermore, she stated that Byron was going to jail for a long time. "There are commandments: Thou shalt not kill." She was telling me how she and a friend sat and cried about being asked some questions by an investigator. I could feel I was losing a friend over my support of another. I hung up with her and had a small meltdown myself. I closed my office door, and the tears started streaming for several minutes. All the stress from this situation, from the media, and from supporting our neighbor all came to a head. If God could have placed me on a different part of the earth, I wanted to go now. I did not want to cause my friend all this distress, but I also would not be judged by helping someone in their darkest hour. Her ultimatum that I could no longer be her friend if I supported Byron Smith ended the friendship. These situations are so difficult because everyone has such strong opinions and judgments are formed only by what media has printed. John was in the local Walmart and a friend approached him in the store and a near-physical encounter ensued because of his support for Byron. There is so much more to the story, and not all residents were understanding nor wanted to. Friendships were lost and might never be repaired.

Over the next weekend, we had a visitor to our home unexpectedly. It was John's longtime friend, Irv. We call him Elvis because he loved Elvis Presley and imitated him by quoting and breaking out in an Elvis song every chance he got. When he came to the door, Byron quickly ran to his bedroom. At this point, he didn't want anyone to know where he was or to be seen here. As soon as Irv stepped in the door, he says, "Quick, let me in before I get shot." And then he started laughing. I just smiled a little knowing that Byron could very well hear what he said as his bedroom was one wall away. Irv went on to talk a little about the incident, and then we quickly changed the subject to other things. I quickly needed to get him out of the house, so I suggested lunch at a nearby restaurant and I would treat. He took the offer, and we averted any further conversations to the restaurant. The same scenario happened the next weekend. Some other friends dropped by on a moment's notice, just to visit. Byron quickly went to his bedroom and shut the door. To avoid uncomfortable conversations, we did the same and went to a local restaurant to spend time with our friends and give Byron some comfort level.

On February 9, 2013, the article came out in the Morrison County Record identifying Cody Kasper and Nick Brady as two of the teens who burglarized Byron several times. The public would finally know that these kids were attacking him and his property. This should affect a change in the community's attitude, especially those feeling sorry for burglars. The county prosecutor was finally bringing charges on Nick's friend Cody Kasper. Cody had been questioned by the police a few days after the shootings. The initial evidence came from his cell phone, and then he started confessing to some things. Cody claimed to never have been in the house but acted as the lookout. He could now blame his friend, who was dead and couldn't speak for himself. According to Cody, Nick bought him an ATV with all the cash they took from Byron, along with clothes and shoes. Colt had seen them in the mall in St. Cloud with a fistful of cash. The news article also had quotes from Meshbesher saying, "If you can't be safe in your own home, where can you be safe?" Public safety was a responsibility of the sheriff. Sheriff Wetzel had retained an attorney to get a raise from the county commissioners the previous year. He believed his salary wasn't in line with other sheriffs in Minnesota, so he sued Morrison County for a raise. Also, Mr. Kosovich, one of the county attorneys, misinformed the *Record* about the October break-in being solved. The sheriff's department didn't solve anything. Byron Smith was left to protect and defend himself, and that's how the burglaries were solved. Byron Smith received no help from the sheriff's department under Wetzel's leadership. As noted earlier, Byron had been thawing out a turkey for Thanksgiving. When he was taken into custody, the turkey was left thawing in his shop. A couple of days later when a neighbor visited Byron in jail, he told him to get the turkey and take it down to John and Kathy's. When the neighbor went to retrieve the turkey exactly where Byron had left it, the turkey was not there. The pail with slightly pinkish water was there, but not the turkey. The only people who had been in Byron's house were members of law enforcement. To this day, the mystery of who took the turkey is still not solved, and when the BCA was asked about it, Chad Museus claimed to know nothing about it. Again, where did the turkey go? They were the only ones with access to the property. What else was taken and not reported? Byron had stated that he was questioned by the deputy about something around Nick's waist and something in the girl's boot. Did they take something else to insure Byron's conviction? Who would ever know what was taken or who took it? The sheriff had another search warrant about six days after they had finished with the crime scene. Bruce, Byron's brother, had left the property, and they brought the warrant over to one of the neighbors. They assumed the neighbor had the key to Byron's home now as they knew Bruce had left (which had only been a few hours ago). The neighbor told them that he didn't have a key. At this same time, Bruce had a cancelled flight, so he came back and was able to monitor the deputies as they took more computer equipment out of Byron's home. Byron thought it was because they were looking for dirt on him. Byron did not have a Facebook account, nor did he do text messages, so he believed they were looking for electronic messages he sent that might have incriminated him. For instance, if he would have been on Facebook talking to a friend about the break-ins and had written something like, "I'm going to kill whoever is doing this," that would give the sheriff all the evidence they needed to prosecute him fully. Byron said they could take anything they wanted to out of that house, and there would never be anything found that would incriminate him in that regard. But this was a day to be thankful for as there was finally public knowledge of another side to his story.

Before Byron retired to bed last night, he said he was going to get up early in the morning and check on his home. There had been a snowstorm that day, but he was going to get up at 4:00 a.m. to do some work there. I thought this unusual, but I was sure he was remembering many projects and things unfinished that used to be part of his normal routine. I was worried about this because John would be gone all day and I would be at work and he was going all alone. When I got home from work, he was not back yet. I asked Dilan to walk down to his home with me. I didn't feel comfortable going alone in case something had happened, although I didn't know what. We walked all the way down Elm Street in the heavy snow and just missed him as he had taken another path back to our home. I asked him how his day went, and he said it was time for him to get out of there. "My home is like a shipwreck," he said. He said he called his brother while there, and they had a long talk, which helped. I was glad he did that as I wondered what he was going to do there all day long. Maybe he needed to come to terms with what happened there. He said he could never live there again. He was going to board up the windows, and people would know it was just an abandoned home. That is sad, that his family home endured such a tragedy that no more happiness could be found there. The bad choices of two young people on Thanksgiving trickle down to forever change the lives of so many people.

The next day, I talked with Ann, who had lived across the street from the Kaspers when they rented a home in her neighborhood for about a year. She read the local paper and couldn't believe all the things those teens had taken from Byron's house over the last year. She also has a son in high school and asked him if Cody Kasper was in school now that he went to court last week. Of course I knew he was back in school because at his hearing, the judge had only demanded that he keep away from Mr. Smith's property and behave in school. I wonder what his school day was like being named in the local paper as the thief that introduced his best friend to Byron Smith's property and then was shot to death. Ann stated that she had called the police to the Kasper home nineteen times for suspicious and bad behavior. There was noise and suspicious traffic in and out of their driveway, which looked like possible drug involvement. She also noted the day the ATV (that Nick had purchased for Cody) came into their neighborhood. An elderly lady was taking a walk, and Cody and Nick were spinning wheelies and swerving down the street with this ATV. Ann called the police and was told there was nothing they could do. One day Cody's little brother had come over to her house as he had been left home alone after school for hours. He was only in the second grade. There was not a mom in this home. It was near dinnertime, and Ann's youngest child was telling her that the young boy didn't have any food to eat, so he was invited to eat with them. Around bedtime, the boy walked home, assuming Cody or his dad would have come home by now. They could see the curtains were open to the house, and the boy could be seen jumping on the sofa and then running to the window possibly to see if his dad was returning home. Finally, at 11:00 p.m., the dad got home. Ann was so glad when they finally left the neighborhood. She had been starting a petition to get that family out of the neighborhood, and they finally left last summer. Her interactions with Cody Kasper led her to believe that he was a con artist and a manipulator. He would come across charming and delightful, but it was a disguise. He was the same with Byron. Byron actually liked him so much that he wanted to take him under his wing and teach him to deer hunt. Byron was deceived by him too. Ann was very concerned that Cody should pay for his crimes and agreed to talk to Byron's investigator, Ross. Another fact she told about were all the items the Kasper family had left behind when they moved out of the neighborhood: knives stuck in trees, garbage in plastic bags left in the woods. Not wanting her kids exposed to anything harmful, she picked up everything. She agreed to talk with Ross and explain everything that happened in the neighborhood. The next hearing date for Cody was February 26, 2013.

People at work came up to me today and were shocked by the local news article. Not many had known that Byron's home had been robbed so many times. As you read the story, it's so astonishing about how much he went through, the memories they stole, and the fear those kids instilled in him. Cody, of course, was blaming most of it on his dead friend. He also stated that he was just the lookout guy while Nick broke in. It's likely that he confessed only to a small portion of what they actually did. As Byron read the article, he discovered things he didn't even realize he was missing. As a music collector, his basement was filled with thousands of album covers. He purchased many things overseas because, for the most part, they were a lot cheaper. One of those items was an SUV, which he rarely drove. He had it custom-ordered in Germany while working over there, and it had all the features he wanted on a vehicle, plus it was less expensive to buy it overseas than to buy in the United States.

A letter came to Byron for another hearing on a juvenile who was also involved, Jesse Kriesel. He was found with one of Byron's guns in his garage. Since he had been in trouble before and not allowed to have weapons at age sixteen, this was a felony charge and would be heard on March 20 at the Morrison County Courthouse.

At dinner one night, I started to ask Byron about his work with the Boy Scouts, just to make dinner conversation. I knew he had been quite involved with different troops and went on out-of-town trips to be an adviser to them. I was curious as to what he talked about with the scouts and what specific advice he gave to them. He began to talk about how he made the boys think about their goals in life and finished by saying, "I ask them what they would be most proud of when they're 25, 45, and then what will you be proud of when you are 65." He started to cry and could not finish talking. I felt bad that I had stirred such emotion in him. But I knew that he was almost 65 and was not feeling proud at that moment of the situation that he had been placed in. Out of concern for his emotional state, I mentioned this incident to his attorney. I felt it important that a jury know who Byron really is and who he was before this happened. Unfortunately, none of that was allowed in the trial.

CHAPTER 3
LEARNING MORE

As I was getting ready to leave for work on Valentine's Day, I noticed a small wrapped box on the kitchen counter with my name neatly written across it. I knew it wasn't from John as he didn't write that neatly. It was oddly wrapped in two pieces of colored printing paper. I opened the box carefully, and inside a paper towel was a leaf pin exactly like that from the *Lord of the Rings* movie. The hobbits wore these pins on their cloaks. I had noticed them when Byron and I were watching the series of movies as they seemed too glamorous for a hobbit who roamed the earth with hairy, bare feet. I was touched that Byron was so thoughtful to leave me a gift on Valentine's Day. When I got home, I thanked him in person for the lovely gift and told him that it made my day. He said that it took him a while to find it. He had gone into his home to retrieve some personal items but hadn't remembered exactly where he had put it. Byron had vacationed in New Zealand not long ago and spent several days touring the area where *Lord of the Rings* was filmed. We had watched the three movies over the last couple of weeks. Typically, they were not movies that I would go to, but I actually enjoyed the photography and the captivating story. Dilan, too, enjoyed the movies. We felt it important to take an interest in something Byron enjoyed so much and had even made the long journey to where they were filmed.

Our lives had taken on a different routine since Byron moved in. Friday night was our go-out-to-eat night. Byron came along but preferred we always go out of town so we would be unnoticed. I think it was easier that way for all of us. He didn't want to be pointed at and whispered about. To prevent being noticed, he would get in our car while it was still in the garage, and not until then would I lift the door up and we back out. I called him Mr. President sometimes as it seemed like we were protecting the president of the United States. When someone came to our home unannounced, he would go to his bedroom and shut the door and didn't come out until they were gone. I guess they say you don't really know someone until you live with them, so some positive, interesting things became apparent as new conversations were held over this time. One important factor being that Byron had received several war medals from his service during Vietnam: a medal of commendation from the United States Air Force and another medal for twenty-seven combat missions in Vietnam. A medal was awarded for the completion of twenty-five missions, but he went beyond the twenty-five. (A sidenote here was that the prosecutor, Pete Orput, had stated to the jury during trial that these medals were merely ribbons acknowledged for service.) Byron didn't talk about that part of his life much, but he was proud that he served four years in the Air Force. With his sixteen years of service with the State Department, that allowed him to receive a full government pension that fulfilled the requirement of twenty years. He talked most about this college life in San Luis Obispo, where he graduated from Cal Poly. He was the member of the ski club and they went on different trips and partied as college kids do. He was telling me one day that they ordered beer by the palette for these trips. He had a California ID that showed his age as ten years younger than he actually was. It made him fit in better, and no one was the wiser. It was actually the DMV's fault anyway. They had typed the year of his birthdate wrong, and it went uncorrected until the next time he renewed his license. Most young people would want to have an ID to be older, but he had one to be younger. He was in his thirties when he attended this California college, so by being twenty instead of thirty made him feel better. He also attended college at the University of Minnesota and then later decided to finish his degree at Cal Poly. His degree was actually in physical science, but his minor was electrical engineering, and his love of electronics got him the job with the State Department. He was proud of the fact that he had paid for his own education without the assistance of his parents. He talked fondly of his college days and his friend and roommate, Greg. He talked of going back to California and spending next winter there at his friend Mark's cabin in the mountains of California. Mark was a good friend from Cal Poly, and his father was a forensic psychologist. Byron was amused by the fact that he had two good friendships with forensic psychologists as he was a small-town boy from Little Falls whom no one would ever think would have those connections. He dated a couple of times but didn't have an interest in any one woman. He did tell me once that he had always wanted to get married, but it just never happened. Since his work demanded he live in a new country every three years, it made long-lasting relationships challenging. It's too bad, because he would have made a great dad and things would have turned out very different for him. Byron volunteered for military service in 1968 and was inducted on April 21. He attended basic training in Amarillo for eight weeks and was transferred to Denver to technical training. He qualified for a forty-eight-week course in one of the most complicated and critical systems—the bombing and navigation systems of the B-52. Airman Smith worked at Fairchild AFB for one year and then volunteered for duty in Vietnam. There Sergeant Smith volunteered for combat mission in-flight support. His work was comprised of in-flight repairs on older, heavily used equipment. Most bombing flights occurred at thirty-five thousand feet, where SAM missiles and MIG fighters were encountered and could not be replicated on the ground. Half of the men who tried out to be a launch technician dropped out due to failure or stress of the flight or not making the minimum number of flights to qualify. Sergeant Smith volunteered to extend his combat duty from twelve to eighteen months. He made twenty-seven flights, exceeding the required minimum of twenty-five to be awarded the Air Combat Medal. He was also awarded the Personal Commendation Medal.

He is an easy houseguest. He is very quiet, does his own laundry, and spends very little time in the bathroom. (As a woman fighting for bathroom time, this is a great attribute.) He combs his hair quickly, brushes teeth, and is done, with no fussing about his look. I made a comment one day on how he should strive to look his best, always, and he commented, "For who?" When he first moved in, he wore the same green shirt for days until I bought him a new one for a Christmas gift. Then he wore that one for a few days. He prefers no scents, perfumes, or aftershave colognes. One day he received his credit report in the mail and asked me what he thought his credit score was. I really had no idea, but I assumed it was a high number. The score was 820. He received a report because he had applied for a credit line for his rental property just in case he needed the extra money. He has moved into our extra bedroom and keeps his files with his mail and court papers in a file chest. He spends much time on paperwork: gathering receipts for insurance claims from all the things that has been stolen from his home. He makes and sends copies of news articles of interest to his attorney or investigator. He studies Minnesota statutes as he is desperately trying to catch the neighbors who own the adjacent property to him, breaking as many laws as possible—even videotaping the Stop sign and speeding violations. He stated one day that their three vehicles have run the Stop sign on Elm Street more than ten times each. He makes his bed neatly every day. He has everything neatly folded and organized. He does not usually get up in the morning until after I have already gone to work. He eats rather light, but has a huge sweet tooth. Just as I was getting into the habit of not eating so many sweets, he likes dessert after every meal. He said they usually had dessert as he was growing up. I am amazed that he doesn't weigh more because of his huge sweet tooth. John has been gone most nights now that it is ice-fishing season. I was a little uncomfortable with this arrangement and told John that he should stay home due to our new houseguest. But John's reason for existence is ice fishing! He considers Byron the new protector for his family. (Last year we didn't have a protector, so this is a new concept.) One night, shortly after he moved in, I suddenly awoke to hear Byron talking to someone in the middle of the night, possibly on the phone, I wasn't sure. I heard him open his bedroom door, which he always closes for the night, and was talking with someone. I couldn't understand some of his words, but what I did hear alarmed me. I heard him say, "Have you come to apologize for breaking my window?" He wasn't talking upset or angry, but saying this in a quiet tone, like he normally talks. After that I heard his door close again and couldn't understand the rest of his words, but he was still talking to someone in his usual tone of voice, not an angry or upset voice, but a kind, mentor-type voice. This incident startled me because I wasn't aware that he was a sleepwalker, but the words I heard made it very clear that he was dreaming about the break-in. Finally, it became quiet, but I had trouble falling back to sleep, wondering if he would wake again or what other dreams or even nightmares would occur. When morning came, he was up before I left, so I asked him if he was a sleepwalker. He said he didn't think so and quickly changed the subject. I never brought it up again and it never happened again.

The next Friday I took the day off from work to go to Minneapolis. Byron had mentioned that he wanted to take a day trip to go to Trader Joe's and a tool shop. He thought John might appreciate this huge tool store near Plymouth.

The first stop was Acme Tools. I was actually the only person that bought anything. I had been looking for something to cut slabs of candlewax with and they had the perfect tool there. The next stop was a woodworking place where I purchased new guides for dresser drawers. Byron had been using this dresser and the drawers had broken guides, so we found some nice replacements so the drawers will slide smoothly. I needed an hour of mall time, so we headed to Ridgedale Mall. I needed to find a gift for my daughter's birthday and my mom's birthday, which are two days apart. Byron wanted to purchase a new cell phone, so he would go to the T-Mobile store while Dilan and I did a little shopping. Next, we headed to lunch. He wanted to go to the Mexican area in South St. Paul. He had taken us down there before to eat authentic Mexican cuisine at one of his favorite restaurants. When Dilan's band had played at Station 4, Byron had driven down that day to hear them, so we all went out to dinner after they played. Although authentic Mexican is not my first preference, it was very good. We were the only non-Mexicans in the whole restaurant. John and Byron ordered the buffet and it looked like food I had never seen before: cow stomach lining, etc. I played it safe and ordered fajitas, and Dilan ordered tacos. John, who typically can eat anyone under the table at a buffet, ate two bowls of the soup and decided the food wasn't for him. Working our way back toward home, we stopped at the Sportsman's Guide store. It is a sporting goods / clothing store with discounted prices. Byron bought a beautiful stained glass Tiffany lamp for about $100, and I purchased some mixing bowls that matched my *kitchen. It was the type of store that you had to dig around to find a treasure. As we proceeded on, I took over the wheel and mentioned to Byron that I had never been to Burlington Coat Factory and had always wanted to go there. I asked him if he knew where one was located as he seemed to know the cities like the back of his hand. He said there was one right next to the Micro Store where we were headed. He wanted to pick up some printer supplies and had visited the store as it had good prices. I purchased a new coat and called it a great shopping day. We had one more stop left to Trader Joe's in Maple Grove. Byron loves to go to Trader Joe's for the unique foods that you can't find in any grocery store in a small town. As we headed to the cashier, the lady behind me commented on what a gorgeous coat I was wearing. Byron made small conversation with the young cashier, who seemed interested in his work as an electrical engineer. When we left the store, I was headed for a cup of coffee for the ride home. Dilan, Byron, and I walked into Caribou, and I told them to order as it was my treat. After I came out from the restroom, Byron was having an interesting conversation with the barista, and in the process our drinks became mixed up. After figuring out who ordered what, he looked at the barista and said, "And I have to eat her cooking!" I smiled back at the barista as we left, thankful for the light conversation. Byron always seemed to be making conversations with everyone he encountered.*

The next Monday, February 18, I got home from work, and Byron was not there. I was home late as I had attended our annual employee awards event. I was receiving my 15-year award certificate so wanted to attend. I knew that Byron must have gone to his house and he went alone. I was always worried when he went there alone as I knew it bothered him to be there. Maybe he needed to work on things and come to terms with what happened so he can move on to some normalcy. I finally saw him walking back to our house around 7:00. I could tell when he walked in the door that it was a hard day for him. He talked about needing to get his license plates for his car and the correct tabs got on the wrong plate. His face was all red, and it might have been from the very cold walk back to our house, but I think it was from the stress of spending a few hours in his house. He seemed irritated the whole evening and finally went to bed a couple of hours later.

The next evening, he was in a much happier mood. Other than the fact that his neighbor, Bill, had been spouting off about how his attorney and the private investigator weren't doing their jobs, he was laughing at the jokes on the Big Bang Theory. *Byron had never seen that show before. I told him once that he would remember living with us because we got him hooked on watching the* Big Bang Theory. *Byron didn't have cable TV in his home because he thought it too expensive. He got irritated about the bill and had it disconnected. Upon first moving in with us, he seemed irritated with the fact that we have TVs everywhere in the house. He is very conservative and had been raised that way. He even drinks day-old coffee because he doesn't want it to go to waste. He will eat moldy food so it doesn't go to waste, removing the mold first. The* Big Bang Theory *is a show about intelligent, nerdy guys with few social graces, especially the main character, Sheldon. One night as we were watching an episode, Byron spoke out the exact words right before Sheldon delivered the same line. I looked at him and he looked at me and we both started laughing hysterically! It was the episode where Penny was down on her luck, standing at her apartment door, locked out, and carrying groceries when one of the paper bags falls apart and the groceries fall to the floor. Sheldon comes out of his apartment to a crying Penny, and she is sobbing and telling him about how everything is going wrong and that last, but not least, she just swallowed a fly. Byron said, "That's okay, flies are all protein and good for you." Two seconds later, Sheldon delivered the same line! It was one of his first times watching the sitcom!*

At times, when I looked out our living room window and down Elm Street, I felt sad and somewhat eerie. It was a tragedy for everyone. Misguided kids lost their lives, and a neighbor and friend's life would never be the same. This should be the prime of his life enjoying retirement, but instead he was facing murder charges. The neighbors living on Elm Street had reported that he liked to scare the neighbors with gun shots. They complained of his shooting. It was actually to keep the beavers from destroying the trees along his river property. At one point, beavers had eaten thirty-five trees that he and his dad planted, so Byron needed to thin out the beaver population on his property. He had suspected the neighbor's daughter of coming on his property as he came home one day to find the garage had been broken into with boxes opened and glass broken all over the floor. He had purchased a collection of German beer steins, and many were missing and broken. There was a trail of clothing back to that neighbor's property. Since our front room window faced Elm Street, Byron, now living with us, had a perfect view of the traffic going down to his property and the neighbor's. Vehicles would stop at their house for a few minutes or so and come back out. It was so unusual and so consistent that he started filming the cars and logging dates and license numbers. My sister-in-law told me once that she and a friend were driving together and her friend said she had to make a stop at that house and it was that very neighbor living next to Byron. Her friend came out with a small brown paper bag, but my sister-in-law never questioned the contents. Byron had also heard stories while he was in the county jail awaiting a bail hearing about drug activity in the family living next door to him. Byron mentioned this to one of the deputies, and he was told that the DEA had to deal with that. It is very suspicious yet timely. Thursday seemed to be the day the supplier drops off the product in a small maroon truck, and then the parade of activity started with about twelve to fifteen cars. They would stop in for a few minutes and leave. Some of the vehicles are very predictable and scheduled. He spent several hours each day writing all the license plate numbers down and recording the type of vehicle and how long they stayed at this home. Their daughter was also a babysitter for Dilan after school when he was in kindergarten. One day my jeweled calculator was gone, too, along with some makeup. I called her mom to ask if she happened to have taken it by mistake. Her mom looked, and it was in her backpack. She said she would return it to me. Byron was told from another inmate while in the Morrison County Jail that the neighbor girl was referred to as the Pill Queen. Byron had wanted to try to capture some documentation on their unusual traffic for a long time but couldn't get it. Living in our house had given him a golden opportunity to keep track of all the traffic going down his street. License plates were recorded along with timelines. All was turned over to the local police. Eventually, he was told that no license plates matched the known drug dealers in town, and nothing was ever heard after that. Also notable is that after Byron reported this activity, the unusual traffic ceased down Elm Street.

John came home after talking with some people downtown that a Little Falls business owner had an encounter with Nick Brady about two months before the shooting. John had run into Scott at the courthouse while attending Cody Kasper's hearing on aiding and abetting theft at the Smith residence. Scott said that Nick Brady had driven to his house in September (2012) at fifty miles per hour demanding to see his son, who had been talking with Nick's girlfriend at the time. Now Scott weighs 275 pounds, and Nick came to the door demanding to see him right away and stated that he "was going to kill the kid." Scott, of course, told him to leave immediately. Nick would not leave and started calling Scott an old man and told him to get out of the way. During this time, Scott's wife called 911. When the deputy arrived, he assumed for some reason that Scott was the one causing trouble, but when his wife explained it was Nick and company (there was another carload of kids with him in another vehicle), the sheriff's deputy told Nick, "You are lucky to be alive. The homeowner could have shot you for coming onto his property like a maniac, and I wouldn't have so much as issued a citation to him."

Scott and his wife were reluctant to get involved in Byron's trial because his wife was afraid that their son would encounter retaliation from certain friends of Nick Brady. After giving it some thought, Scott wanted to help Byron and asked for the incident report of his encounter with Nick Brady. He was told by the sheriff's department that there was *no* record of this incident ever occurring. Other incidences of calls with threats to Byron by friends of Nick Brady when he was out on bail were also requested, but records were not available. The incidences occurred, and law enforcement intervened, but records of those incidences involving Nick Brady and friends were never presented.

Byron and I often looked at information on Facebook. He didn't have an account, so I did searches through mine. One night he requested to look at Cody Kasper's page. Chase Fortier was listed as one of his friends. It was verified in an investigative report that Chase was in possession of one of the guns stolen from Byron's home in October. In fact, we also heard a rumor that Chase Fortier had a garage full of stolen goods from other burglaries that he and his friends had committed. One day, allegedly, a van came to his home and emptied the garage. It was also rumored and later proven that he had disposed of one of the guns by burying it near the river by his home. He finally took the sheriff to that location after his mother found out and made him call Sheriff Wetzel. Chase's mother was a close relative of the sheriff.

So far, Byron had not received a letter that they were prosecuting him. It could possibly be the fact that he was related to Sheriff Wetzel. The county attorney promised that all those involved in the burglary of October 27 at the Byron Smith residence would be prosecuted to the full extent of the law. To date, no one has been prosecuted for stealing about fifty thousand dollars' worth of gold and valuables on that day. On Cody's Facebook page, we find that he had a girlfriend who had posted comments on his page about how she loved him and that he was so sweet to her. Classmates overheard her one day talking about how she hoped Cody wouldn't get into any more trouble because she needed a prom date. This was during the time he had been issued a summons to appear at Byron's trial. His name was splashed all over the front page of the local newspaper as the one who had committed burglaries at the home of Byron Smith. His sister commented on FB, "This bull—— will all be over soon!" Cody Kasper admittedly stole from Byron, who took an interest and wanted to help him in life. Cody introduced his friend Nick to Byron, and their choices and actions caused this tragedy.

The next afternoon, Byron went back to his house again to check on things. This is the third time he has gone there alone. He usually comes back in a very quiet, nonsocial mood. He was gone about three hours and when he came back, he was surprisingly talkative, in fact overly talkative. He was working on some video equipment and cleaning up some things. He calls his brother there from his landline as he feels safer talking on a landline versus a cell phone. He is always thinking about security and privacy. He shared that he had been talking to Bruce about buying some neighboring property to Byron's homes. If they own a certain amount of acreage, they can remain rural and not part of the city, ultimately saving tax dollars.

One evening Byron is helping Dilan study for a biology test. They have been absorbed in homework for almost three hours. He is grilling Dilan with question after question. It's amazing how much brain knowledge he has about plants, which is what the test is on. I remember very little detail of some of the things I learned in high school. Who does? This morning right away he had asked me a question that would probably stump me, and it was, "Who was the one pope that was not elected by the people?" I thought for a moment and said that it had to be the very first one. I was right and I think he was surprised that I got it right. Most of the time he uses such unusual words that I have to ask him what the word means. He helped Dilan study for three hours without a break. I thanked him after they were done, but he seemed to enjoy and even thrive in that opportunity to work with a young person in that capacity.

The next Friday night brought in snowy weather. "The roads are too slippery to drive out of town in this weather," I said. We decided on Cabin Fever, since it is right down the road. Byron didn't want to go. He said, "There are too many locals." I thought he may be getting more comfortable as he did go to the West Side Café once for breakfast without incident. He still does not want to go anywhere local. His life has completely changed now. He mentioned over dinner one night that he wasn't invited to judge a science fair in Minneapolis this year. He was always invited every year. He wasn't invited to a Boy Scout retreat as he has been in the past. His life very much had revolved around being a Boy Scout adviser and mentor. "That part of my life is over," he said one night. We all felt very sad for him.

John took him for a drive on Sunday (March 17) to visit his mom in Crosby. They left while I was in church on Sunday. John is very diligent about visiting his mother. They took her out for a chicken dinner at Coach's, a bar and grill restaurant in Deerwood. They have a chicken special every Sunday and all the locals go there. It is a noisy place, but the food is excellent, so you can overlook the noisy environment. When they got back, Byron was telling me that he mentioned to my mother-in-law about Indian finger weaving. He had instructions in his home somewhere, and he would retrieve them and teach her how to do this. Being she is part Native American, this would be a perfect craft for her. She loves to crochet, and this could be something she could do in conjunction with that. He also brought a brochure for a Scandinavian Festival in June at the Nisswa Pioneer Village. He seemed like he really wanted to attend, so we will have to make sure we are free that weekend. He also mentioned that there are several powwows held during the summer and one, in particular, is a good one with a craft and food festival near Bemidji. Byron then informed us that he knows the dance of this ceremonial celebration as he has had the opportunity to dance in several powwows. He has the full ceremonial dress and everything. All three of us, John, me, and Dilan, looked at each other in amazement. Byron, dancing in a powwow, was a bit of a surprise.

I was watching the Good Wife *on Sunday night, and Byron came in, sat down, and turned on the lamp. "I have something to show you and I showed them to Dilan as a contribution to his education," he said. He told me to open my hands and placed two unusual looking gold coins in it. They looked like foreign money but inscribed in English and were quite heavy. He said they were just like the others that had been stolen. (He had about $25,000 worth of gold coins stolen in the October 27 burglary.) The coins in my hand were worth over $2,000. He had purchased them when gold was $300 an ounce and now it was at $1,200 an ounce. Each of the coins was a pure ounce of gold. I asked him what Dilan said when he saw them, and of course, he was amazed. I can't imagine what high school kids did with 20 gold coins worth that much money as they have never been recovered. The thought of pawning them or selling them would certainly raise questions. What happened to 20 gold coins worth about $25,000? I asked if he could get reimbursed from his insurance company for the loss. He said, "No, the coins would have had to be covered under a separate policy and are not traceable anyway." He would never recoup the loss of them.*

One Sunday afternoon Byron wanted to go for a walk in the woods. It was a sunny day, but windy and cold. We went to check out his rental property, which is what he calls the house he just bought in

July. He bought the 5,300-square-foot home in July (2012) as it adjoins his family property. He had wanted to buy it for years, but the owner wanted too much money and they finally settled on a price that was agreeable. At one time she had wanted $450,000 for it. It is a grand home with two fireplaces, six bedrooms, five bathrooms, a huge kitchen, and a sun room. When I first saw the home that was tucked back in the woods, I thought it was a dream home. The burglars had broken into the detached garage of this property too. Byron has the doors double bolted and double locked too. The padlocks are readily visible sending a message forbidding entry. As Byron toured us through his home, he showed us the bedroom that he would be sleeping in as soon as all the snow melts. He is planning to live there permanently and board up all the windows in his other home. We walked over to his Elm Street home. He was looking for a camera so that Dilan could use it for one of his classes. He proceeded to tell me all the things he had wanted to change some day, the floors, the laundry room, and the kitchen remodeling. We went downstairs where the shootings took place. This was the first time I had ever been down there. You could see the bullet markers in the cement wall—about six of them with numbers assigned to each hole. The carpet looked clean, but he said he had cleaned best he could one day. He seemed nervous to be there as he was quickly moving about. He stopped to show me some of the souvenirs he had purchased from all his travels while desperately looking for that camera. The basement is filled with many electronics parts and stereos and record albums by the thousands. In his shop area is where the monitors were for the outside cameras. He had to be in that room to view the cameras. On Thanksgiving Day, he was in a different room in his reading area. There are shelves of books and a chair centered in the U-shape of the shelves with a lamp. It's like an intimate, cozy spot to quietly read, but I knew that was the chair where he was reading when he heard the glass break on Thanksgiving Day. He still seemed a bit uncomfortable and uneasy there, but I could tell he wanted to find that camera and quickly get out. Then he started talking to me about the shootings while we were there. "You couldn't see their faces as they were coming down." The stairway is narrow, and his chair faces the stairs from the side. He went on to tell me that if he is found guilty, he will make a public statement that lets all criminals know that they can *be safe in the city of Little Falls because criminals are welcome here and are protected declaring that a homeowner is not protected by the sheriff's office. His motto for criminals was, "Come to Little Falls! Nothing will happen to you." I was standing there thinking how sad it would be if he really was found guilty. It is not a concept I had given much thought to. Sadness and anxiousness overcame me, and I just wanted to immediately leave his home. On the walk back, I noticed that the neighbor girl was outside smoking a cigarette. This was the same girl that Byron suspected of stealing his military jacket and leaving a joint in one of his cars. She had been there when we walked by upon entry and had stood there and took a picture of us walking by with her camera. For what reason, I am not sure.*

Byron has stopped the video recording of the Elm Street traffic this week. He says he has enough information to submit to the DEA.

On Easter Sunday 2013, Byron is recollecting the event of his Thanksgiving Day events to Mr. St. Onge, who is visiting our home this evening with his young son. Here is how he tells it: He is downstairs reading. He hears someone trying to get in the door. It rattles. The intruder tries another door. It rattles too. He has double locked them because of previous break-ins. He sees the shadow of a person moving across the wall downstairs. Maybe they will go away because all doors are locked and dead bolted. He hears them now upstairs, running across the wooden deck. He hears them try more doorknobs. Suddenly a window is breaking. He hears glass shatter now. He is in fear for his life. "This is gonna be bad," he says to himself. He stops the story there and says the rest will come out in court. George St. Onge came over to visit because he, too, has been burglarized many times at his business where he sells motorcycle parts outside Little Falls. He actually has trails leading outside his property where thieves have entered his property so many times. He has called the sheriff's department only to be told, "There is not much we can do." Mr. St. Onge could identify with Byron's frustrations with being burglarized so many times as Byron had with no results in finding out who was committing the crimes and getting the property back.

CHAPTER 4
COPING

On April 23, a grand jury was summoned to decide if there was enough evidence to change the charge from second-degree murder to first degree. It seems as if the lead prosecutor, Pete Orput, wanted to make a name for himself, and rumor was that he wanted to run for attorney general, so this case might gain him the public recognition he might be seeking. It was stated by several locals in the bakery one day that he said this little town was going to make him famous. Upon hearing all this, Byron felt he had been literally bullied by a bunch of thieves and now he was being bullied by the local justice system. Byron wished he had remained overseas in his retirement. The only reason he came back to Little Falls was to take care of his mother, who had broken her hip, so he took an early retirement. He told me, among others, that the most unsafe place for him ended up being Little Falls, Minnesota. The criminal teens who took part in the burglaries of his home were still attending school, running around town, going on with their lives, seemingly without much punishment. Byron Smith had to be relocated out of his own home, and his old opportunities to be a Boy Scout adviser and judge science fairs were no longer a part of his life. They were his life before last Thanksgiving Day. Cody Kasper went to court again on Wednesday because last week he had a test, so the judge rearranged the court schedule to accommodate him. Byron hired a lawyer for his neighbor, Bill, who had been served with a subpoena to appear in front of the grand jury to upgrade his charge. The neighbor was going to be questioned about Byron's phone call to him on the day after Thanksgiving when Byron asked him to call a lawyer. The prosecutor was allowing this attorney into the courtroom but was not happy with the situation. Meshbesher seemed to think the prosecutor wanted to discredit the neighbor as a witness for the defense or possibly charge him as an accessory. None of us ever knew any details about his previous burglaries. The reason Byron never mentioned anything to us was that he wanted to see if law enforcement was doing their job. If a neighbor had a fifty-thousand-dollar burglary, would one not expect an investigation in the neighborhood to see if any of us had seen a strange car or suspicious people in the neighborhood?

During April, I had the chance to travel to San Diego for work. Dilan was bugging me about never going anywhere or taking family vacations, so I asked him if he wanted to go along with me and have a few fun days in California before my conference. Without hesitation, he was on board. In some ways I was shocked that a fifteen-year-old would want to vacation with his mom, but he needed a break from the winter and the recent events that had unfolded in our household. He hadn't really flown anywhere since we went to the Bahamas on a family vacation in 2008. We would fly out together, and then I would send him home so he could get back to school and I could attend my conference. We had a wonderful four days of sightseeing and eating in great restaurants. Aside from the fact that the weather was warm and sunny, it was nice to bond with my son. We spent a day at the San Diego Zoo and Balboa Park, where we lingered in the photography museum. There was a tarot card reader in the park, so we decided to have some fun and have a reading. As I chose the cards carefully, I picked every card that meant happiness and good fortune. The card reader told me I even had wealth coming my way, and who doesn't like to hear that! When Dilan chose his cards, the adventures/travel cards were displayed. Dilan had fallen in love with California and wanted to move out there by this time, and the reader told him it would eventually happen. He was elated! How fun was all this! I then asked the reader if our friend who was living with us would have a good outcome for his life, too. All I hinted to was that his life was in a bit of turmoil currently, and then I started choosing cards. The first card to be turned was the death card. We were in disbelief as our cards had all been positive and it was fun to listen about the future. With the death card presenting itself, both Dilan and I thought it best not to tell Byron. The card reader did add, though, that he would be okay, but after a long time. We took a taxi back to the hotel and then went on to Mission Beach, Coronado Island, and Coronado Beach, where *Some Like It Hot* was filmed in 1958 with Marilyn Monroe. I felt lost the day I had to put Dilan in a taxi at 5:30 a.m. that morning. He found the gate at the San Diego Airport and headed back to the cold, snowy Minnesota. As he had purchased a couple of California shirts to wear, at least he had some good reminders of sunny California. The Grand Hyatt had a kind concierge who gave me a hug the day I left and told me and my son to come back and see them again. It would be a trip we both would remember.

Back in Minnesota, a huge snowstorm followed me home. I was so glad to see a snow-free tarmac when we landed. I knew snow was close and coming, so at 9:00 p.m. I left the airport and hurried the two-hour drive back home. I would say it was great to be back, but things were basically as I left them, plus I had a ton of work to catch up on because I was gone for eight days.

While we were in California, Byron had moved all his electronics packages from the basement to one of his garages. Over the last several months, he has ordered security and electronic equipment at bargain prices. He told me he wants to install security systems in homes so others won't get robbed like he did. Boxes were piled high to the ceiling in our basement, so it was nice to see my painted walls again. I don't think he spent much time inside his home, but the other night he couldn't sleep so he went down there at 3:00 in the morning to check on things. I think he is still afraid of being burglarized. Byron continues to talk about life after the verdict in a positive way. Tomorrow night he says he is going to try sleeping at his other (rental) home. He has a mattress set up with electric blankets. The window to a bedroom downstairs is covered in cardboard so no one can see in. He's going to give it a try. This will be his first night sleeping away from our home.

The next evening, I attended our hospital's volunteer banquet. I agreed to help serve dinner to the volunteers who were honored for their work at our hospital. Another employee from the clinic was late in coming to help. As she dashed into the banquet, apologizing for being late, she stated that she had just come from grand jury duty. After we served the volunteers, we were invited to sit down and eat. Someone had asked her kiddingly about being on a grand jury for *a murder* case. She just stated she couldn't discuss anything, but she told us to just think about what happened in Little Falls last year. I sat there in silence, not knowing if I should speak about it and just tell my opinion and how those kids should have been home with family instead of robbing people. But I continued my silence. I later learned that she had told many about how she voted. She was talking about it on her breaks from jury duty during lunch. I couldn't believe how she was talking about this to everyone. Each juror was to abide by confidentiality in these cases, and she absolutely had not done that. She later told an employee that her son had been stabbed to death at a young age by a friend, so from that experience she confessed that she voted for a first-degree murder indictment. Another grand juror was an elderly woman who had lost a young daughter as well. This incident and revelations were reported to Byron's attorney.

As I was drove to work this morning, I prayed for Byron that it would all be okay and they would not indict him of first-degree murder. I had given him a big hug before I left for work today. I saw tears in his eyes as I left. This was the first night since December 18 that he is not staying in our home. It was April 23 that day. I called him to make sure he was okay. I was worried about him. I had called Bruce to let him know that he was staying alone, and Bruce seemed to think it was time for him to get into a different routine. Calling him set my mind a little more at ease. He didn't seem to be worried at this point and seemed convinced there was no way that they can indict him of first-degree murder. I hoped and prayed that he was right. I didn't realize it at the time, but Bryon stayed the night elsewhere because he was afraid law enforcement would find him more readily in our home. If he was indicted, there was a chance he would be arrested again. If he stayed in his rental house, no car could get there. John built a barricade so no traffic could go down to his other property. He didn't really want to be alone. He just wanted to protect himself in case there was another arrest warrant if the grand jury favored first degree.

The next day I called Dilan about 4:00 p.m. I knew he was home from school. I told him to not answer the door. I had called Byron to see if he was joining us for dinner. He sounded fine but declined and added, "You don't know anything." I knew exactly what he meant. He was going into hiding in case he was indicted and they wanted him back in jail. When I got home, I explained to Dilan to not say anything to anyone. I had driven past the courthouse, and there were no extra cars to indicate a grand jury was still in session. In fact, at four forty the lot was almost empty. Either the members were let go early or they had made a decision. We locked down the house and shut the drapes so if law enforcement came to our home looking for him, we would not respond.

I got up at six o'clock the following morning as usual and noticed Byron's bedroom door was closed. If the door was closed, that meant he was sleeping. He left the door open at all other times. Then I noticed his hat and shoes. This was a good sign. That meant there must have been a decision or he just didn't want to be alone this morning. He usually slept until about eight o'clock each morning, so John called me after I pulled into the parking lot for work and said that the decision was a first-degree murder indictment. I sat in my car for a bit when I heard the news. I couldn't believe it. I was in tears walking into the hospital, trying to figure out how this happened. My friend Renee was there, and we talked for a bit. It helped to discuss it with someone who was understanding of his situation and supported me. She was always concerned about what was going on, and since she didn't live in Little Falls, she was like a godsend, and I felt safe talking with her. Luckily, Byron's attorney had blocked a subsequent arrest and another request for more bail. Judge Anderson ordered that bail would be continued as is. Byron called me around 3:00 p.m. and needed a ride from the courthouse. Since I was too far away, I called John to pick him up at the courthouse. When I got home from work, he seemed in a fairly good mood considering the day's events. We all ate dinner together as if nothing had changed. He wasn't talking about it.

Byron still seems to be taking this bad news in stride. The temperature is finally warming up, so he can go down to his property regularly and do some yard work and not be bothered by anyone. He has a makeshift bedroom set up on his adjacent property and is camping out. John has gone to Pipestone for the weekend and Dilan is going to prom. A senior girl asked him because she didn't have a date and wanted to go, so he agreed to go. There is a group of them together. They went to St. Cloud for dinner and came back to the house, and we went to Maple Island Park down by the dam and took some pictures. They all seemed to be having fun. When we arrived back at our home, his friends notice Byron's camera set up taking pictures of his street, and they were wondering about all the spy stuff we have in our home. I guess I am used to it as being part of our décor these days, so I don't give it much thought. There is the video camera set up facing Elm Street, binoculars on hand, a speed gun, and a telescope. I guess one would wonder about all that stuff. One of his friends even asked if we were spies. I had to laugh. Well, we actually were watching the suspicious activity of the neighborhood.

His attorney would try to get the indictment dismissed. There were a list of many reasons, including the prosecutor's opening statement to the grand jury. The prosecutor was not to represent the victim but to represent justice. The prosecutor failed to present the grand jury with specific evidence: text messages, criminal history of both burglars, and the defendant's internet usage were untruths told to the grand jury. The prosecutor also invited irrelevant testimony from the decedents' mothers in an effort to impassion the grand jury to indict.

According to the grand jury transcript, the judge began by giving specific instructions. A grand jury was selected randomly and was rare in rural communities, so he pointed out the extreme importance of their service. He specifically asked if any of the jurors had personal reasons that they could not serve for the next two days and, finally, if anyone believed they could not be fair and impartial. There was no response from any of the jurors. He then administered an oath.

The jurors had to stand, raise their right hands, and swear that they would inquire and decide this matter to the best of their ability and according to law would *not* discuss these grand jury recommendations with anyone, so help them God. The grand jury responded with "I do." Judge Anderson explained that he would not be present and was not required to be as well as the bailiff. The county attorney would be present as a legal adviser to answer any questions. He also explained that twelve jurors must agree on the indictment, but the decision did not need to be unanimous. Witnesses would be called, and each juror was entitled to ask questions. The judge instructed each juror that they were not to disclose the testimony given to any other person. The proceedings were entirely secret, and the judge repeated this. He also stated that no juror should report to anybody how they voted or what was said or done in the grand jury. It was to be an entirely secret proceeding. Again, the judge reiterated the secrecy of the proceedings: "Each grand juror must keep secret everything that occurs during the grand jury proceedings and everything said or discussed during grand jury deliberations." Finally, each witness was called and raised their right hands for the oath, and Prosecutors Pete Orput and Brent Wartner gave jurors their numbers so they could be addressed by number. There were twenty-three grand jurors. So on April 23, 2013, this grand jury would decide whether there was enough evidence to upgrade his second-degree murder charge to a first-degree charge.

To begin, Orput, again reiterated the judge's instructions of complete secrecy. He told them that some of the evidence might be disturbing and they might want to talk with others about it, especially if they were having emotional problems. The judge's instructions must be followed. Orput then began his opening statements taking the jury back to October 27, 2012, when Byron Smith had been burglarized. On page 37 of the transcript, he stated that Byron had set up some surveillance video cameras throughout his home. (Actually, cameras were not set up throughout his home. There were four exterior cameras: three pointed at two out of three doors and one aimed at the sidewalk approaching the main door.) Also, on page 37, Orput stated that Smith said, "There goes the bitch," as he and his neighbor saw the neighbor girl drive by. This was a false statement. Byron Smith did not know what the neighbor girl even looked like. Orput goes on to say that when Smith heard the doorknobs rattling and someone peering into the picture window that "he had access to that information, knowing who is there, the size of the person, and essentially what they looked like." This was also untrue. The monitor deck for the cameras was in an entirely different room from where he was sitting and reading when Nick Brady peered through the window. Byron would have had to go through two doors around two corners about fifty feet away from where he was sitting to view the monitor. He did not get up from his reading chair to look at the monitors. Rather he was hoping that with all the dead bolts he had installed on each door, the intruder would give up and leave. On page 39 of the transcript, Orput stated that after Byron shot Haile Kifer, she screamed, "I'm sorry." This was also a false statement. According to Byron, there was no screaming at all. Her only words were, "Oh my god, oh my god." Orput also told the jurors that after he shot Kifer, he tried to clean up the mess. This was not true either. He spread a rug as a cover to reduce the psychological stress of the scene. There was no cleaning. He was thinking more intruders might be coming and he would have to defend himself against them as well. Orput continued to tell the jurors that he spent the rest of the day moving around the house, surfing the internet, on eBay, and then went to bed. This, also, was untrue. Special Agent Cheung's report later verified that computer activity was only that of normal automatic updates. The statement "went to bed" was totally false, and even when Smith was admitted to the county jail, he stated how thankful he was for the safety of a cell, and after two days without sleep, he might be finally able to feel he can sleep safely.

On page 42, Orput continued his false statements to the grand jury. He told them that he called his neighbor Bill Anderson to find him a criminal defense lawyer. Anderson had testified that Byron asked him for an attorney. By saying "a criminal defense lawyer," it implied the defendant's admission of guilt, which was not what was said. On page 44 of this transcript, Orput stated that the BCA (Bureau of Criminal Apprehension) learned Byron had a significant amount of computer and electronic equipment, and they called Special Agent Janet Nelson as they investigated his home and saw a DVR, a digital video recorder, that was recording the surveillance video. This falsely implied that the investigators observed this. However, Byron had told Deputy Jeremy Luberts about the recorder and the necessity of turning it off immediately. Byron gave Luberts the password and told him how to operate it.

When Jeremy Luberts took the witness stand, Orput asked him if he had reported a previous burglary. Smith specifically told Luberts on October 27 that his adjacent property had also been broken into. (This report was lost by Sheriff Wetzel's office until mid-December, when it appeared, but still no formal investigation until this day.) Also, Deputy Jamie Luberts had received notice of the previous burglary on or about September 10, in which two guns were stolen, and also a burglary around the first week in July, when $3,200 in cash was stolen. There were four burglaries, two of which he had certain knowledge and two of which his fellow investigator and twin brother, Jeremy Luberts, had certain knowledge from Byron Smith's previous interviews.

On page 134 of the transcript, Juror 23 asked if the children had any prior problems or been caught vandalizing other people's property. Sgt. Jeremy Luberts responded, "Not that I am fully aware of." Between the reporting of this event on Thanksgiving Day and up until April 23, 2013, it became well-known in Little Falls that Nick Brady had vandalized and burglarized Dick Johnson's residence. Furthermore, there was reporting that his prescription medications were found in Brady's vehicle after they had broken into Smith's home on Thanksgiving Day. There was also a police incident report naming Haile Kifer as a shoplifter at Coborn's Superstore. All incident reports were supposedly read by law officers daily.

As Special Agent Nathaniel Pearlson gave testimony, he explained that when they entered the Smith property, they had two priorities. One was to secure the video equipment as it only had so much memory and would start overwriting and they might lose evidence. This substantiates that Byron was cooperating with law enforcement as he had given Jeremy Luberts operating instructions and the password for the equipment.

When Agent Janet Nelson was on the witness stand, Orput asked if Byron's laptop was located next to his reading chair. Nelson replied that it was not and that it was next to the sofa. Orput then again remarked, "Which is adjacent to the chair." This, too, was a false statement by Orput. He was trying to establish to the jurors that the laptop was within reach of Byron sitting in his chair, and it was not. The laptop was on the other side of two bookcases, which were between the chair and the sofa, far out of reach.

It's also interesting to note that seven law enforcement vehicles, several with more than one officer, followed later by the sheriff's vehicle, for a total of eight, came to Smith's house with a search warrant for more computers three hours after Byron's brother, Bruce, had left the property. This happened on November 29, 2012, six days after Byron's arrest.

Agent Nelson also testified that the camera outside Byron's home captured him entering his home at 11:45 a.m. Nick Brady was seen on the camera at 12:33 p.m. There was no activity in between those times. Nick was seen on camera 1 and 2. He walked down the stairs (outside on the deck) and appeared on camera 3. At 12:34 p.m., Nick Brady tried the door and was peering into the window. He had a hood pulled over his face to try to conceal his identity. At 12:35 p.m., he was seen walking in front of camera 3 with both hands over his face. He apparently had observed the other surveillance cameras. He went over to move the other camera. He then peeked around the side of the garage, and you could see Haile in the trees. At 12:51, you could see Haile running across the driveway and the grass from the trees on camera 4, and then she would walk around the back of the house and appear on camera 2. She, too, was holding the hood over her face. She was also on her phone. At 12:52, she walked off the deck to the west into camera 4 and was now in front of the house. At 12:53 she would walk out of the breezeway and continue across the front yard in the direction of the sheds. Agent Nelson also explained she created a marker list from the audio recording. She created a disk with selected audio clips from the six-hour, twenty-four-minute file.

She stated she could hear the sound of the setup, the device handled and set in place. After about a half hour she heard a thump and breaking glass. She heard someone walking around inside a house. Then she heard several shots being fired. After that she stated that she heard a man's voice making statements randomly. She created a written document and called it a marker list, a four-page document. She created another disk of marker 6 through marker 40, which captured the shootings She explained how she reduced the sound of background noise so she could hear more of the vocal statements, which made some portions sound more hissy in the background. It was digital compression. Juror 13 asked why the markers were not in order. She explained that going through visual representation of the audio, when she heard the spoken word, she created a marker at that point. Then she would go back to the previous area of audio that hadn't been marked and would create a marker for that. The software creates markers in numerical order, but it places them in the chronological order they were made. That was why they were out of order.

That was the end of testimony on day 1 of the grand jury proceedings. Day 2 began at 9:20 a.m. on April 24, 2013. Haile Kifer's mother, Jenny, was the first to testify. Jenny admitted that Haile had been in treatment for chemical dependency in October or November. When Haile returned, she was just turning eighteen and wanted to live on her own or with her cousin Rachel Brady. Jenny then showed the jurors a picture of her daughter in her junior year of high school, another with a trophy she had won in gymnastics from the tenth grade, and a family picture that had been taken last summer at a cousin's wedding. Juror 23 asked if Haile had any prior convictions with law enforcement. Jenny stated a minor consumption, but nothing else. In fact, Haile Kifer did have a shoplifting violation at Coborn's in August of 2012 and was released to home with her mother according to the citation report. The next witness was Nick Brady's mom, Kim Brady. She told the jurors he was in the eleventh grade at Pillager High School and that he loved the outdoors and working on his cars. She, too, showed pictures of her son. Juror 3 asked how Nick and Haile were related. Nick's father, Jason, and Haile's mom were sister and brother. Next BCA Agent Chad Museus was on the witness stand. He testified to the search for more electronics at the Smith home, along with a laptop computer they hadn't seized. He confirmed that Byron Smith's toxicology report showed no signs of impairment and he had made calls to his brother on November 22 and 23. He confirmed that he searched the Kifer home and found a few empty containers that had contained cold medicine. When asked by Juror 3 if he had searched her current residence in Sobieski, Museus said he had not. Grand Juror 5 asked if there was ever a search done at the Brady home. He responded that he had not done one. He was also questioned on the text messages by Juror 8, and Museus stated that there was no information on the text messages that would indicate anything regarding the Smith residence at all. (Note here there actually was a reference to Bryan's [spelled wrong by Cody Kasper] in a text between Nick Brady and Cody Kasper about when they were going again. Also, a text between Rachel and Haile referred to items taken by them in a previous burglary.) Museus states that their text was just a "Hi, how are you doing" kind of text. Nothing relevant to the investigation. (Actual text message is outlined in Chapter VIII).

Dr. Kelly Mills, a forensic pathologist for Ramsey County, was the next witness. She explained the autopsy process on Nick Brady. He was fully clothed, a bit of blood on his face and paper bags on hands in order to preserve evidence. Brady had gloves on his hands, and there was a gunshot wound defect to his hands and gloves. A second bullet wound was to the right side of his head and another to his abdomen. She described in great detail the amount of residue around the wounds, which showed proximity of the firearm and reentry wounds. She concluded with the fatal gunshot wound was the one that went to the back of his hand and proceeded through his head. She conducted Haile's autopsy next. Again, Haile was fully clothed, with jeans, shirt, and a black hooded sweatshirt. A gunshot wound was identified on the left side of her face, but no evidence of close-range fire. A second gunshot was discovered behind the left ear with no close-range gunfire. She stated that this would have been the fatal one. Another was under the right side of her chin or front side of neck. There was another gunshot to her abdomen and then one to her arm. Another to her left chest wall through left lung and ended in the back posterior chest wall. Again, she detailed at length for these grand jurors the size, amount of soot, stippling, and close-range indicators of all gunshot wounds and those fragments she recovered. Haile also had healing, incised wounds on her forearms. The types of wounds one would see in different types of personalities but sometimes with those who have committed suicide. Classically, these were cutting wounds of trying to feel pain. She had thirteen on the front of the right forearm, seven on the back of the right forearm and thirty-two on the front of the left forearm and fourteen on the back of the left forearm. These wounds all occurred before the shooting. Her toxicology report showed negative for alcohol but positive for marijuana metabolite or THC metabolites and dextromethorphan in her urine. In Dr. Mills's opinion, she would have been intoxicated at the time of her death. With the level of marijuana, she had, it stayed in the blood for roughly two days after smoking or utilizing marijuana. Jurors began to ask questions about the fatal shots and if it would have rendered either of them disabled. She answered that in her opinion, an individual getting any of those types of wounds that would strike vital structures, it would have altered, to a degree, but not rendered them unconscious or unable to move.

The witness testimony concluded around 1:15 p.m., and grand jurors were given final instructions. At approximately 3:15, they were ready to vote. Twelve or more grand jurors favored an indictment according to the jury foreman, and so it was issued.

On August 5, 2013, Meshbesher & Associates filed a Petition for Discretionary Review to the Court of Appeals of the State of Minnesota, which described the mistakes made by the prosecution in the grand jury proceedings. In question specifically were the prosecutor's opening statements to the grand jury, which misstated the evidence, was argumentative and unduly impressed for an indictment. The prosecutor's troublesome statement regarding that Smith was viewing the monitors and could see "who was there, the size of the person, knowing essentially what they looked like" was the most troublesome. Besides being inaccurate, these were comments aimed at defeating a self-defense claim. The factual inaccuracies did not end there. The prosecutor specifically stated to the grand jury that Haile Kifer told Smith "I'm sorry" before she was shot. That statement was not on the recording. Next, the prosecutor stated at the end of the day on November 22, 2012, Smith surfed the internet and went to bed as though nothing out of the ordinary had happened. Not only was there no evidence that Smith went to bed, but there was ample evidence that he remained awake and in fear for his life as he thought more attackers were coming to break-in. The phrase "went to bed" further eroded any chance of the grand jury giving serious thought to any self-defense claim. The mothers of the deceased were called as witnesses and typically might voice grievances at sentencing. Their testimony was calculated to impassion the grand jury against Smith and indict on emotion, not legal grounds. Meshesher cited another case in *State v. Grose* 387 N.W.2d 182 (Minn. App 1986), the court of appeals addressed a plethora of improper documents, misstatements, and procedural violations by the prosecutor. In upholding that dismissal of the indictments, the court held that the actions may have improperly influenced the grand jury.

Of course, the State filed a response in opposition to dismiss the indictment. In that document the prosecution stated that it was not improper for him to describe what he believed the evidence would show as long as the grand jurors were instructed to make their own decision on the evidence. The jurors were instructed to make their own decisions on the evidence. The prosecution also argued that having the mothers testify was proper. In a homicide prosecution, the state might offer information about a victim's life but might not use as an attempt to influence the jury's decision on the basis of prejudice or passion (*State v. Buggs*, 581 N.W.2d 329, 342 [Minn. 1988)]. The prosecution might present spark of life evidence so long as it did not inflame the passions of the jury or invoke undue sympathy. According to the prosecution, the testimony of Haile's mother was only seven pages and Nick's was five pages. The length and content of the testimony with photographs was well within the limits set by the Minnesota Supreme Court (stated in the state's memorandum in opposition to dismiss the indictment).

After the grand jury proceeding, I had emailed a gentleman from North Dakota that had contacted us after Byron was let out of jail. His name is John "Jack" Ertelt, and he had a similar situation happen to him in North Dakota with the constant burglarizing of his property, including the stealing of guns. He wants to help Byron and offer his experience in dealing with law enforcement and the courts. At first when he called, I thought he might be one of those crazy people that had called us wanting information, but he turned out to be a good and concerned friend. He wanted to meet Byron, but this attorney did not want him talking to anyone outside his support group. I told Jack that it would have to wait until after his next court appearance, which was July 1.

The next night as I made dinner, our conversation with Byron centered around other things in his life, and he mentioned that he went out with this girl one time who was rather loud, overweight, and had a huge Southern accent. Three things he did not appreciate in a woman. (I had to laugh at that, and he in turn started laughing hysterically as he continued to talk about this date with her.) While riding the train back home after their outing, she leaned into him and "smothered" (his term) herself into his arms and lay like that for the rest of the ride. He absolutely hated it. Dilan had a girlfriend who also smothered him, and they broke it off because Dilan needed his space. He didn't care for any smothering. We both laughed at the story. Then the conversation took a more serious turn as we talked about parents not bringing up their children properly, such as the teens who started terrorizing and burglarizing his home. He asked me what I would have done if my home had been broken into so many times, with my house ransacked, drawers all gone through, everything turned upside down, and particularly my guns stolen. When he did call 911 in October, they basically said there was nothing they could do. They advised him to put up lights (even though the burglaries all occurred during broad daylight) and security cameras. Even the one fingerprint they had, they never sent in. So on Thanksgiving Day when he heard people on his deck rattling door handles and saw a shadow of a person looking in the window trying to gain entry and not ringing the doorbell (supposedly they knew he had left), he asked, "What would you do?"

The sentencing hearing for Cody Kasper was coming up in June. The letter Byron received from the court encouraged him to come as the victim and have his say. John told him that he should definitely attend, but Byron wanted no part of it at this time. Adam Johnson would represent him in this matter. Adam was Meshbesher's assistant attorney. But we decided John should go and tell the court that Cody was the ringleader of this whole gang and that his friend would not have been shot if Cody had not introduced his friend to Byron's property. Maybe Adam was aware of all this, but someone should go and voice their opinion at this hearing on Byron's behalf.

CHAPTER 5
DISCOVERIES

Last evening there were three sheriff's cars and one state trooper in front of our home that had someone pulled over searching his truck. He was a long-haired man in a ponytail with a boxer dog and a young girl. I came back from my walk as he had just been pulled over. The young girl, maybe seventeen years old, looked Hispanic. She was standing at the passenger side of the trooper talking with him as he was proceeding to the truck. I came in the house and told John that a trooper had a guy pulled over right outside our home. Both he and Byron were just sitting on the sofa watching TV. By this time, the trooper had donned gloves and with a flashlight was searching the inside of his truck while the guy and his dog stood outside watching. I had stopped to talk with our next-door neighbors, who were doing yard work, before I headed in, and they had no idea what was going on either. As we watched the trooper search, he pulled out a beer can and a cardboard box, which he placed on the lawn. He then pulled out a plastic Ziploc bag, which looked like a powdered substance. The girl and guy, along with the dog, were each placed in different sheriff's cars after that.

Another odd coincidence was that the suspicious neighbors had left their home, followed by two other strange cars, about a minute or two after all the sheriff's cars had arrived on our street. A friend of John's had heard about this going all over town and assumed that it had something to do with Byron as all this occurred right in front of our home. Byron, in particular, got a chuckle out of that. The rumor was that Byron had committed suicide. Byron would never do that. It was not who he was, although he had every reason to feel defeated and hopeless. Byron was the most disciplined person I had ever met. It was amazing that he had handled these interruptions in his life with a rather accommodating attitude. I don't know if I could move in someone's home and just feel at home right away. But he seemed to be like part of our family, and that happened rather quickly. I told him one day when he finally did move out that I would miss our conversations. He said he would miss that too. We had had a few nice weather days, and he had spent them at his rental property and had stayed overnight there a couple of times. I thanked him the other morning for letting Dilan use his nice camera. Dilan had a photography class this quarter, and he'd taken some impressive pictures with Byron's camera. He said all the other kids were cropping and editing all their pictures, and his were perfect from the start. Byron's camera was about a three-thousand-dollar piece of equipment, and he was letting Dilan use it as he wished. The camera that was stolen was a custom order and he had waited for over a year, it finally arrived in August, only to have it stolen in October. The camera with the lens was worth six thousand dollars. The other night Dilan was doing algebra homework, and Byron had typically helped him throughout the winter. What adult could help a youth with sophomore algebra homework and instantly know the material? Byron could and did. It was almost like he was instantly drawn to youth and being a mentor.

Cody Kasper's sentencing was on June 7. Byron wanted to help Cody when he first met him and while Cody was working for him. Byron received an Affidavit of Restitution, and I told him he needed to fill it out and make Cody accountable for the things he did. Cody's father was in the newspaper for possession of drugs, and nothing was written about him being sentenced or fined, so not sure how he got free from those charges. Rumor had it that he knew all about his son's crimes and advised him to not get caught. Cody betrayed Byron in the worst way anyone could: by bullying and terrorizing a retired man who lived alone. He gained his trust and then stole from him without any thought of hurting the very person that had only good intentions to help him. Because of Cody, Byron's home became unlivable to him. Cody needed to attempt some restitution, but as of yet, none had taken place even though it had been court ordered.

One Sunday morning Dilan and I got up early to drive to visit my mom who lives in Big Stone City, South Dakota. I hadn't seen her since Christmas and was looking forward to the visit. My sisters would be around as well. Byron was telling us all about Big Stone Lake and Lake Traverse. He knew all about their depths, and the fact that if you took a canoe down the river, the only place you would have to get out is at Big Stone. We have a nice visit with many of my sisters and brothers. All were there except Kari and Staci, the youngest in my family. I still did not tell them about our guest and that he is living with us. We will still keep the secret. My mom would be somewhat apprehensive and just worry anyway. It gave mother and son a chance to talk on the two-and-a-half-hour car ride. We talked about his future and his upcoming birthday. He wants to have a birthday bon fire in the backyard next week. He will be 16 years old. I told him to tell Byron so he knew that there would be friends around that night. Byron still doesn't want to be around a lot of teenagers right now. A year ago, he would have relished and flourished in the buzz of the teens and their antics, but now it is very different for him. Dilan is very mature for his age and understands how he can't have friends over much anymore and that he made that choice when asked if it was okay with him if Byron lived with us for a while. We talked about how our lives as a family have changed and how we do things differently now that Byron lives with us. We take Byron out to eat with us, but we don't go in the town of Little Falls. If he needs something, I have a shopping list on the refrigerator that he can write items down if he wants me to pick up anything for him. He doesn't go into stores downtown, although he did take a nice photograph into the local paper one day. He had the photo taken so the paper wouldn't always print the mug shot when they wrote about him. We go out of town for dinners so no one knows him and even gives us a second glance. We have run into people I know only twice, and I have always come forward to say hello and then retreat back to our table. Byron has pretty much made himself at home throughout our whole house. He has shipments from UPS come almost every day with electronics and security equipment. Big boxes collect and are stored in our basement until he has the chance to remove them. I hadn't been given but a day's notice that I was getting a guest long-term, so didn't have much of a chance to prepare. When I knew he was staying, I had cleaned out four drawers in a dresser there so he could store some things. I have only been in that room once since he's been here and that was to vacuum the carpet. I want to respect his privacy and know that his possessions are safe once again. He came back on Sunday evening as he had spent the last two nights at his rental property. I had brought him a piece of strawberry pie from a restaurant that Dilan and I had eaten dinner at. He started talking about strawberry patches in California and how abundant they were. His father had come to visit him while he lived there, and they had gone to a strawberry patch. Now his grandmother Smith was addicted to berry picking. His dad made a comment that Grandma Smith would have been in heaven at this berry patch. It brought Byron to tears talking about this. He talks fondly of his parents and grandparents, even mentioning that Grandpa Smith would go fishing just to get away for a while. His grandmother would pick whatever berries were ripe, even chokecherries, and pick for days.

Byron began to work on his list of stolen items for Cody Kasper's court hearing. It was a project that took him most of the day. He then drove to the courthouse and delivered the list to the correction's officer. If he hadn't completed the form, he feared the county could keep all unclaimed items from a search in connection with a suspected crime. He didn't want Morrison County to auction off his possessions for the coffee and doughnut fund, so that was enough motivation along with the urging of his attorney.

When he was finished, Byron showed me the completed list of all items stolen that he turned into the court: July was $3,100 in cash while he was mowing lawn on the island near his property. In September, a chainsaw, gas-siphoning kit, and copper wire were taken valued at $1,000 and another $1,000 in damages at his rental property. In October (2012), the following items were taken: Nikon camera, $3,315; lens on the Nikon camera, $3,500; gold coins (depending on market), $31,200; video camera, $1,725; military medals, $100; Rolex watch belonging to father, $2,500; gold chain,

$1,100; gold ring, $300; (2) iPods, $430; Chinese GPS, $770; and an American GPS, $300. All totaled in merchandise, cash, and damages was over $52,000. The sad part was that State Farm Insurance only reimbursed certain items. Reimbursement checks totaled under $15,000.

The transcripts of Cody's hearing came in the mail today. As Byron read them, he said he was only confessing to the little things that would not be considered a felony. He did not admit to any gold, medals, or guns, only a video camera. He stated he took part in three burglaries at the Smith residence. The statement also claimed that he would be sentenced to ninety days of EMH (electronic home monitoring) and two hundred hours of community service. He would also be ordered to pay restitution in the amount of $3,900. To date, he attempted one payment of $65. No other attempts had been made.

Jesse Kriesel's sentencing was the next day, and he seemed a little concerned about that. Jesse was a kid who received one of Byron's guns and admitted being on Byron's property on one occasion. Cody was sentenced on Friday, June 7, at 9:00 a.m. The following was what I wrote for John to read at Cody's sentencing on June 7:

> Byron Smith is my neighbor and friend. Last summer he was telling me about a kid named Cody who had worked for him. Byron spoke fondly of him, telling me how he wanted to teach him to deer hunt with a bow and arrow. He felt sorry for him because of his bad family life and wanted to help him. When Mr. Smith found out that Cody Kasper was one of the burglars that came to his home, he was in shock and disbelief. You, Cody, were the one that introduced your friends to Mr. Smith's property and brought yourself and your friends to steal from Mr. Smith in July, September, October, and again on Thanksgiving Day. Because of you and your friends, Mr. Smith feared for his own life and can no longer live in the home his father built. Because of your actions, Cody

Kasper, a kid that Mr. Smith only wanted to help, your friend Nick is gone.

Your gang's consistent attacks on Mr. Smith's home led to a fatal conclusion. You and your drug gang made the decision to keep attacking Mr. Smith's home, which changed his life forever too. His father's Rolex watch gifted to him by the French government in 1944 for being a POW is sitting somewhere in a pawn shop, so that you and Nick could buy drugs, cigarettes, and an ATV.

And to Cody's parents, are you aware that your neighbors called the police 19 times due to your destructive and suspicious behavior in the neighborhood? If home monitoring is the recommendation for punishment, your influence surely will not change the decisions Cody makes. You need to be sent somewhere that will change your behaviors and choices and truly think about changing your life. You certainly changed Byron Smith's life forever.

Byron had called me and wanted Dilan and I to come down to his yard, where he had been working that afternoon. He had caught a toad for Dilan to take to school to feed a snake that his science teacher was housing. If a toad was brought as a meal for the snake, you get extra credit, so Byron was helping Dilan gain extra credit. They gathered pine needles this winter because the science teacher decided a good extra credit project was to bring in a million of something. Dilan first brought in a computer printout with a million pixels, but the teacher wouldn't accept that. He decided a million pine needles were better, so Byron and Dilan collected these for that extra credit project.

Later that evening, I saw Byron's silver truck go into town. I wondered where he could possibly be going at 7:00 in the evening, plus he still had his lawn mower in the back of the truck. It was odd that he didn't unload it before he drove to town. He came back around 9:00. We found out when he got back here on Wednesday that he crushed his forefinger on a log and had to go to the emergency room. His finger was all wrapped and he needed stitches. It was going to rain for the next couple of days, so he can take it easy on his hands. He received a letter from the court regarding Jesse Kriesel's sentence. He only received probation until he is 21 years of age and some continued education in Red Wing for a previous offense.

We all went to Dairy Queen one night. I noticed when we pulled up that there were a lot of kids around and I didn't know if Byron would feel comfortable getting out of the car. He did so and it seemed that he never gave it a second thought. He seems to be getting more comfortable around people, and that is a good thing. For the most part, we have been his only people, along with a few friends that come over. He went to lunch today with John Monahan and a classmate from high school that came to town for a visit. His classmate is retired from his forensic psychology career. He and Byron were at the top of their high school class.

Byron was talking about his travels tonight. He went on a vacation from Tazmania to Bangkok to New Delhi to Cairo to Los Angeles and then to Minneapolis in the stretch of about a month's time. He didn't have reservations when he went to India, so he ended up staying in a hotel dining room on a cot for four days. They thought one of their guests was leaving, but he chose to stay additional days, so Byron paid 1/3 of the regular cost for a cot in the dining room (he couldn't sleep until all the guests had eaten and left). Fortunately, a shower was included with the cot!

This Saturday we went to the robotic farm open house near Albany, Minnesota. I had told Byron about this farm as I had a personal tour last fall. Steve and Lisa Groetsch milk 240 cows 24 hours a day. They have four robotic arms that track the weight of each of their cows, the pounds of milk they produce at each milking, the pounds of food they eat each day, and the gallons of water each cow drinks. It's all very high-tech and interesting, especially since I remember the days of milking a cow by hand. The cows of today rest in beach sand as it is better for their udders and their hooves. Everything is automated, including the precise amount of feed and water. Byron had wanted to visit as soon as I returned from my visit. Lisa is the daughter of a hospice volunteer in Albany. Norb is a very special, spiritual man. He comes to my office to bless it. He so appreciates the work I do for the hospital and believes that people who have extra money should share. If all people thought like Norb, the world would definitely be a different place. Byron enjoyed the day at the farm, and then he and John went to pick up a boat at John Monahan's home. John told me that Byron got a little teary-eyed when John Monahan mentioned that he couldn't imagine having a murder charge hanging over your head and how does one cope with that.

Dilan had a big birthday party last night with about 25 kids over with no issues! Byron went back to his rental property during the birthday festivities. But when he came back to our home early in the morning, he did visit with a couple of Dilan's guests that had stayed the night. It was the first time he had really talked with any youth (other than Dilan) since the shootings. He visited with Jesse and Kendall. He seemed as natural with them as a friend would be. I sensed the boys were somewhat uncomfortable because of who he was, but their nervousness was short-lived and it was good to see him talking with youth again. Jesse had been with Dilan's band in the beginning, so he knew Byron well as the band had practiced in Byron's garage during the summer of 2011. Byron said that he didn't even recognize Jesse, but he hadn't seen him in nearly two years. Kendall was talking to Byron about his family and how they had a strawberry farm and raised strawberries but now they had sheep and the sheep had destroyed most of their bushes. Kendall went on to say that the strawberries were difficult to keep from spoiling and they were thinking of getting out of that business. He talked with Kendall about the strawberry fields in California, and after the boys left, Byron mentioned that it would be nice to take Kendall on a trip to see those strawberry fields.

Byron had told us that he had bought a canoe in Clearwater right before Thanksgiving and hadn't had a chance to pick it up. John offered to take the trailer down to Clearwater and they would finally pick it up this week. I asked him why he hadn't picked it up, and he said, "Well, I got put in jail." He is very careful not to drive too much because he doesn't want to jeopardize losing his $50,000 in bail money. That's why he rarely drives. He takes little chances.

On Sunday I headed to Brainerd to check out a couple of plant places to put the finishing touches on my flower beds. Byron called around

2:00 and was wondering if I wanted to go over to the island and dig up wildflowers. There were tons growing on his island, but we have to take a rowboat over to it. I was excited because I have wanted to start a patch of wildflowers but the only way I could do it was from seeds, and that would seem to take forever. After I got back, John and I walked down to Byron's, where he had been working since yesterday planting a rather good size vegetable garden. John brought a fishing pole, and he would fish while we were digging up the flowers. We got in the rowboat to head across where he had cleared and mowed brush so that there was a path to walk through. The day he was mowing on this island just off his property was the day he suspected Cody and friends came to his house to steal. As long as they could hear the sound of the mower, they knew he would not come to the house. This would have been the first burglary. On the island, there were tons of wildflowers, so Byron took me all over and showed me the different varieties and helped me dig up some of the roots, and we put them into pots he had brought for me and a pail that I had brought. He showed me the other plans he had for this island as far as cleaning it up and having a little camp where he could have a fire and camp out. We explored for the best wildflowers for about an hour or so and then headed back. We got a little stuck with the rowboat on the way back, and I got my shoes and jeans wet halfway up my knees. I wish I would have brought more pots because I collected some beautiful wildflowers, but I am sure I could go back again. A skink invited itself into one of the flowerpots on the way home. John was waiting for us in front of Byron's house. He hadn't even had one bite, and we walked back home. Byron would be back to our house later that day.

On Monday we were discussing the upcoming sentencing of Cody Kasper with Byron. I finally mentioned that I had written a statement for John to read. I had previously not shared this with him until now. I told him we were concerned that his attorney might not be aware of all the important connections. Important in that Cody was the kid who initially started this whole event. The judge needed to know that, and so far, the judge had only heard what Cody had admitted, to which was only being the lookout for his friend Nick. Cody claims he was never in Byron's house, and law enforcement, as far as we know, had only found the six-thousand-dollar camera taken on October 27. Byron wanted to look at what I had written after we ate our dinner. He was talking about two friends that he had known for twenty years that both happened to be forensic psychologists. He also stated that they would be potential witnesses in his trial. One of the friends knew of his background helping teens and would attest to that in court if needed. He got teary-eyed when he talked about how this friend had recommended him as a judge for state science fairs and different academic events. He again expressed dismay that he would never do that again nor would he be a part of the Boy Scouts. He himself, as an Eagle Scout (the highest honor bestowed upon a Boy Scout), always took pride in this accomplishment. I am sure his tears were not only sadness but frustration because this was such a huge part of his life. We worked on his victim's statement for a couple of hours until John could read it smoothly enough. Surprisingly, Byron was all in favor of John reading this. Byron edited my version a little, but the content, he kept the same. In preparing this statement, he was very insistent that Cody be given a serious punishment and not just a slap on the wrist. His victim's statement said that the court's recommendation was probation, electronic monitoring, and two hundred hours of community service, along with some restitution. The punishment was standard for a first-time offender.

CHAPTER 6
BIRTHDAY MONTH

Cody Kasper received his sentencing on Friday, June 7, 2013. John went to Court as representative for Byron. Byron just couldn't bring himself to attend. We were not sure if his attorney would be present, so John took the speech I had written in case it was needed. When they got there, John asked if he would be allowed to say something, so he went into a room with the prosecuting attorney to talk. The prosecutor for Cody was Todd Chantry. He read the document and said that he was glad to know how this all happened. It would do no good to read it because his sentence, as a first-time offender, was already set. The only benefit to reading it would be to make oneself feel better. Todd did indicate that he would put this information in the judge's ear, though. He was speaking about the fact that Cody was the kid who started this whole incident by bringing his friends repeatedly to burglarize Byron. Byron's attorney, Adam, did appear in Little Falls and was a little dismayed that John was speaking with the prosecutor. Adam asked who wrote the speech, and John told him that I had written it, along with Byron's edits. Byron really wanted it read. Adam was worried that since the court documented everything, this might be brought up in his trial in a negative way and he didn't want to take the chance. So the victim's statement went unread. The one thing that we wanted to accomplish was accomplished. The fact that the prosecuting attorney would tell Judge Anderson that Cody started it all was one thing we wanted him to finally know. Judge Douglas Anderson went to the same church I attended. I actually worked for him when we first moved to Little Falls. His legal assistant was out on a medical leave, and I applied for a temporary job there and worked with him closely for several months. He had been a judge for a few years when this event occurred. He was known as an easy judge, which was the reason why Byron's first attorney, Greg Larson, had his case changed to Judge Anderson versus Judge Freeberg. Doug Anderson was a very likable person. He was easy to work for, very nice, and I enjoyed working for him. Even after his assistant came back from medical leave, he kept me for a while to work on some small projects.

On Friday afternoon after Cody's sentencing, John and Byron headed to the Little Falls Police Department to talk with the police chief about the incessant speeding down Elm Street, and as they talked, Byron reported to him that he had videotapes of all the neighbor's family members running the Stop sign continually at the end of Elm Street. The chief said that he could easily issue a citation on that documentation alone. Byron was getting comfortable talking with him and then was telling him the whole story of how many times the kids had come to his home to burglarize it and how little the sheriff's department did to help him. He told him that they had never even investigated the incident at his rental property. When Byron told him that the kids in high school were waiting to see if Chase Fortier ever got into trouble over this (because all the kids knew he was involved, too, and also a relative of the sheriff), the chief of police was concerned that the sheriff was clearly making seemingly intentional, grave errors in this whole case. He added that all this bad publicity would reflect on the police department, too, even though they were two different entities. Chief Schirmers was going to turn over all the evidence Byron had collected and make sure it would get to the proper authorities and they would be thoroughly investigated. It was a good day for Byron even though John said he again was very teary-eyed when he told his story to the chief of police. At least he felt he found a friend in law enforcement after all this time. So that Friday night, we headed to the casino for their seafood buffet. It had been about a year since we had been there. It was a little costly and a forty-minute drive, which was why we didn't go very often. Dilan had also been listed on the A honor roll, so we were very proud and it would be a celebration. Byron had helped him considerably in achieving this. I think, deep down, it was important for Dilan that Byron be proud of him. I told Byron one day how much Dilan looked up to him as a mentor. Dilan never hesitated in the beginning to want to help Byron, and I believe he strove for excellent grades. When Byron caught that toad for Dilan as an extra credit project in science, it brought his grade to an A.

The next Saturday we drove to Nisswa, Minnesota, to the Scandinavian Music Festival. Byron had seen an ad last spring, and we had this little flyer on our refrigerator ever since. It seemed important to him to go. We try to do everything we can to take Byron's mind away from his troubles. This festival is probably not something that I would have chosen to attend, but it seemed important to Byron. We left around 11:00 a.m. It was a nice, sunny 70-degree day. As we approached, we could hear the sound of fiddlers and people dancing in colorful costumes. There were five stages of music and many of the musicians were actually from Denmark and Sweden, and some from the Twin Cities. One of the members of the T. C. Nykleharpalog took the time to show us her harp and how it was made and how very few of the instruments are actually in the United States. She gave Byron a flyer for a store in Minneapolis on Lake Street that he wants to visit soon. The store sells only Scandinavian items. He seemed to enjoy the whole festival, taking in the live music without the aid of electronics. He came up to me and told me that I needed to stand closer to the musicians to really hear the music and appreciate it. He was right. There were fifteen musicians gathered around a tree playing fiddles and nykleharpalogs and it sounded beautiful. Another violin player would stop by and join in and soon there were a group of 20 or so playing. We didn't meet anyone from Little Falls, but I think he is getting more comfortable around people and not so concerned with what they think anymore. During the first several months, he was talking of changing his name and never coming back as soon as this was all over with, but I see that slowly changing. After several hours of music, we called it a day and headed for Zorbaz on Gull Lake for dinner. He had never eaten there before and they had a live musician on the patio and watched the boats pass by on beautiful Gull Lake.

On Sunday morning I was making cinnamon rolls for breakfast and suddenly spotted Dilan's friend Rachel in the backyard coming up to the door. Byron and I had been talking about the music festival and how he wants to spend next winter in California among the redwood trees at the cabin of his friend Mark. He even said that we should come up there too. Anyway, Rachel was looking for Dilan, and it was already noon by this time, and he had slept in because he didn't have to work at the local Dairy Queen that day. Byron had mentioned this several times about Dilan still sleeping. I had baked the cinnamon rolls and was then starting sloppy joes for lunch when he suggested that I take a plate full for Dilan because that would surely wake him. We didn't get that far because Rachel was there to talk with him. Byron had laughed about the unusual protocol for a friend to be coming when Dilan was not even out of bed yet. I went down to Dilan's room and told him he had a guest. He said they were going to Perkins for breakfast and Tristen was also going. Byron is gradually gaining some comfort with teens again. He told me once that he is very uncomfortable around them now. I was a bit startled by that comment and I shouldn't have been after all he's been through. I then asked him if he was uncomfortable around Dilan then too. He told me that was different and it was better if it was one on one. I think he is slowly getting back his enjoyment of youth.

June 11, 2013, is Byron's 65th birthday. I planned a small dinner party with friends and it turned out to be a beautiful day so I decided to grill ribs for an outdoors cookout. I left my office early to begin the preparations. I worked in Albany that day and rushed home to make a quick grocery stop for some potato salad and also a liquor store stop for some dark beer. I have noticed when we have been out for dinner that Byron enjoys a dark beer, so I thought some would be nice for his birthday. Before I left for work, I had left him a gift to enjoy for the day: some bottles of different flavors of lemonade, another favorite drink he orders in a restaurant. I also tossed in some of his other favorite treats: a big bag of Hershey's miniature chocolate bars and a bag of mixed nuts. I had marinated the ribs all day so they would be full of flavor. I threw together baked beans, baked cornbread and put the potato salad in a big bowl. I had baked him a cake on Sunday because I knew I wouldn't have time on this day. As the guests arrived, the conversation started with the shootings, but then took on a lighter tone. Byron told us that when he was in the 9th grade, he won first place in the Minnesota Science Fair. His project was doing arithmetic in Roman numerals. Byron stated that he was ranked third in his high school graduating class of 253 students. A friend of his was ranked #2 and they ended up rooming together at the University of Minnesota. He also told us that he ended up at Cal Poly when he had gathered enough money to finish his degree. Cal Poly is well noted as an engineering school, but not as expensive as some. He chose to attend there because it was a college that was not devoted to an athletic program. Then Dilan came outside to join us with the cake with two candles, a 6 and a 5, all lit up. Byron made a wish and blew them all out. I had purchased a CD of music from the year of his birth—1948. He made us guess some of the singers from that year. Since he enjoys all music, I thought a CD of music from the year he was born was a great idea and he seemed to enjoy it. The guests left after a few hours of celebration. He thanked me for the great party, and we all went in and watched America's Got Talent *and went to bed. He was going to get some yard work done the next day. He hadn't done anything on his birthday because he said he didn't want to get dirty that day.*

On Saturday he left about 10:00 a.m. after he and I had a little breakfast conversation. A little while later I notice a blue Prius in his yard. It sat there for a couple of hours. I was a bit concerned at first, but then he had the gate to his property locked, so he had let them in. After a few hours, an elderly couple left his property. It must have been someone he knew well because they locked the gate after leaving. We later learned that it was his cousin from Florida just passing through on vacation. They stopped in to support him and couldn't believe it when he told them that the drug gang of kids had stolen over $50,000 in cash and property and that nothing had been done about it.

CHAPTER 7
SUMMER OF 2013

Since it was now June and the weather was nicer, Byron had been going back and forth to his rental property. He was clearing brush and killing poison ivy and other weeds from the property. The previous occupants had left gallons of garbage, and he bought the property at a decent price knowing he had much work to do there. I had mentioned to Byron one day that I saw a young man wearing a pair of green shoes and they looked really cool. He was sitting at the computer in our dining area and right away started looking online for men's green shoes. We couldn't find the exact ones, but we found out that there were many green shoes for men. One pair I had mentioned that Dilan would wear those. Thinking he was just curious about my men's fashion sense, only a couple of days later when I got home from work and walked in the door, he told me to take a look at Dilan's shoes. He had ordered those green shoes that I had commented on. They were a nice pair of Vans bright green in color with green trim. He must have had them shipped for the next day. Dilan really liked the shoes, as I knew he would, but was very surprised that Byron had ordered them for him. He didn't typically buy clothing online, rather lots of security equipment. His plan was to start installing for others and various electronics that were of musical orientation. One commercial piece of electronics that he ordered was worth twenty-five thousand dollars in its day, but now was worth only two hundred dollars. He ordered different things that TV and radio stations would have used years ago, but now the technology had changed, but the items were still in great working condition. The FedEx delivery man and the UPS delivery man would bring all the packages addressed to him to our home. He loaded them in his small truck every week and took them over to his house to store them for future use.

The next day, Byron and John had an appointment at the Little Falls Police Station with the police chief and two members of the Minnesota Drug Enforcement Agency. They had reviewed the videotapes that Byron had turned over to them and had run some of the license plate numbers. They were told that none of the plates were from other drug rings that they were currently investigating, even though there was unusual traffic: multiple cars stopping for five-minute intervals. The problem was that the traffic down Elm Street had stopped. Maybe it was because they discovered they were being watched or because they had been questioned by law enforcement. Unfortunately, nothing came of all the tracking, recording plate numbers and suspicious deliveries.

We were sitting at the computer one day looking at the summer music schedule in the area. He is telling me about one of his favorite bands, Whiskey Tango, was playing at Red's Irish Pub in Swanville. They were playing on June 22. I told him that I had always wanted to see the Fabulous Armadillos and they were playing in Swanville the next weekend. He googled them to read more about them and said that we should go listen to them. The next day right beside my computer was a print out of a map to Swanville with the date of June 22 handwritten on it and Reds was circled with the street number. I got a good laugh out of this because I knew exactly where Red's Irish Pub is located and certainly didn't need a map to get there, but Byron is always precise. This attribute may have been to his detriment as he tried to assist law enforcement to catch the burglars and that security plan was used against him.

I was surprised that our recent dinner conversations have again been about the shootings. We had a short break from those conversations for several weeks. Maybe it is because his next court date is looming on July 1. He mentioned that it would have been cheaper for him to just open the door and let them take whatever they wanted. His attorney fees were mounting and he saw no end in sight. We began talking hypothetically, what if they would have been injured or incapacitated for life, he would have possibly been made responsible for all their medical bills. It seems no one takes responsibility for their own actions and there is always someone else to blame or file a lawsuit against. I actually brought up this topic, he didn't. He said that after he had to shoot them, he never even thought of anything like that. His only thoughts were about whom else was coming to his home and how should he prepare for more people coming. If three people came at once, he said he could have never handled all that. He said that he went back and forth in his mind waiting for others. He didn't want to even go upstairs for fear if someone saw him through a window, they would shoot him. He unscrewed light bulbs when it started getting dark so if anyone broke in during the night, the lights wouldn't work if they turned the switch. (Remember, there is a broken window, so anyone could come in.) He said he had no idea that they had a car parked anywhere. He also stated that although he had plenty of liquor downstairs, he never touched a drop. He said he never even thought of it. He keeps his best liquor downstairs, where the shootings occurred, and his cheaper liquor is upstairs. Law enforcement did test him for drugs and alcohol, which were negative.

Mr. Meshbesher has hired a professional jury selector to interview Byron and help in his jury selection. They needed to ask him about his past work and if he ever had post-traumatic stress from his Vietnam days. He hadn't, though. He never saw death there. His hearing was only a week away, and the Morrison County prosecutor had not given him the transcript of the grand jury indictment yet. His attorney was anxiously awaiting that document, so the hearing might be delayed depending upon the arrival of that.

At 8:00 on this Saturday evening we headed out for Swanville to listen to Whiskey Tango. I wondered in the crowd of people that might be there, would he be recognized as the man who shot the burglars in Little Falls? This would be his first large-crowd public appearance. As we arrived there was a good crowd already assembled. We found an empty table and sat down. The band started playing the best of the 80s music, some Bon Jovi, Michael Jackson, Rick Springfield, and Journey tunes. Soon two of John's friends that he had worked with a few years back came over to our table. They started asking him about the guy in Little Falls who shot the teenagers breaking in. They were wondering if he is still friends with him. John said, "Well, he's sitting right here." They both gave a shocked and amazed look and the one friend came closer to me and asked me if I was really sitting next to that guy! So I introduced him and they shook his hand and started talking to him. Since the music was loud, it was hard to hear, but they sat and chatted for a while and then one of the guys asked me to dance, so we went on the dance floor for a couple of songs. When we sat down, I asked Byron if he wanted to dance, and he said he eventually would. About fifteen minutes later, they played Lita Ford's song, "Deadly," and he said, "Let's go." It was nice to see him cut loose and have a really good time. We stayed 'til around midnight. The band was on a break and some rappers came out to entertain for the next 10–15 minutes or so. Byron had escaped to the back of the stage to check out all the equipment and chat with the band members. He mentioned that he would like to take some video of them playing. Byron has taken quite a few videos of bands playing, especially while he lived in China. He has them all stored on his computer and frequently goes back to look at them. He has done some amazing photography snapping band members in challenging positions. After a few shots of the band, he started talking about his security work and mentioned that he always carried Necco wafers in his tool bag. He used them to write down potential combinations for security equipment and then ate them to destroy the numbers or combinations. His coworkers used paper and then had to find a way to properly dispose of the paper they had written the security code on. Byron just ate the Neccos to avoid the risk of someone taking any information.

Since I had been up since 5:00 a.m. that day seeing Dilan off on a mission trip to Grand Rapids, Michigan, with our church's youth group, I was glad to be home before midnight. The group finally arrived after a 12-hour car trip, and he called me twice on that day and then twice on Sunday. I had to ask if he was missing me, but he only confessed to be checking in. Byron gave me a gift for Dilan the day he left on his trip. He told me to give it to him sometime. It was a shark-tooth necklace that Dilan said he wanted. "Oh, did you have one and find it?" I asked. He said, "Not until yesterday." I was a little taken back that he had ordered yet another thing for Dilan just because he knew he wanted one.

One of Byron's friends had visited the cemetery near Swanville where Nick and Haile are buried. They took some pictures of the graves to send to Byron's attorney to prove that the graves did not seem to be cared for, but more importantly, their graves did not have stones yet. Nick and Halie were buried together, and the rumor around town was that the family was turned down by Oakland Cemetery and Oak Lawn in Little Falls as burial places. The reason was unknown, but they were buried at Bear Head Cemetery near Swanville.

As July 1 draws nearer, Byron seems a little more agitated. He came back last night from working at his rental property. He came walking in our backyard with his bag and a bouquet of fresh cut wildflowers. He gave them to me and said he had picked them down by the river. He had spent the day doing yard work and unpacking boxes and sat down on our patio and started talking to me about getting his $250,000 back and why God had picked him to take care of this mess. He decided maybe God had selected him because he knew he could do it. He has a new name for the burglars: terrorist drug gang. He went on to say that they are worse than al-Qaeda because that group has a religious, organized mission. These teens just steal from people for their drug habits without any thought or consequences. If he had to do it over, he would have been smarter. He wouldn't have shot them with a gun. There was too much blood and it was too messy. He would have done something cleaner. He said, "I don't like the bullet holes in my home and I can't fix them. I can't clean up the blood." His attorney may want the jury there to reenact how the burglars were looking in all the windows and trying each door to break in. He was wondering why it had to be him and was demanding of God that he give his retirement back. He had stated earlier that if he hadn't killed them, he would have had to pay their medical bills for life had they been handicapped in some way. He didn't see any way out. I sat there silently and listened to his frustrations and encouraged him to pray that this would be over for him and he would somehow get the quiet retirement life he had come back to Little Falls for. I assured him that God had some divine intervention in mind to help him and everything would be over soon. He had an electronic security system installed in his home so no one could get in without a code or an alarm sounds at the sheriff's office. His *other property doesn't have security, but there is nothing in that home right now. He is working on the interior, painting all the rooms and trying to secure furnishings for it. It will be his new home after the trial is over. The house is over 5,000 square feet, so there is a lot of work to do. It has a huge, beautiful kitchen and large fireplace in the living room with a sunroom decorated in true Minnesota-cabin style. Byron doesn't much care for the house. He only purchased it because it's adjacent to his other property. He says it's not built very well. The other fireplace in a huge great room is a fake and he's not fond of that aspect. When he sleeps there, he says it's similar to camping out. He usually stays one night at a time as long as the weather is warm and then comes back to our home. There is no water or heat in the home right now. He has decided not to mow the lawn this summer. He says there is no point because he is not living there. He wants the public to know that the burglars have taken away his home.*

Jack Ertelt from Valley City, North Dakota, continued to stay in contact and asked if he could come to Little Falls and finally meet with Byron. He had wanted to visit Byron, but their meeting had been delayed. He was coming through the area, and Byron agreed to sit down and talk with him. I was cooking roast beef and vegetables that evening, so instead of going out this Friday, we would eat at home so they could visit. I told them it would be best if they weren't in public so no one could overhear all this conversation about the shootings. Mr. Ertelt was not at all what I pictured him to look like. When he talked on the phone, he had a deep, slow tone to his voice. Therefore, I pictured him to be an older-looking gentleman. He was a nicely dressed man who was very concerned about Byron's case as he had been following it since the beginning. He had been having thefts and vandalism to his property for several years with losses over fifty thousand dollars. When he heard about the case, he called to express his concern and wanted to help Byron. I knew he was an intellectual man as I had emailed him several times and he never had any misspellings in his communication along with a real knowledge of the legal system. He had represented himself twice in court proceedings and continued to study laws. He found a Minnesota statute, number 609.065, that states "A person has the right to take whatever means necessary to defend himself and his property." He thought this castle law is the best written compared to any other state. Since the George Zimmerman trial was currently underway, he was comparing the self-defense right and pointing out the similarities to Byron's case and Florida law. Byron seemed appreciative of this, but tended to not get too excited about the comparison. He had put his faith in his attorney and respected his knowledge of Minnesota law to shine through. After all, Meshbesher was well-compensated for his services.

We took Byron to the Swanville Carnival on Saturday night after Mr. Ertelt left. There was a band called the Fabulous Armadillos that I had been waiting to see for a long time. We didn't arrive until after 9:00 as I was waiting for Dilan to get home from his Michigan mission trip with our youth pastor. There were 19 youth that went to Grand Rapids, Michigan, for the week to help the homeless and do other various activities in that city. I had called Dilan and told him we were heading directly to Swanville, and even after the long drive that day, he wanted to attend with us. The small town of 600 was filled with young and old as we headed straight to the stage to listen to their lively music. Byron had never heard them before either and very much enjoyed their style too. We started to leave around midnight and noticed someone had left a cell phone on a picnic table. Like a shot, Byron picked up the phone and said, "I am going to take this to the police," and he darted off. John and I just looked at each other in surprise and right away tried to catch up to him. He walks very fast. We couldn't catch him and couldn't locate him after we searched the area where the police had been located. We looked in the three police cars that were positioned there and no sight of Byron. I told John we should split up because as I tried his cell number, there was no answer. I wasn't even sure if he had it with him as I remember it being plugged in to charge before we left. John didn't want to split up, so we continued the search until ten minutes or so had passed and we finally saw him. We just felt it was odd that he was that concerned about a lost phone and making sure the owner got it back. It was possibly the loss of sentimental awards and gifts of his own that were stolen, so it was important to him to see that this person got his possession back to him.

On Monday morning, July 1, was the day of his Rule 8 hearing. It was originally scheduled to be the Omnibus Hearing, but since there was a new indictment, his attorney rescheduled that hearing for August 30. This would be my first court attendance with Byron. The others had been very short, so I felt no need to be there. This was his third court appearance since being charged. Byron seemed quiet that morning, taking his time about getting his suit on as we all waited for him to get ready. He had been sitting at his computer and then all of a sudden realized that he had about 30 minutes to dress and get there. I commented to him that he looked very nice in his suit while walking into the courthouse. Adam, one of his attorneys, was there waiting as we passed through security. He and Byron stood aside and were talking while John and I took a seat in the hall. After several minutes, I noticed a dark-haired woman enter the waiting area with a T-shirt with Haile's picture and the back of her shirt said "In memory of Haile Kifer." I assumed it was her mother, but not quite sure. Coming to join her were several other people: a young girl with short shorts and a tank top, two middle-aged men wearing old T-shirts and loose pants with sandals, and others with T-shirts and blue jeans. They all looked like they just got out of bed. My first thought was that they could have dressed better, especially out of respect for the court. Then this group was accompanied by two women with county ID badges. I learned they were from the victim's rights advocacy group. They were helping explain the court proceedings to the Kifer and Brady families. I had no idea that there is a group that supports families of criminals. The family members were led by one of these county employees and sat silently waiting for the hearing to start. As the attorney's made their decisions and the judge asked questions about the proceeding, two members of the media were taking quick notes. Terry from the Morrison County Record *was present along with a gal from the* Brainerd Dispatch. *The prosecution attorney wanted clarification as to the records of the juveniles and any possible delinquency that they had to present. The judge gave them until August 7 to turn over those discoveries to the defense and then the judge gave the defense two weeks for review. The Omnibus Hearing would be set for August 30, and nothing more was determined that day.*

When Byron got up from his seat, he stepped back so the family had to pass within two feet of him. (He told me later he did this purposely so they had to walk close to him.) We all filed out of the courtroom while his attorney met with us afterward. He began by thanking us for supporting Byron. He further thanked me for keeping this altogether. He talked about how Orput wants this to be done and over with quickly, how Orput does not care about those teens, he cares about making a name for himself. He also stated that he wants to further his career by winning this case, and that's the only thing on his agenda. Steve Meshbesher wants us to meet with this professional juror selector next week and discuss Morrison County and what type of jurors should be selected. He is debating yet if the trial should be held in Morrison County or moved to a different county. He further stated that he wouldn't have a choice in the location if he decided to move it, so he is being very careful about this decision. I mentioned my work schedule to him, and he said we would work around my schedule to meet with this professional. Our discussion further continued for about an hour about his strategy and how he was going to present this case to a jury. As we walked out, I asked him when he thought a trial would take place. He stated that it would probably be later this winter or next spring. We were then informed that the family had gathered in front of the courtroom, so we were escorted by a deputy to the back lot, where we were parked in case there were any issues. Byron requested we stop at his bank. His attorney had mentioned that he needed Byron to transfer some money to him to pay the professional jury selector. He also wants him to be seen about town doing regular business.

Byron has been attending our Fourth of July celebrations for the past few years too. This year in 2013 is no different. John decided to leave on the 3rd, and he and Byron could set up the tent in his mom's backyard as she has no shade trees. My mother-in-law goes all out for this annual event. She cooks more food than she needs to and plans for a huge crowd. We usually bring our own drinks and everyone brings a dish to share—like a huge potluck. The parade starts at 11:00 a.m. and usually lasts over an hour. There is music in the park next to Serpent Lake and then fabulous fireworks at 10:00 p.m. Dilan had to work at the Dairy Queen at 6:00, so he had to head back early. I stayed back with him while John, Byron, and Kenny Dean, John's cousin, went fishing for a couple of hours.

Kenny Dean lives with his parents in a suburb of Minneapolis. Kenny, my mother-in-law's brother, has Alzheimer's and is currently residing in a veteran's home. Last year he remembered my name, but this year he doesn't know anyone. Their son, Kenny Dean, helps take care of his dad. He was also very interested in the fact that we had Byron in his presence. Byron's story has been all over the Minneapolis and St. Paul newspapers. As we ate dinner, he kept asking Byron question after question. I thought at first it might irritate Byron, but he answered as best he could. Kenny Dean asked him why he waited to call 911, and Byron told him that it would come out in the trial. Kenny Dean stated that he could hardly wait to tell his friends back in Minneapolis that he had had a Fourth of July celebration with a "famous criminal." He then apologized for calling him a criminal, because he stated that he would have done the same thing in those circumstances. After they left, I got on the boat with Byron and John and went cruising around the lake until it was time for the fireworks.

At 10:30 p.m. the fireworks display finally started. Crosby puts on the best fireworks display I have ever seen and many others agree. Even Byron said it was rated the third best he had ever seen. The first being in Washington, DC, then followed by a Boy Scout Leadership Camp event. I sat next to him during this time, and we talked about his plans after the trial, which include going away for two weeks where no one could find him. He also stated that he was tossing around calling for a county commissioner's closed-door meeting to have Sheriff Wetzel resign and demand the termination of Deputy Jamie Luberts. He also continues his plans to pursue several civil lawsuits to those who have referred to him as a cold-blooded killer.

CHAPTER 8
LIFE'S LESSONS

I had a phone conversation with my mom the other day, and she was asking about Byron. I told her that we had taken him to Swanville to listen to a band, and she was very concerned about my safety. She literally told me not to go anywhere with him because some nutcase could shoot at us and I might be in that line of fire. My mom did not know that he actually lived in our home yet, but I assured her that nothing like that would happen. Sometimes I had second thoughts about safety, but I certainly didn't let it consume me. A gang of teenagers decided his home was a prime site for multiple burglaries. They weren't smart enough to think that if you kept going back to the same house, sooner or later it would end badly. They seemed to be without fear of any consequences. Byron was subject to the worst fear imaginable: not feeling safe in his own home for months. One of Byron's friends from high school who still lived in Little Falls asked me if I had to do it all over again, would I let Byron live at my home? I did not hesitate and told him that this could have happened to any one of us. Byron was a human being in need of kindness and support at the lowest point in his life. I could only imagine the despair he felt when he didn't feel safe in his own home and he didn't know whom to reach out to. Our family helped a friend in his darkest hour. We all need to live by example so our children learn the same. It's important to teach our children how to be the best humanitarian they can be, so we need to start by setting a good example. Several people mentioned to me what a great kid Dilan was after their mission trip. Byron seemed to push Dilan to be better. Byron expressed his opinion to me once in a while about how I raised Dilan, but was sure to state that was all it is. He referred to some forms of discipline as to how his father did it. In one instance, his father made him walk home five miles instead of picking him up from an event. I told him if he had had his own children, he would be more of a softie. He just looked at me with an "I don't think so" look and shrugged his shoulders.

The last week had been rather quiet, but things changed in this neighborhood in a hurry. As we were watching *America's Got Talent* on a Thursday around seven o'clock, we saw two cars driving down Elm Street in a big hurry. One was an older silver Ford Thunderbird and the other an older, smaller hatchback-style car blue green in color. The cars caught my eye because of their high speed around the corner. I mentioned to John that it looked like we have suspicious cars in the neighborhood again and he should get license numbers. Byron happened to be down at this rental home this evening as he had been working in that yard all day. John got excited and was trying to locate a pen and paper while both cars had stopped at Byron's locked gate. Both cars just sat there for about two minutes and then decided to turn around and come back down Elm Street. By this time, John was outside about in the middle of our yard watching the cars come down. The hatchback car sped down the street and headed south. The silver car with his window down slowed enough to ask John what he wanted, and John replied, "Get out of here. You don't need to be here. Get out!" The driver, whom we later found out to be Devin, replied, "I am going to kill that old son of a bi——." John quickly came in the house and told me what he said and called 911. Deputy Larsen arrived in about five minutes. During this time, I was on the phone with Byron telling him that two teens were at his gate and they threatened his life. I suggested that maybe he come back here, but he insisted upon staying. He acted very calmly, while John was an excited maniac. The deputy wanted John to call Byron and ask if he could come on his property to check things out. Byron had no interest in the deputy checking the property. Byron remained calm through this event, but it was unsettling to me because now there was another troubled teen ready to cause harm. The deputy did take both of the teens into custody for questioning along with the Devin's passenger, his girlfriend, Tori. The other car was driven by

Shelby. Shelby did not have a history of being a troublemaker. Devin did. The deputy brought up Devin's information on his computer as he recently had been charged with a burglary. Deputy Larsen called John after he spoke with them and told them to never go in that area again. He told John he could put a restraining order on him if he so chose. When Byron's attorney heard about the incident the next morning, he advised John to get a restraining order. He was concerned that more teens would want vengeance still. He recorded everything and thought it was important to Byron's case that these teens were still looking for revenge.

George Zimmerman's verdict finally came down on Saturday, July13, late in the evening. We didn't hear it until Sunday morning. We intently watched the case as we thought it might make an impact how a jury felt about Byron's case. I left the TV on so when Byron got up, he could hear the verdict. He was quickly taking notes and recording the details of what the media said. Byron felt really good that Zimmerman was acquitted. This might help his case as this was truly self-defense. George Zimmerman had lived in Florida and had followed this boy as part of a neighborhood watch group. This felt like a little victory for Byron, and he felt really good about it.

Tuesday morning, July 24, we headed to Meshbesher's office in downtown Minneapolis. He wanted to gather all of us to be interviewed by a professional juror selector. She would decide if the trial should be held in Morrison County or be relocated. We left about 8:30 that morning and made a stop for a little breakfast as the meeting was set for noon. Along with the juror selector would be Ross, the private investigator, and Glen, a retired policeman who specializes in the psychological aspects of shooting a person, the fear and the adrenaline. He will be an expert witness as Byron goes to trial. We arrived about an hour early, so we had the chance to sit outside and enjoy the downtown area of Minneapolis. It was a nice, sunny day with a temperature of about 75 degrees. His office is downtown on the corner of Hennepin and 5th. It is in the old Lumber Exchange building and has been refurbished for office space. The office area itself is not large, but has marble floors and beautiful woodwork. We were given lunch catered from the Green Mill and were met at the door by Lori, a paralegal and member of his staff. I had spoken with her many times on the phone, so it was nice to meet in person. When lunch was delivered, we all gathered in a small conference room and were introduced to Dianne, the juror consultant, who conducted the meeting. Meshbesher would be coming soon as he had been called out to Wright County on another case. Dianne wanted to gather our knowledge of the community of Little Falls and what people were saying. Right away she thought it would be better to stay in Morrison County due to the fact that there are a higher percentage of conceal-to-carry permits compared to neighboring counties. Last time Meshbesher asked for a change in location, it was changed to Stearns County. He does not have a choice once you ask for a different location. It was discussed that Morrison County was where Byron's parents lived and raised their family and were good, hardworking citizens. Byron's dad had served in World War II, and his mother also served as a nurse in that war. They built their home here and worked for many years raising a nice family. Both Bruce and Byron had completed four years of military service. One of their sisters, too, had also completed military service. Of course, most of the people who spoke with us were in support of Byron. It seems the more people hear the real story, the more they come to the conclusion that he was justified in his reaction to multiple burglaries. At first, the community was shocked about the death of these kids, but they didn't know all the facts, so there is a complete turnaround in some of the people that were against him at first. The discussion with the juror consultant then turned to the case itself. Byron shared with us that when he shot Nick in the hip, Nick's facial expression became so angry toward Byron for shooting him that in fear Byron could only do the only thing he knew to survive this altercation before he himself would be killed by a younger, stronger man. Byron had not shared this before, but Dianne felt that would not help his case, but Byron thinks it significant to self-defense. It was later discovered that the neighbor's phone was a go phone, which was not with a regular carrier, so no records could be obtained. The neighbor girl was seen on Thanksgiving Day driving down Elm Street, quickly turning her head while Byron was talking with his neighbor Bill outside his house that day, according to Bill's statement. Both Bill and Byron believe that she is the neighborhood reverse watcher that gave clearance to go into Byron's home on Thanksgiving after seeing him drive away. His attorney decided to try again to get her phone records. They have the phone log of Haile, which reveals before the burglary that she was texting her cousin Rachel Brady that her and Nick were a team today. Miscellaneous items were discovered in Nick's car possibly from other burglaries. Among the items were sex toys, prescription pill bottles, foreign coins, an older gold watch, collector baseball bat, and other tools. Haile also tested positive for marijuana and Triple C drugs according to her toxicology report. There was DNA from Haile in the backseat of the red car according to Ross, the investigator. Other discussion was held about the grand jury indictment. According to the judge's instructions, each juror was to not talk about the case outside the courtroom and to not share with anyone how they voted. An employee of the clinic was revealing how she voted to several coworkers and her reasoning was that she had a son that was killed (in Florida) about the same age. There were also many untruths that Orput told during the proceeding. One was the fact that after Byron shot them, he was on the computer shopping on eBay. Byron distinctly said he was not and could get a log of his computer activity to prove it. (This fact was later verified that Chad Museus had told the grand jury that Byron's computer was active. The activity was later proved to be automatic updates only and not eBay shopping from Byron Smith.) Meshbesher is looking to get this over turned on August 30 as he presents evidence to dispute all Orput's claims. He is also going to ask for a dismissal of the charges against Byron with the evidence that Ross gathered. At the end of discussion, I presented my opinion on the fact that Morrison County is the eighth poorest county in Minnesota and it would be more feasible to have the trial in a county, where there are more professional people from which to select. A jury of his peers needs to be those who have worked hard to obtain financial success in retirement. In Morrison County, that may be challenging. Still, the choice by the attorney and professional were to have the trial in Morrison County.

On Thursday we left early in the morning for Duluth to see the Tall Ships come through the harbor. They had been there three years ago, and this time we would see them as they went through the harbor. We got there before 2:00 p.m. to see the first three ships come through. It was a very warm day there, so we didn't wait to see the rest as there was about a half hour break for the rest to come through—about nine in total. We walked along the peer to see them up close. Byron seemed to enjoy conversing with all the people involved in the ships' history and ownerships. One of his favorite bands, Matthew Sweet, was playing in the parking lot of Grandma's Saloon & Grill, so we attended that. The weather had taken a cold, rainy turn, so we stood in the mist, listening to them. The next day John and Dilan wanted to climb a rock wall, so Byron and I decided to go to Grandma's Saloon while they climbed the wall. We had a nice conversation about his younger days and his family. He talked about his friend Greg and his wife, Nancy. Greg was his friend from college, and they had roomed together for two years. He was telling me that he went into this flower shop close to their apartment and had bought a beautiful purple velvet plant. The lady in the flower shop had told him as he purchased it that it was the most beautiful plant in the store. When she saw he was on motorcycle, she felt bad that the plant would be brought home in that manner. Little did he realize that this was the same lady his roommate started dating months later, and when they met, she had remembered Byron as the guy who purchased the purple velvet plant on a motorcycle. She was so glad to see that it had made the trip and was still as beautiful as ever. Nancy had moved in with Greg and Byron for a short time until they got their own place. Byron started working at Hughes Air Craft in California shortly after that. Greg and Nancy eventually got married, and they had a son, Jesse. Byron is his godfather. Jesse is now married and in his early 30s. He talked about wishing that he had found someone and got married and had his own children. There was a 28-year-old woman in China a couple of years before he retired that her father wanted Byron to take back to the US and marry and have children. But they couldn't communicate well due to her lack of fluency in English language, and also, he didn't want to change diapers at his age. He talked about adopting children and decided he would enjoy being a grandfather instead. In fact, he wrote on the Caribou Coffee Shop's wall: "I like to dream about talking with my fifth grandson 100 years from now, if I could." (It was one of the store's challenges of the day questions where you could write your answer on their chalkboard.) I told him that would be a difficult dream because he didn't have any children, but he stated that anything is possible.

The next day we drove up the North Shore to Gooseberry Falls State Park and enjoyed walking in pouring rain. The North Shore is still beautiful in the rain, but certainly would have been more enjoyable in the sunshine. We stopped at a little candy shop along the way and then headed to Two Harbors and viewed the largest locomotive in the world. Byron gave us the whole history of this train and knew as much about the train as the museum curator. Before heading back home, we talked about driving across the big bridge into Wisconsin. Byron reminded us as part of his bail agreement he had to remain in the state of Minnesota, so we headed home on the Minnesota side.

The following weekend we went out to the Landing for a Friday-night dinner after Byron had been working in his yard all day. He burned some brush he has been clearing over on his rental property. The flames grew 30 feet high, and the neighbors called to make sure it was contained. He had a burning permit, and the fire was contained, so no concerns for safety. He goes into his family home for things he needs and then leaves quickly with never thinking to spend another night there. After spending more than a few hours there, he starts feeling ill. The next day John noticed a red, rather noisy Ford Cougar car that drove down Elm Street and went down to Byron's gate and then stopped there like he was deciding whether to walk down the driveway, paying no attention to the No Trespassing signs. As the car paused, John tried to get a picture on his cell phone and tried to get a license number. After a couple of minutes, the car came back down and left Elm Street. John promptly called the sheriff's office to report that two boys were seen in a red Cougar leaving Elm Street. A deputy and policeman immediately responded to the call to check out Byron's property. We were sure that no passenger had left the car to hide in the trees, so after the deputies checked the property, all was clear. Byron had actually been in his yard during this time but saw nothing. He showed two of the deputies where his path was to his house in the woods and let them know that's where he stayed at night when he wasn't at our home. As we talked with one of the deputies, he told us that the license plates on the red car were registered to a girl named Christine, except there were boys in the car. The deputy also revealed that he had Chase Fortier in his car yesterday for another incident. John was reporting to him other friends of both Nick and Haile that could possibly be involved in crimes. The deputy was talking about trying to catch all the drug activity in Little Falls, but due to the liberal prosecution, they basically get little jail time and a small fine and keep doing it over and over again because it's so lucrative. The deputy encouraged us to continue to call-in with any vehicle that goes down Elm Street that shouldn't be there.

I was curious about the owner of the car so did some research through Facebook. It seems the owner of the car has the same friends as Haile and Nick. But I also discovered that she belonged to a group called the Haile Kifer and Nick Brady Memorial Fund. I clicked on this group and saw that there were 1,055 members. It had been started by a friend of the family to help pay funeral costs. Most of the people who had joined this group were not even from Little Falls. In fact, one gentleman posted that although he did not support what the kids were doing by breaking into someone's home, he wanted to help with their funeral costs. There were only a few surprises in this group, namely, two local businesses. There was also the VFW, of which Byron was a member. This infuriated him that they would give memorial dollars to teens using drugs and breaking into homes when he was a Vietnam vet and member of this organization. I told Byron about these few locals that had donated to their funeral, and he was intrigued that such a Facebook page existed. Byron still believes that the drug activity on Elm Street is related to Sheriff Wetzel's staff not exploring his burglaries. He also believes that his next-door neighbors are a key component in Nick and Haile's knowledge of him being away from home on Thanksgiving. Byron's cellmate, Matt Berry, told Byron while they were in jail that he knew of his neighbor and she was known as the Pill Queen.

As Byron waited for the August 30 hearing, he received a large envelope in which his attorney had filed all the motions. He was asking the judge to dismiss the first-degree murder charges due to prosecutorial misconduct, grand jury misconduct, and prejudice. He was also seeking suspension and discipline from the Bar Association for Mr. Orput's unethical conduct with the grand jury. Byron seemed more confident than ever that this might be the start of the end for him. Here's what happened in grand jury testimony: BCA Agent Chad Museus had interviewed Cody Kasper on November 28, 2012, in which Cody admitted participating in three previous burglaries with Nick Brady at Byron Smith's residence. The burglaries occurred in the summer and fall of 2012. Nick Brady was always the one who drove, Cody acted as the lookout, and they were connected by cell phones in case someone was approaching. The last burglary was two weeks before Thanksgiving. He also told Agent Museus that Nick was committing other theft crimes with a person named Jesse Kriesel and that Nick had even stolen coins from his own grandmother. Agent Museus asked Cody for his SIM card in his cell to analyze data. This is the actual text message (misspellings included) retrieved from his phone:

> Kasper: Where you been?
> Brady: What do you mean you dident txxt me back ass face!
> Kasper: I know I'm sorry byrans!!!
> Brady: When
> Kasper: Soon!
> Brady: Yes we keep saying that and not doing it!!
> Kasper: Well let's do it!
> Brady: Tomoro?
> Kasper: Yea

Agent Museus told the grand jury that his review of the above text message did not yield any information about Mr. Smith's house (even though one can see that Byron's name was mentioned but spelled wrong). Byron Smith was burglarized the next day after this text.

Additional text message data from Cody Kasper on October 26, 2012, also revealed his use of marijuana. This was exhibit I in court documents.

> Kasper: Sup?
> Britt Bloom: I'm commin to school btww
> Kasper: Bring weed!!!

Cody Kasper's statement to law enforcement also included that items stolen from Byron Smith's residence included an envelope with hundred-dollar bills and fifty-dollar bills about an inch thick. This was their first burglary, which occurred in mid-July of 2012. After which Nick Brady took Cody shopping, buying shoes and clothes and also a four-wheeler. Cody told Kimberly Brady, mother of Nick Brady, about a search warrant issued at Kasper's house to warn her that they might be coming to her home. Nick also had stolen guns and swords in Kim and Jason Brady's home. Kim Brady contacted Cody telling him that she got rid of guns. When testifying at the grand jury hearing, of course she did not admit to any weapons of this type that her son possessed, nor did she mention her removing evidence in an investigation. In mid-October, somewhere between the eleventh and seventeenth, Cody and Nick went to the Smith residence to specifically steal copper wire. Also stolen was a gas siphoning kit and a chain saw. Cody had seen Nick break in through the basement door twice. Nick had stolen guns from Mr. Smith's house on a separate occasion with another boy by the name of Jesse Kriesel. Cody did not confess to participating in that burglary. Cody did not confess to participating in the burglary of Mr. Smith's residence on October 27, 2012, even though he planned it in that text message with Nick Brady. During that burglary, a Nikon camera was taken, and later, Matt Kasper, Cody's dad, was allegedly trying to sell the camera to another Little Falls resident who admitted that he came to him along with other items for sale. Also taken on October 27 were firearms: a twelve-gauge shotgun and a Ruger Mini 14 rifle. Cody described both of these items to the police. The shotgun was given to Chase Fortier in trade for a bicycle, according to Cody. Chase buried it after Cody told him to get rid of it because it had been stolen. (No charges were ever filed against Chase Fortier.) On November 24 when Cody was questioned by BCA Agent Ken McDonald and Deputy Dave Scherping, he was asked why Nick and Haile would choose to burglarize Byron Smith's house, and he stated that he had no idea. But yet he had already participated in three burglaries at Byron Smith's. Cody Kasper also stated that Rachel Brady, Nick's sister, would pawn the stolen property. He stated that she pawned coins at a pawnshop in St. Cloud. Nick also went to several pawnshops.

Kim Brady was questioned by BCA Special Agent Brian Marquart about Nick's weapons and if he had any in his room. She told him only a shotgun he had purchased at Walmart, a BB gun, and maybe a pocketknife. He also asked her if she had seen any unusual property in her home, and she replied, "Only a couple of knives a few months ago." Agent Marquart asked permission to search his room, and Kim and Jason Brady refused. Again, she removed evidence but has yet to be charged for obstruction of justice and destruction of evidence. Kim and Rachel Brady were part of a *Dateline* airing in May of 2014, in which they claimed they had no idea of Nick's activities. The *Dateline* episode went on to attract audience sympathy for these two women and showcase their grief for Nick Brady. In a statement taken on November 27, 2012, from both Cody Kasper and his dad, Matt Kasper, more came to light as to the events leading up to Thanksgiving Day. The interviewer was Ken McDonald, special agent, Minnesota Bureau of Criminal Apprehension. KM was McDonald, CK was Cody Kasper, and MK was Matt Kasper's responses.

> KM: When you went and did that burglary [to Byron Smith] in the summertime, what were you driving?
>
> CK: He [Nick] was driving his. I don't know if he got his white car there or not. So it was either the white or the red one 'cause he didn't have the black one.
>
> KM: Did he talk about going back and doing it again?
>
> CK: No.
>
> KM: So he got the cash and the camcorder, he never said...he'd like to go back there again?
>
> CK: No.
>
> KM: Is there anything else you're not telling us?
>
> CK: [Negative response.]
>
> KM: That's a no?

CK: No.
KM: You understand that's the most important thing, right?
CK: Yeah. I don't know if he went back there by hisself sometime or I don't know that he got so he was [inaudible] he went, just went by hisself flat out or...I just don't understand why he'd walk right up there.
KM: How did Haile get hooked up in doing burglaries with him?
CK: I don't know. I mean those, those two, I don't know. They were kinda close, but she went to treatment and he started hanging out with her again. And then I didn't really talk to 'em. It was only those. It was usually only her and him doin' some'm.
KM: So you've already admitted some'm in front of your dad now. Is that camera and those coins or any of that stuff at your house?
CK: No, there's a camera that Nick gave me.
KM: There's what?
CK: A camera that Nick gave me.
KM: What camera is that?
CK: There's a um, I don't know it's black.
KM: Where, it's in your house though?
CK: Yeah.
KM: Where, it's in your house though?
CK: Yeah.
KM: Where's that at?
CK: It should be in the house. It should be right in the kitchen.
KM: It's a black camera?
CK: [Positive response.]
KM: Do you know the brand name?
CK: [Negative response.]
KM: No? Anything else?

CK: No, that's all.
KM: Just a camera.
CK: Yeah.
KM: No coins?
CK: No, there's no coins or anything.
KM: Any, any foreign coins?
CK: No, [inaudible] a fifty-cent piece, but that's not from Byron's house.
KM: What would Nick do with all his burglary stuff?
CK: Sell it.
KM: To who?
CK: I don't know, the pawnshops.
KM: Which pawnshop?
CK: Ah. Rachel.
KM: Was Rachel doing the pawing?
CK: Ah, she only did the coins, that's the only time I know of. But I don't know if he took those coins from his grandma or [inaudible].
KM: Where did she pawn the coins?
CK: I don't know, some, it's on the, it's a ways going over the bridge in St. Cloud. Over by it is a civic center [inaudible] what is it…
MK: Security Pawn [inaudible] down there…
CK: What's the, what's the center there or whatever right, civic…I don't know.
KM: It's by the river.
CK: No, it's on the left side of Lake George, that side of town.
KM: Okay, but in St. Cloud?
MK: Should just be able to run her name there. Don't they got a database for that stuff?
KM: Well, it's like Chad's talkin'. The main, the main thing we are here today is that murder. What aren't you telling us about that?
CK: I told you everything now.

The private investigator that was hired through Meshbesher and Associates went to Security Coin and Pawn located at 623 West St. Germain in St. Cloud, Minnesota 56301, on April 1, 2014. One of the managers there located a record of Rachel Brady/Schaeffel that showed she brought in a ring in September of 2012 that they paid $250 for and another necklace they paid an additional $250 for along with three US quarters that they paid $15 for. The ring was a fourteen-carat gold ring with a pink opal, a lady's ring. The necklace was a fourteen-carat gold link chain that could have been either male or female. The three quarters they paid for was just the weight of the silver. Byron had purchased gifts for his mother that matched the description of items pawned. The manager indicated that his records showed that they did not have anything picked up by law enforcement officials at his pawnshop.

On Thanksgiving Day, Nick Brady drove a red 1998 Mitsubishi Eclipse, license plate XPH-777, to Smith Avenue, just off Riverwood Drive. He was accompanied by Haile Kifer. He parked the car facing east on the south side of Smith Avenue. The car was registered to Jason Michael Brady of Randall, Minnesota. This vehicle was known to have been used just prior to the deaths of Nick and Haile. Items that were seized inside the car include a red box containing miscellaneous items of jewelry inside the glove box, two-dollar bills in plastic sleeve in the glove box, a Louisville Slugger wooden baseball bat in the back seat, six prescription pill bottles in the back seat belonging to a Little Falls resident living near an area that Haile's parents resided; a Kodak digital video camera in the front passenger seat; a black Calvin Klein bag containing sex toys in the back seat; a red-and-black hand crank flashlight found in center console; a Truper brand hedge clippers with Tony written on the handle found in the trunk; a Minnesota driver's license application for Haile Kifer in the glove box; a Pillager public school schedule for Nicholas Brady found in a back pack in the back seat; many misc. collectible coins, including foreign found in the center console; a ceramic Nick container, which included foreign bills and more collectible coins; and a gold Pulsar brand watch in the center console.

A look at Jason and Kimberly Brady's court case records reveal an extensive criminal history. The public information from the site, mncourts.gov, reveals that Jason Brady, father of Nick Brady, had criminal records starting in 1999 with a DWI, followed by numerous traffic violations, a loaded, uncased gun charge in 2002, an assault charge and two domestic abuse charges in 2005, and drug sales and possession in 2008. Kimberly Brady, mother of Nick Brady, had a criminal history that also began in 1999 with disorderly conduct. In 2002, she was charged with a DWI; 2003, trespassing; 2005, possession of marijuana and drug paraphernalia; 2006, another DUI; 2009, open bottle in motor vehicle; and in 2014, possession of marijuana and drug paraphernalia in Hennepin County.

On January 25, 2019, the Morrison County Record reported in the Morrison County Arrest Warrants section that Rachel Brady was on now-Sheriff Shawn Larsen's list for arrest warrants for January 27, 2019. In October of 2018, the Morrison County Record reported that she was facing a felony third-degree drug possession charge in Morrison County. The charge stemmed from a September 28, 2018, incident with the Little Falls Police Department locking the restrooms at a park for the evening when he found Rachel and another individual appearing sluggish. The officer allegedly found a syringe and bottle with white powder residue and she allegedly said it was heroin. She was later apprehended and sent to the Morrison County Jail. She has two small daughters.

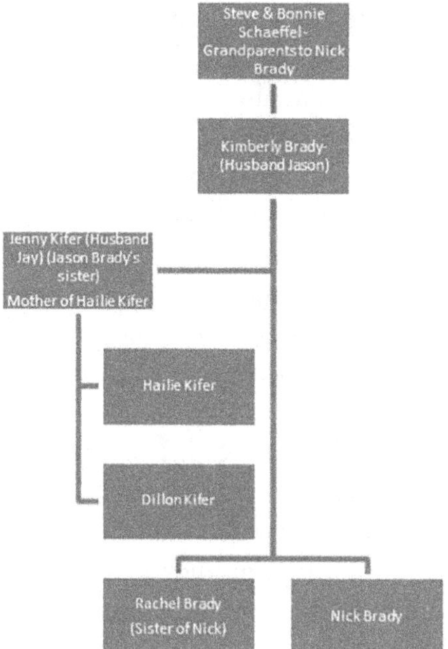

During the grand jury testimony of Deputy David Scherping, he stated that he was first to the scene when Byron Smith asked his neighbor Bill Anderson to call for assistance to his home. Scherping explained that when they arrive on duty, they check the ICR's (Incident Command Report), which indicated the activities of the previous shift. (Note: Both Kifer and Brady had prescription medications in the red car parked near the Smith residence. This was a fact after the November 22 shootings.) When Scherping was asked by one of the grand jurors (on April 23, 2013) if Kifer and Smith had any previous criminal activity/convictions, he stated to them that he didn't know of anything.

Sgt. Jeremy Luberts testified to the grand jury that the burglary reported by Byron on October 27 was acted upon by law enforcement, but it was not until after the shootings that they actually did any type of investigation. In fact, according to Byron's neighbor Bill, Sheriff Wetzel told him, "We botched it," referring to the investigation of October 27. Since Byron Smith had somewhat unusual items, a quick trip to St. Cloud to check pawnshops would have been fairly easy. One particular item was a Chinese GPS, which Byron used while living in China. No one could use it unless you could read Chinese. Jeremy Luberts was also asked by a grand juror if he knew of any other vandalisms to other people's property that the two had been involved prior. He answered, as Scherping did, "Not that I am fully aware of." Again, Brady's red car contained prescription drugs from a homeowner living near the Kifer's home, along with foreign coins and currency, a gold watch, among other items.

Another text message was never brought forth either. It is the Thanksgiving morning text between Rachel Brady and Halie Kifer:

> Rachel Brady: Heey its Rachel, my phones dead. I miss you!
> Kifer: Omg J I have so much to tell you! Ha me and nick are a team right now.
> Brady: I can't wait to hear all (: and nice(: what you guys doin?(:
> Kifer: Driving around went back there from last night J lol
> Brady: Oh nice!(: you go in? Was someone there?
> Kifer: Yes and no.
> Brady: Find anything? (:
> Kifer: Some stuff a huge black dildo I took to show you and some anal beads J ha
> Brady: No way?!?(:
> Kifer: Ya! J
> Brady: That's so fucked! (: I love it!(: mehr (:
> Kifer: I wish you were with :/ were doin it tonight if you wanna
> Brady: I wish I was too!/: and Well yeah!(: I think im just gonna tell him spending the night with family er what?:p
> Kifer: Yea J
> Brady: Mehr.(: I hope 2nite is fun and works out!(:

The text message shows substantial forethought by participants with respect to burglaries. Furthermore, law enforcement knew of these text messages yet denied any knowledge that the Kifer or Brady had committed any previous crimes.

After the grand jury indictment, we tried to stay positive, even though this was a hard blow and it was difficult. We went out to Texas Roadhouse for dinner on Saturday night for the first time. We got a waiter named Benji, and he was very entertaining. Byron showed him some magic: If you find the hook on a peanut and press against the hook's vertical line, the peanut shell cuts straight in half and you can pop the whole peanuts right in your mouth. Benji was very entertained by this newfound trick. He went and told his co-workers about a magician at one of his tables. We were all trying to guess what his major in college was because he let it slip that he minored in music as he sped away to do the line dancing routine as short entertainment for the customers. I thought it may be English as he seemed like the creative type. Byron thought theatre and I agreed with that as well. When he got back to the table, we asked him. He majored in creative writing and has written three poetry books. We talked back and forth as he brought our food. Benji told us that he had our group down to a T: John was the tough one because he was always complaining about something—the service, the food, etc. Byron was the intelligent magician and I was the stunning woman. We all laughed about our quick observation of the group. Then as we left the restaurant, he even gave Byron a book recommendation. Byron said it was the only time a waiter had ever given him a book recommendation.

Byron met with the Colombe family today. He is trying to buy the adjacent property to both his homes. There is a family of four children who own the four lots adjacent to his. They wanted $100,000 for all four but he went to the county assessor's office and there is no available electricity and gas to the property with additional problems due to an easement of the front lot. The family wanted to keep the front lot they valued at $40,000 and Byron would have to pay the remaining $60,000 for the rest. He discussed the problems with the family and is waiting for them to respond. He wants the property as an investment and to ensure that it is never subdivided into separate lots so that he has screaming *neighbors beside him. Due to the hot weather the last few days, Byron is staying inside until a cool down occurs. When we got home tonight Byron was listening to Carl Stalling music. Carl Stalling wrote all the music for Warner Brother's cartoons. It seems odd listening to that, as you can almost see the animation as you hear the melody. The other night he was listening to 30s music along with some Roy Orbison. He continues to hear little about his case.*

What he did know was that Meshbesher wanted the audio thrown out after the second gunshot to the girl. According to the medical examiner, that shot fatally wounded her and the fact that he shot her again would not matter. At the height of his fear, he had to shoot her again to make sure she wasn't a threat. He did one final shot to end her suffering. Nick was shot three times, but with a higher-caliber rifle. He was also wearing gloves, which Byron did not remember. Meshbesher wanted Byron's discussions with law enforcement after he was jailed to be thrown out. He had hired Greg Larson, a local attorney, that very day, in the beginning, he was not informed that he could consult with an attorney when they knew in fact that he had retained one. Those discussions or confessions should not be admissible. Mr. Orput had misled the grand jury. The BCA agent later admitted he had given the wrong dates of computer use to the grand jury. One of the grand jury members talked about the case during breaks and told others how she was voting. Judge Anderson was explicit in his instructions to the jury that they were not to do this. With all the inconsistencies, Meshbesher was hoping to relieve Byron and at least attempt to downgrade his charges. There are three types of homicide in Minnesota: first-degree murder, which is premeditated; second degree, which is not premeditated; and involuntary manslaughter. Throughout this process Byron kept repeating to all who would listen and his mantra became how parents are not teaching their kids ethical behavior. He cited this in is a one-page sheet he had written and that we were instructed by him to hand off to the reporters. He felt that this was the root of the problem that caused the deaths of these two people: they were not taught ethical behavior from their parents.

CHAPTER 9
THE OMNIBUS HEARING

On August 30 at 10:00 a.m., the Omnibus Hearing began. The main purpose of an Omnibus Hearing is to determine the evidence, including testimony and evidence seized at the time of arrest. The counsel for the plaintiff (or the people) and the defendant attend the hearing to discuss pretrial matters pertaining to the case. Any motions are also made at this time prior to the trial. Jack Ertelt drove down the night before to support Byron and attend the hearing. As Byron's case drew more media attention, we wanted to be assured of a seat so we left early. Byron seemed confident that things would start to go well for him in this process. He had been gone from our home a few nights before as he was preparing for the decisions that would be made on this day. He drove his car over to our home in the event that his case would be dismissed by the judge. He was prepared to leave town for a couple of weeks until the media attention died down. Byron, John, and Jack rode to court together that morning. As I sat waiting, I asked the bailiff if there was a huge crowd who would get into the courtroom, and he told me that it would be up to the judge. A gal I knew that had worked at the local Subway for years came with her husband to support Byron. There were a few media present already: the local newspaper reporter, Terry Lehrke; a reporter from the *Brainerd Dispatch*; and a local radio station reporter. Later, *Kare11* news reporter Dave Bergmann showed up in the afternoon. I was surprised to see him shake the hand of Rachel Brady. As the sister and the pawner of Byron's property, according to Kasper's confession, he must not have known of her involvement yet. It was somewhat frustrating to watch the Brady family during the court proceedings.

They laughed at Meshbesher's questions of the witnesses, and they seemed to think that this was a big joke. Rachel Brady, once again, appeared into court very casually dressed with a low-neck tank top. One of the Brady relatives comes with a ripped, white, dirty T-shirt and some type of jogging pants. Haile's mother, who looked young enough to be her sister, shed tears during some of the testimony.

There were three investigators who would be on the witness stand today: Chad Museus, Jeremy Luberts, and David Scherping. Chad was with the Minnesota State Bureau of the Drug Task Force who was on duty over Thanksgiving and was called to investigate the shootings of the teens. I find it ironic that the primary investigator was also a drug task force supervisor. I wonder if he realized how drugs had everything to do with this case and he was helping prosecute a man who was consistently attacked by those using drugs. Meshbesher had three issues to address today to dismiss the first-degree murder indictment: (1) the evidence was not sufficient, (2) the evidence was not properly processed, and (3) errors in the process, including prosecutorial misconduct, along with argumentative evidence and prejudicial evidence.

Meshbesher started out by talking about the text messages between Nick, Haile, and Rachel Brady. These stated that they were a team, referring to Haile's message to Rachel Brady on Thanksgiving morning. The fact that Byron had unscrewed light bulbs indicated to law enforcement that he was planning an ambush for the perpetrators, when in actuality he unscrewed them because he was afraid that more burglars were coming yet and he didn't want them to turn the lights on so he would be seen. In all actuality, the reference to light bulbs was not even relevant. This break-in occurred in broad daylight, as had the others. The drapes were open to a large north window, which allowed Byron to see a shadow while the burglar was searching for a way into the home. The drapes were still opened three days later when his home was shown on a TV news report. Investigators working at night were not sufficiently observant to realize the presence of the large, open window.

Meshbesher also pointed out that the indictment showed internet usage on the evening of Thanksgiving, which was a false statement. As the defense had an expert test the computer, there was no evidence of computer usage that evening, yet the prosecution claimed he had used his computer after he shot the teens. Byron had told us that there was no way he used the computer that evening. He was hiding in fear in case others were coming. He had used it the day before and then nothing after that.

Meshbesher also stated that the investigators referred to their positions as catching bad guys. He objected to Byron being referred to as a bad guy when he was defending his own home. According to Minnestoa Statute 609.065, "A resident can use any means, even deadly force, to defend his property and himself." The obligation to flee did not apply in Minnesota as in some states. The irrelevant testimony of the mothers was also mentioned by Meshbesher as they did not have any evidence to present. Their only job as witnesses was to gain sympathy with the jurors so that they would vote for a first-degree indictment.

The search done on Byron's property was done during a time frame not approved by the judge. They were to search during the hours of 7:00 a.m. and 8:00 p.m. The search was done after 8:00 p.m., so any evidence gained after that time would not be admissible at trial.

Chad Museus was the first witness. He was questioned about the 911 phone call he placed downstairs. Byron had stated that the phone was not working, but yet he claimed a call was made from it, but did not take it into evidence. Century Link did not have any record of that call made either. He was on the stand for about an hour. Meshbesher also asked him about the text messages, and again he stated that he did find any relevance to the Smith property. (Even though Byron's name [spelled wrong] was specifically mentioned between Kasper and Brady.)

The next witness was David Scherping, who was the first to arrive at the scene after the neighbor Bill called for them to come to Byron's home that Friday. He stated that he arrived around 1:00 p.m. and found Byron at the side door with his hands up as he told them to come in. He showed them a bedroom, where a window was broken, and then took him in the basement to where the bodies lay.

Scherping then called for additional help. He testified that he did not question Byron during this time. When Jeremy Luberts came on the scene, he was the one that questioned Byron. They both entered the home around 1:30 after Jeremy arrived and put Byron in a squad car and placed him under arrest, handcuffs in front, at 1:45 p.m. At no time was he read his Miranda rights when he was taken into custody. He sat in the sheriff's car until 2:30 and transferred to Scherping's car from Mattison's car. Scherping transferred him to the jail. There was no talking between them and no Miranda rights given. At 2:59 p.m. they arrived at the sheriff's office and began to record and question Byron. He remained in handcuffs. They interviewed him again at 4:20 and woke him at 1:00 a.m. for another interview with Jeremy Luberts. Scherping had also testified to the grand jury that he had no knowledge of Nick or Haile's previous burglaries. Meshbesher pointed out that this was a lie because during the grand jury, which convened in April, and it was a well-known fact that pills and money from another home were in the red car that Nick and Haile had driven to burglarize Byron. Meshbesher pointed out that he had lied to grand jurors and wanted the judge to note that in the record.

Judge Anderson then ordered an hour break for lunch and then the last witness would testify: Jeremy Luberts.

Adam, cocounsel working with Steve Meshbesher, would be asking this round of questioning. Jeremy Luberts's testimony basically consisted of the fact that he issued six search warrants and claimed to not recall any time he did anything that day. At the very end, though, Adam asked him what time he received the search warrant to go back into the home. He stated it was on the warrant (he couldn't remember) and that showed 6:30. The warrant was issued by Judge Carlson for the hours of 7:00 a.m. to 8:00 p.m. He then stated that they actually didn't go there until 9:00 p.m. that evening. Adam noted to the court that they were not authorized to go into the home after 8:00 p.m.

The hearing ended about 2:30 p.m. The judge ordered by October 15, the defense would respond to the transcript of the hearing. The prosecution would have until November 14 and then the judge would take all under advisement and make his decision after reviewing.

Outside the courtroom, Meshbesher wanted us to wait to proceed outside so that any news media would be gone. *Kare11* was still on hand, and they took some video of Byron leaving the courtroom.

Later that afternoon, John Monahan came over and visited along with Jack. I took Dilan to St. Cloud later to buy new jeans for school and when we got back after a few hours, they were all sitting in the kitchen eating fish that John had fried. They were all drinking beer and eating and having a casual time. Byron may have been a little disappointed that no decisions were made, but he didn't really seem too upset. He has a meeting on Tuesday with Meshbesher to discuss his case. He and John will drive together on Tuesday.

In the next few days, Byron seemed extremely quiet. He told John that Meshbesher had asked for more money in the trust account. He was worried that the costs were getting out of control for his defense, stating that Meshbesher would need twenty thousand dollars each week during the trial. His retirement funds and personal savings were running low, and there seemed no end in sight. He was asking why God picked him to take care of those kids. He repeats, "Why did he pick me?"

Another reason for his depressive mood was the fact that nothing seemed to be happening with the neighborhood drug traffic. The suspected drug delivery still occurred on Thursday evenings in a small, maroon pickup. Different cars continued to proceed down Elm Street on Fridays with numerous trips in and out lasting from five to eight minutes each. It was very routine and had been for months. The chief of police had seemed to stop taking an interest in this. Calls to him go unanswered with no call backs after numerous messages.

CHAPTER 10
NO BREAKS

On October 27, 2013, Dilan was getting confirmed. George and Lynne, my sister and her husband, and Dilan's godparents came from Sioux Falls on Saturday to be a part of the ceremony. My mom, along with my other sisters, traveled together from South Dakota, and John went to pick up his mom in Crosby. Byron decided that he wanted to go to church with us as well. He told me this last week as I had talked with him about the weekend plans for confirmation day. I was quite surprised he wanted to attend church because he had not taken an interest before, but I think he really wanted to be part of Dilan's big day. As the day arrived, I began to really stress out about having him attend church with us. I wondered if anyone would recognize him there or give him long stares or say anything to him. I called both my sister Lynne and my sister Cheryl. Neither of them knew that he had been living with us. When I told them (by phone), they were a bit surprised. They both expressed concern about his presence in church. Lynne brought out the fact that his story was such a big deal in a small town. Cheryl thought so too. I wondered if I should call the pastor and tell him, but then I thought, after all, it's church! I called my mom, and I was hesitating to make that call because the last couple of times I had called her, she seemed overly concerned about our safety. I had mentioned that Byron had talked about taking Dilan to China and showing him his favorite city. He had really enjoyed working and living in China. She explained she was not in favor of such a trip. When I called her the Friday before, I told her I needed motherly advice. I wasn't sure how to handle the situation. Should I talk to the pastor? Would anyone notice him?

Would there be a bad scene? Would people stare or say something? If I didn't tell the pastor, would he say something? After all, the Sunday after the shootings, the pastor prayed for the burglars at the services and had not prayed for Byron. All these thoughts were going through my mind, and I was really stressing about it. But I kept telling myself that "it's church!" Maybe I was overthinking the whole situation. I stressed out so bad I started feeling ill. I caught some kind of bug or virus that zapped my energy, but I had a huge meal for twelve people to prepare, so I had to shop for groceries, clean the house, and plan a meal. I took a day off from work to prepare for the day. When I called my mom, she said I shouldn't say anything to the pastor, so I decided and even due to a lack of time on my part not to say anything. His daughter was getting confirmed, too, and I finally thought the less of a big deal I made of it, the better off we would all be. It turned out to be the right decision in the end. We had a great family time. I was proud of Dilan for his smooth reading in church. He had the first Bible reading of the day and then played guitar for the praise session. When he was blessed, he took the first turn (of the class), and we all went up and put our hands on him. I put my hand on his hair, and the pastor made a mention about his hair, how he wanted to have great hair, like Dilan. Everyone got a good laugh at that, and the pastor put his hand right on his head. One of Dilan's middle school teachers was present in church. Ray was suffering from colon cancer, and I am most certain it took all his energy to go up to each student as they were being blessed. As I put my hand on Dilan's shoulder, a hand was placed on my hand. I knew it was Ray's, and it was. Among Dilan's confirmation cards was a card from Ray. I told him to be sure to write thank-you notes and write that one first. He went above and beyond that by visiting him at his home the next Tuesday afternoon. He brought the thank-you note in person to him. He told me when he got back that he was shocked at how happy Ray was even though he was fighting cancer. Dilan also noticed how happy his daughters and wife seemed to be. Ray told him that he didn't want anyone to feel sorry for him. He was happy and going on a new journey.

I was proud of my son as he had made a special visit to a very special teacher and human being. But I also am grateful to Ray for teaching my son not to be afraid of what life passes to you, because in the end we will all die and all we can hope is that someone will have loved us here on earth and remember the good things that we accomplished.

The rest of our Confirmation Sunday was spent as a family, enjoying our meal and good conversations. Byron seemed to enjoy visiting with my mother and John's mother. He actually seemed to feel at home with all my family around. At about five o'clock, everyone had started their travels back to their own homes. Lynne and George left for Sioux Falls, and my mom and sisters headed back home too. Byron sat down on the sofa and said, "Well, that seemed quick, and now it's all over." He then started in about how he wondered what my dad looked like because he noticed that neither me nor my sisters looked like my mom. I picked up a photo album on the bookshelf and showed him a picture of my dad. He looked at it, put his hand over it to cover the hairstyle, put his other hand to cover the 1940s suit, and asked me, "Now who does this look like?" I couldn't believe it. Dilan was a spitting image of my dad. I had never really noticed before. We showed it to Dilan, and he smiled and agreed. The picture I showed him was my dad at about twenty years old. Dilan posted it on Facebook the next day, and everyone thought it was so cool that he looked like his grandfather. My mom sure got some laughs about it as she remembered how my dad could touch his tongue to the tip of his nose for a joke. Dilan can do the same thing, so we had a good laugh together about that talent.

Byron and Dilan were talking about colleges the other day, when Byron stated that he actually had 418 college credits. He knows of no other person in this 400 Club, as he calls it. I asked him why he never got a master's degree and he said he just didn't want to pursue that. He paid for his own tuition and split his college years because he ran out of money at the University of Minnesota and then moved close to his brother in California and finished his degree at Cal Poly, in which he earned two degrees, a physical science degree and an electrical engineering degree. He worked for Hughes Aircraft for two years and then went to the State

Department for the next sixteen years. He refers to himself as an electrical engineer which is actually his minor degree and more of his passion.

Byron brought over a waffle griddle one morning that he had purchased at Gopher Supply which is a wholesale supply house with overstocked items for discounted prices. He likes to shop in those discount houses because of the prices. So, the Saturday morning before I started my cleaning routine, we made Belgian waffles for breakfast. He had brought a mix from home that Bruce had bought when he was visiting. They were really good and fun to make. I got Dilan and John both up from their slumbers so they could enjoy a waffle morning. The conversation started when John had found out that some kids that were possibly stealing from Byron were also almost caught on the west side near Peterson's Body Shop. Peterson was telling John that Nick's red car was seen a few times and these teens were combing the neighborhood to see which homes were vacant and had the "good stuff" to take. They would ring doorbells and pretend they were out of gas so they could go inside and use the phone. The sheriff's department had been alerted to the red car, but had not been able to catch them in the act. Byron was astounded that law enforcement was aware, but yet when the grand jury convened, they stated that the kids had not been in any previous troubles with the law.

Last Friday night while John was in South Dakota deer hunting, Dilan and Byron and I went out for our usual Friday night dinner. When I got home from work though, Dilan was gone. I called him on his cell and he told me that he and his friend, Ahn, were off to St. Cloud. Byron then reminded me that he had promised Dilan a meal of his choosing as a reward for losing 25 pounds over the summer. Byron wanted to take him to Fuji, the Japanese Steak house in St. Cloud. I called Dilan back and asked him if he wanted to meet us there with Ahn. He didn't hesitate at all and was totally excited to be going. Byron and I left immediately to meet them in St. Cloud. The four of us were seated with another family of about eight people and we watched the chef create our awesome food right in front of us, along with a few magic tricks, such as tossing bowls of fire in his hat. I was seated on the corner, next to Byron and then Dilan sat next to him and then Ahn. I could see immediately that Byron was in his element by talking with both Ahn and Dilan. It was never more apparent that day than ever, how he enjoys the company of the youth and wants to guide and enjoys deep conversation with them. As we finished our dinner, Ahn and Dilan were headed to the Mall and Byron and I would do a little shopping at Aldi. After we got home, I asked Dilan if Ahn had said anything about Byron. Dilan said that he had told Ahn that his grandfather was joining them for dinner, but when Ahn heard me call him Byron in conversation, it had dawned on him that this was Byron Smith, the man who shot the teens breaking into his home last Thanksgiving. Ahn told Dilan that he was aware that he was not his grandfather and he kept telling Dilan how nice he was. He kept saying it over and over again, Dilan said that he said it about twenty times, so much so that it was annoying to him. Dilan said he lied to Ahn about Byron being his grandfather because he just didn't know how to explain it or want to. When he told Byron that Ahn was so amazed at how nice he was, Byron understood that Dilan didn't know how to explain the fact that Byron Smith would be there at dinner. He was thankful that Ahn appreciated the real Byron Smith and not the Byron Smith that the media and the then-sheriff Wetzel had portrayed.

On November 25, my friend Renee texted me after dinner with "Sorry for the news." I knew right away that the judge had made a decision in his court case and it wasn't good. Judge Anderson did not dismiss the first-degree charge, nor did he suppress any evidence that the investigators had sought without executing the search warrant improperly. The St. Cloud Times *stated that Judge Anderson felt the prosecutor's mistakes were harmless. We couldn't believe it. I am shocked that they outright lied in court and that it was considered harmless. This is all so unbelievable. We were celebrating John's birthday and he had been getting phone calls from family members. Byron seemed on edge because he sought out Dilan and wanted to know where his heirloom nutcracker was and then the DVD remote from downstairs could not be found. He had mentioned that he couldn't find the nutcracker that he brought over and was anxious to find it. It had been in his family for years. I understood his passion for wanting his items returned after all had been taken, but it causes tension in our home from time to time. We also had an insurance agent named Jeff from Combined Insurance who came over to update our insurance policy. Jeff had also been on the grand jury first-degree murder indictment. He told us that he repeatedly asked about the kids and how much previous trouble they had been in and repeatedly asked if Byron was a good citizen. Orput continually got upset with him, so he just stopped asking questions. He also stated that Orput seemed put off when Bill had representation from an attorney during the grand jury proceeding while he was questioned by him. Byron just doesn't seem to get a break with the system at all. When my friend texted me, I quickly went to the computer to check the St. Cloud Times website and sure enough, the article was at the top of the site. I knew that he didn't want to mention it being that it was John's birthday. When Jeff was finally done with his insurance pitch, I asked him a few questions about being on the grand jury. He said there had already been a selection and no one was cut, which is different than a petit jury. Then Byron asked him several questions: If the mother's testimony seemed scripted or authentic. For the most part, he didn't really want to answer or didn't know how to answer. The mother's testimonies came at the end of the proceeding. Of course, everyone is going to remember the very end before they vote. As we got ready to go to bed, Byron was hanging out, talking about simple things, like the cats. I got the feeling he wanted to talk, but I didn't have the words or the energy to bring up the fact that the judge had made a decision. I thought it would be better left unsaid. I saw three sleeping pills on his table in his bedroom. They were not cut in half like he normally takes them. Everything seems to be out of control.*

Another reason I felt bad for Byron is that he had planned a gift for Dilan. Byron ordered the whole set of Breaking Bad *DVDs because Dilan loved the show so much. The box came on Tuesday, the first day of release. When Byron got home from Minneapolis, he directly grabbed the box and asked where Dilan was. He brought it upstairs and let Dilan open the box. Dilan was super excited to receive such a gift!! He took his picture with the discs even hugging them as he went to bed. Byron got a big laugh out of that when Dilan wanted him to take the picture of him and his gift.*

Thanksgiving Day seem to come quickly this year. As the first anniversary of the shootings came, I was worried about the neighborhood and who would be racing down Elm Street and those threats that came with it. We had discussed whether to stay home or go somewhere out of town. We decided to be normal and stay with our usual routine. I invited

John's brother and his family, but they cancelled at the last minute due to illness. Greg and Laura would come, though, so we would have a nice quiet time. I put the turkey in the oven around 8:30 a.m. that morning and started to prepare the rest of the meal. Byron had been fairly quiet the last couple of days, especially with the judge's new decision. A little before noon I noticed that he went downstairs to our family room. I waited awhile and then went down to see if he was all right. The shootings happened around 12:30 p.m., and he had been rather quiet for the last couple of hours. He was sitting on the sofa watching a sci-fi film clip with William Shatner (in his younger days), and I noticed he was teary-eyed. I asked him about the show he was watching, and he explained it a bit, so I stood there with a dish towel in my hand, watching it for several minutes. When he seemed to be very involved in the story, I dismissed myself and went back to cooking. We got through the day by eating a nice meal and afterward played a game of Apples to Apples. The game involves cards with unusual phrases/words definitions and players take turns being the judge of the best description of the card overturned. The person with most cards wins the game. It's helpful to know your group well, which Byron would be the least likely to win, but he won by a landslide! Later in the afternoon, we decided to watch a funny movie, Weekend at Bernie's. *Our day was spent keeping him as distracted as possible so as not to dwell on what happened last year. Both Friday and Saturday the weather was very nice, sunny and in the 30s. Byron hung around the house both days filling his time with mostly reading and watching a little TV. Finally, on Sunday morning, he left at 7:30 a.m. and came back around 1:00. He said that he wanted to check his house and everything seemed in order. "Nothing seemed disturbed," he said.*

On December 13 another hearing was held to ask Judge Anderson for a delay due to a motion before Judge Anderson on dismissing the first-degree charge and the dismissal of the evidence from the search warrant that had been done outside the time limits of the warrant. No delay had been determined as it might not be needed depending on if the appeals court would review the grand jury indictment. Meshbesher seemed confident in the proceedings, which made Byron feel a little more confident. Meshbesher had also commended

Byron for being more friendly in this hearing and smiling for the media instead of looking away. It has been difficult for Byron, such a private person, to be seemingly brought into such a high-profile case. He despises the attention. When we were talking today, he mentioned that he wanted Dilan along with a couple of other scouts to be witnesses for him at the trial. He wanted to show the jury that if a few, nice young men admired and respected him, this would cancel out any ideas of him not liking teens. In fact, the opposite is true. He illuminated when he was around Dilan and his friends.

On Saturday, the fourteenth, we drove to Minneapolis for a Trans-Siberian Orchestra performance. It was a tradition I started a couple of years ago as a mother-son day. With Dilan's vast interest in music, the show's display of lighting and pyrotechnics is like no other. John planned to go ice-fishing for the day and I had asked Byron if he wanted to go with Dilan and I and he jumped at the chance. I knew it would really be something he would enjoy. I always buy tickets early so had scored really good seats, on the floor, row 15. It was a perfect view of the stage without having a sore neck by looking up all the time. These arena-type performances are not something he typically attends because there are so many people, long lines and good seats are hard to get. This is the third performance I have attended and I now make it a point to go every year. I suggested to Byron that next year we fly (somewhere warmer) and attend one of their performances in another city just to see how different or alike they are. The music of TSO is so moving that some of the songs bring one to tears. The vocal and instrumental talents of the group are phenomenal. The show is three hours of amazing rock opera music. Afterward Byron had commented that it was the most technical concert he had ever attended—and he has attended many in the US and abroad. Byron suggested afterward that we walk around downtown Minneapolis and wait for the traffic to lighten before heading home. He and Dilan talked about Christmas break, classes for next semester and college choices. I felt more like the third wheel – but being fine with it. After a short visit to Starbucks we headed straight home. When we got home, we brought out the snacks from the last Trader Joe's trip and discussed the TransSiberian performance. He thanked me for including him and told me he enjoyed everything about the day. We talked about odd, random things: Our picks for a dinner companion if we could have anyone we chose. He would pick Pope Benedict or Queen Elizabeth. I couldn't think of any one person I wanted to have dinner with, but told him I have always wanted to meet Kevin Cronan of REO Speedwagon, my favorite rock band from high school days. I was surprised Byron didn't pick a musician for as much as he collects all types of music. Dilan picked one of his favorite musicians too.

On Sunday morning when Dilan needed a button sewn on his coat, Byron jumped at the chance to show him the proper way to do it. I can see how the Boy Scouts had such a good relationship with him. He thrives on teaching youth and this whole awful event of two youth changing his world is most ironic. Someone once asked me not long ago, if he had remorse about the shooting. I answered that he, of course, was remorseful about the situation. But he still doesn't know how he could have handled it any differently. He shared that after the boy was shot, he was trying to compose himself and get ready to call for help. But when another person or attacker, as he refers to them, came down those stairs, it changed everything for him. He didn't know how many others were entering his home that day. He had mentioned that Haile took several minutes before entering the house after Nick broke-in. As part of his on-going security installment, he had enabled a device that would stall out cell phone usage. It was part of his security training for the government. Burglars would not be able to communicate on their cell phones close to his home.

Another Christmas came and went with Byron in our home. Dilan was still excited about his early gift of the Breaking Bad *series as he had been glued to the whole series about a chemistry teaching making meth to provide for an unborn child he would never know because he was dying of cancer. Dilan and I went to church that Christmas Eve while Byron and John went to Crosby to spend the evening with his mom. Byron was going to attend church with us but at the last minute decided to go with John. We had planned to just have small snacks with some wine and enjoy the evening. Church was overflowing as it always is on Christmas Eve. Judge Anderson happened to be one of the communion ministers at the back of the church. When I told Byron that if he had gone to church with us, he could have received communion from the very judge who was hearing his case. He became a little amused and said he would have gladly taken it from him. We exchanged gifts after John and Byron got back from Crosby. Dilan received a sewing kit from Byron. I received gloves (three styles), a ceramic Santa, a palm tree candle and a premium box of chocolates from Costco. We had given Byron a collection of quarters from every state. It had taken me awhile to put this gift together, but decided it would make a perfect gift for him. He had told me that his sister had taken the collection he once had. I had also given him some wine with wine tools and some lottery tickets, hoping he would have a lucky year in 2014. Byron had given John a set of hot sauces, a stamping set and several other small items. It was a quiet Christmas Eve.*

On Christmas Day we headed to my brother's house for a celebration with my family in South Dakota. The wind was howling and snow was drifting over the roads, but they were clear enough to make driving not too difficult. The almost-three-hour drive passed quickly and we had our usual turkey and ham luncheon with all the trimmings. There were 39 of us there—all my brothers and sisters, including all their spouses and children and my mom. Of course, there were many questions about Byron. They knew him well from him attending our previous Thanksgiving dinners he had attended at our home. Most everyone shared the sentiment of his acquittal. "They were in his house and he has the right to defend his property and himself," stated my niece Brittany, who was 21 years old at the time. My mom agreed, but didn't think he will get a full acquittal because he didn't call 911 right away. I had heard the same sentiments from my friend, Michele, as we had lunch together last week. She looked at me and said, "He is going to do some time." Her words cut like a knife because I don't ever think much about that. I always thought that there would be enough evidence presented about the burglars, their history of crime and the fact they had broken in and he had to defend himself. His plans to go back to New Zealand and go to California to stay in the redwoods would happen for him. I truly believed that.

Byron received a copy of the Gordon Wheeler documents in the mail that day and started telling us all about his case. The *Gordon Wheeler* case is interesting because Morrison County law enforcement shot twenty rounds at Gordon Wheeler. This man had shown himself at a county commissioner's meeting and had threatened to take the county prosecutor hostage along with the county administrator. He was claiming that they put him in considerable debt by not allowing him a license to run his business. After complaining to them for about twenty minutes, he displayed a weapon during the meeting. Then-sheriff Wetzel and a deputy discussed strategy and then started shooting him several times. He went down, and they proceeded to shoot him while he was down to make sure the threat was gone. The following transcript is the statement of Sheriff Michel Gerard Wetzel on June 25, 2008, at 13:05 hours, bureau number 2008000162:

> I saw Mr. Wheeler's head come above the desk and I saw a handgun above the desk trained directly at me. I started firing. I don't remember how many rounds I fired. I was moving while I fired and got around the edge of the desk and I could see Mr. Wheeler had come down. He wasn't flat. I saw his right arm, but I couldn't see his left arm and I specifically remember firing two more rounds. I couldn't see where the gun was.

Before Wetzel fired at Wheeler this occurred: taken from that same BCA investigative report, Lieutenant Motes stated that he first told Wheeler to drop his weapon and for the council members to get down. Wheeler appeared and held his weapon up at the ceiling. Then Wheeler pointed the gun in Motes's direction. Lieutenant Motes fired at least four rounds at Wheeler. When Motes came around the desk, Wheeler was still moving. He could not see Wheeler's hands, so he fired an additional four rounds.

These statements are also part of an investigative report by Special Agent Chad Museus on September 19, 2008. The medical examiner reported that Mr. Wheeler was struck by seven bullets: one to the left side of his head, one to right side of head. The other five bullets hit him the back of his torso. A total of twenty rounds were fired.

Lieutenant Motes also stated in the report that he discussed less lethal options with Sheriff Wetzel, to include tasers and bean bag rounds, but it was determined that those options were not feasible in their situation. Many considered it overkill that Wheeler was shot in the back several times. This was the same word, "overkill", Sheriff Wetzel used in how Byron reacted to his situation, yet he reacted the same! If trained law enforcement personnel were free to shoot until the threat was gone, were average, untrained American citizens not granted the same privilege in defense of themselves? What was the difference between Sheriff Wetzel shooting Wheeler in the back and Byron Smith shooting to defend himself in his own home?

Byron was nowhere to be found when I got home from work this Friday night. John was plowing snow and would be late, so it was my opportunity to have dinner and to talk with Dilan alone. He had seemed edgy lately and talking about losing another ten pounds. I was concerned that he was trying to become too thin. He had assembled a new band and wanted to slim down for better stage presence, but I wanted to make sure there were no other concerns. He had weighed 200 pounds at this same time last year, and now he was down to 155. He was five foot eleven, and he was telling me he wants to weigh 145, and I told him he was thin enough. I also knew that last year Byron had referred to him as getting pudgy, and I remember when Karen Carpenter (the seventies singer) had anorexia because she had seen an article by a music critic calling her pudgy, so she wanted to lose weight for performing, and that was how her eating disorder began. Byron had been concerned because Dilan would again be working at Dairy Queen, which was very tempting. We talked about school and how proud he was of himself getting 101 percent in chemistry because he thought that would be his hardest class this semester. He had been stressed because the Dairy Queen was opening next month, so he had to go back to work, and he was taking a zero-hour class this semester, which meant he starts school at 7:00 a.m. instead of 8:00 a.m. He was concerned about juggling it all as he wanted to keep his grades high so he could get accepted into a good college. He talked with Doug, the owner of the Dairy Queen, and he promised to lessen his hours until summer to he could keep his grades high. Doug was appreciative of the fact Dilan would be working there again. He was the senior student worker there and had been there for a couple of years.

Byron came back to our home around 8:45 p.m. He was in a happy mood and started talking about his afternoon. He had opened a path to his rental property, which he had purchased last July (2012). Dilan told him about his 101% grade in chemistry and told him how happy he was in achieving that! Then Dilan left to pick up Kory and Tremayne—his bandmates. Byron proceeded to talk about Dilan wearing the suit that he wore when he graduated from high school. He had brought it over from his house as he thought it would fit Dilan perfectly. Byron's 50-year class reunion was coming up in 2016, which is the same year Dilan graduates from high school. It is a navy-blue shark-skin fabric with a thin, small-notched collar. He set aside for Dilan to try on as Byron said he had weighed 155 when he graduated from high school. Anyway, he proceeded to show me two other suits, along with the graduation suit, and explained the notch in each collar varies due to the trends and some suit jackets are two button and some are three buttons. The graduation suit he said may be ten years ahead of its time as the collar was so narrow, but still a nice-looking suit. If Dilan would have been back from picking up his friends, he would have received a lesson in suit fashion that night. Byron then brought out a bunch of ties and displayed them to me, pairing them up with the proper look for each of the suits hanging from my dining room chairs. He had a real glittery, silver tie that was unusually showy for a man to wear. I will be curious to see if Dilan would wear it with the navy-blue suit. As the fashion discussion ended, he carefully put away each of the suits and ties to his room and settled in for some reading. He will typically read the Economist *magazine, which is his favorite or some other electronics publication, like Wired. Byron devotes several hours every day to reading. He selects a variety of magazines, books or newspapers. He prefers it quiet while reading which is sometimes difficult in our home with usually the sound of radio or TV as background noise. Byron seems to be able to tune it all out.*

His plea hearing was held on January 23. This was where he actually pled not guilty. They scheduled the start of the trial for April 14, which was actually the day jury selection will begin. I took my lunchbreak for this hearing as I knew it wouldn't last but a half hour at the most, and it lasted about twenty minutes. Directly after the hearing, Meshbesher called us into a small conference room. The trial will cost twenty thousand dollars each week. The judge said the trial should only take one week. Meshbesher said it will take three to four weeks. Byron had to give him a check for fifty-two thousand dollars to start paying all the witnesses and wanted another twenty-five thousand dollars whenever he could get it together. Byron seemed quite down that evening because Meshbesher basically told him that he needed to pay soon because "we don't want to see you go to prison for the rest of your life." Byron was telling me all this as he was sitting at the kitchen counter while I was cleaning and washing dishes. He stated that he told Meshbesher that he had turned over all assets to Bruce, who was working in Nigeria right now, so it would have to wait until his return to the United States.

The next day he went to St. Cloud to go to the John Deere store for a lawn tractor repair and do some small shopping. He seemed in a good mood as we went to our usual Friday night dinner. After dinner we stopped at the Weyerhauser Musuem. They were having a special opening with a candlelit path from one museum to another. As we entered the building, Byron immediately went to a surveyor's drawing of Little Falls in its early days and pointed out the changes that have occurred in the last 100 years. We walked around for about 1/2 hour looking at all the exhibits and then he spoke with one of the caretakers there and asked her if she knew what the tallest dam was in the US. Of course, he knew the answer: Blanchard Dam. His father had worked there for 23 years and Byron proceeded to tell us more information on almost every exhibit in the museum. I had noticed a long row of phone books in one of the rooms and pointed them out to him. He opened the door and pulled out the one from 1964 to look up his old home phone number from when he and his family had lived on the west side of town. Sure enough, Ted Smith was listed as 632-4836. He said that he would always remember the phone number because you just had to double each next number.

A copy of the morning's St. Cloud Times *featured a guest columnist from Grey Eagle who had written an article about Byron's case stating that laws need to be changed in regards to self-defense. The laws in that regard have not been changed since 1963 and basically it says that a Minnesota homeowner should run from his home to avoid any harm to the perpetrator. You could be liable for injuries to the offender if you harm them in any way during the crime. Byron has said this all along. He repeats time after time that he had no choice but to shoot. The columnist also stated that her son lives only two blocks from Byron's home.*

Sheriff Wetzel released word to the Morrison County commissioners that because of the *Gordon Wheeler* case and Byron Smith case, he felt it was time to retire. Michel was only forty-nine years old, but he has worked for the county for about thirty years. Byron felt a victory in this. One of the county commissioners I spoke with said he saw it coming last year when Wetzel sued the county to get a raise last year.

I was reading and watching TV the other night when Byron got back from a visit to his house to check on things. He sat down in the chair next to me and told me that he thought Dilan was annoyed that he was still living with us and he seems very irritated lately. Dilan has been touchy lately but he rises each morning at 5:30 to get to school by 7:00 a.m. It's an American history class he wanted to take this semester. I explained that to Byron. I know Dilan lately has been annoyed with the fact this tragic event consumes our house and is constant conversation over dinner. Byron also has high expectations of youth and Dilan is feeling the stress. Byron wasn't sure that Dilan would confide in me about that, but I assured him that it's more about his new schedule than anything else.

Saturday morning on the 7th of February Byron was up unusually early. I had been up for about 1/2 hour and he came into the kitchen with a suit on. He had an appointment with a psychologist this morning that Meshbesher had wanted him to see. The appointment was at 10:00, so he was getting ready to leave by 8:00. He seemed in a normal mood, but there was some type of test he had taken early on with his first visit in jail. The psychologist wanted to retest him and summarize his progress since that time.

Byron got back at 7:30 p.m. after a five-hour session with the forensic psychologist. This psychologist is planned to be one of the witnesses in his trial. He will explain to the jury about post-traumatic stress and how it affects reactions to certain circumstances. Byron's circumstances are those of being burglarized repeated times and each time closer together with more loss. He went to bed early but shared in the morning what the psychologist spoke with him about. He took another 270-question test—the same as the one he took while he was still in jail. He said the doctor wanted to compare his answers from then and now. Some of the questions were personality type, such as "Do you think your father was a good person?" and then a similar question later in the test was if he thought his mother was a good person. The doctor wanted to understand his background about the fact that he had spent many years overseas in places and cities that some people would not consider safe, but he was comfortable working in them and walking around with never even being pickpocketed. The doctor will also bring out the fact that he came back to retire to a small town where he thought he would always be safe; a town he grew up in. And within a few years he was the target of burglars again and again and again. He was abandoned by the sheriff's department and left to his own defenses to deal with a situation that had no other ending than a bad one. The day was very exhausting for him, yet this doctor is prepared to give a great testimony as to what caused his reaction to the teens that broke into his home for the final time on Thanksgiving Day.

There was more frustration with the suspicious traffic that continued down Elm Street. Byron gave the police department the license number of a maroon truck that made weekly short visits to the neighbor next to Byron's home. Since giving the number to police, the truck hadn't been seen since. Byron had expressed there might be a leak in the Little Falls Police Department unless this truck was keenly aware of an unmarked police car. This was not the first time that license numbers had been provided for suspicious activity and then the activity seemed to stop instantly. This frustration continued because he was certain that there was a definite connection with that drug traffic and the lack of investigation by the sheriff's department in his burglaries along with charging him with murder.

On February 19, 2014, at 4:00 p.m., I visited Little Falls High School and asked to speak with one of the teachers. I happened onto a blog spot this high school teacher had written showing Byron's mug shot indicating that this was the face of a murderer. I was astounded that a professional educator would write that. Normally, I had learned to let these things slide, but I could no longer do it. I had had enough of people feeling sorry for burglars and not hearing the other side to the story. After checking in as a visitor, this teacher was promptly paged. My son was taking her Spanish class next semester. She came down to greet me, and I asked to go somewhere private so that I could speak with her. I told her that my son has signed up for Spanish class next semester and I needed to speak with her about something. I asked her if she knew him, and she told me that she did not make it a practice to get to know future students. We sat down, and I told her I had more of a personal question and asked her if she blogged. She told me that she did not blog and didn't have a blog. I then pulled out my printout with her name and Facebook picture with a blog that contained a posting of Byron Smith's mug shot and above it were her words referring to the media and that they should use this picture so everyone would know what he looked like after he killed those unarmed teens. She became upset and asked me what this had to do with her curriculum. I stated that I couldn't have my son taught by a teacher who would judge someone and write this without knowing the whole story. She asked me again what this had to do with her curriculum. I told her that I wasn't here to argue with her but told her what she wrote (as she was finally admitting that she wrote it now) was very inappropriate, especially because students could read it. I told her that those kids had broken into our neighbor's home repeatedly and had stolen his father's war medals for drug money. I told her that he was a Boy Scout leader and had always wanted to help kids and I wanted her to hear the other side of the story. She got up from her chair and told me we were done talking. I got up to leave, and as she turned away from me walking, she said in a louder tone that she wanted my son removed from her class and that she didn't appreciate being prejudged.

I immediately went down to the principal's office and told him what happened. I wanted to make sure she didn't talk to him first and portray me as harassing and threatening, of which I was neither. I just wanted to tell her another side to this story. He seemed concerned at first that I just marched up to her room, but I assured him that I announced myself first. I explained to him that I was concerned about a teacher that my son was going to have and her written words. He asked to see it. He began talking about the case and how the fact that the trial was going to be held this spring was going to tear this school apart as some of the students here would be named as being involved in some of the burglaries. He was afraid that the media would portray Little Falls high school students as all being bad. He stated that there was a network of fifteen to twenty kids that were friends to the two who were shot that might also be involved in some of the burglaries. The timing of the trial during spring was unusually bad because of how busy it was that time of year. He was wishing it would happen during the summer instead. I told him that Judge Anderson decided the calendar. I asked the principal if this teacher I had spoken with had any personal connection to those kids. He stated that she was Haile's adviser. I expressed my concern about Dilan and his dad being very public in defending our neighbor and that if any bullying or negativity would occur, I would be removing Dilan from school promptly. "I need to protect my son," I told him and left. Certainly, this presented a huge discovery that the school had a deep fear of exposing the reality of students' criminal activities and the effect it would have on the school itself. Also to consider, Judge Anderson's wife was a teacher. Did this fear influence the decision to not allow the testimony of the students involved in the Smith burglaries?

The next evening, Byron, again, came back from his house after checking on things but kept his coat on and asked me to get my coat on to come with him. He said the moon was bright and full and that it shone so blue on the snow that I just had to take a walk with him to see it. He said, "It will only be a quarter-hour walk." I must have hesitated with my answer. It was about 9:00 p.m. already and it was really cold out. The temperature was several degrees below zero. But I began to imagine the beauty of what he had seen, so I grabbed my coat, gloves, boots, hat and off we went down Elm Street for a moonlit walk in the frigid winter. We walked down to his home and around to his other property. He was spot-on as to the beauty of the night. The moon shone a bright blue color across the snow. He talked about how much work he had done to his new property and what his future plans were for it. The conversation is comfortable with Byron. We are like old friends that have known each other for many years, when in fact we have not known each other but a few short years. The moonlight reflecting off the snow made the whole sky bright as we walked along the dark path without even a flashlight. The night was calm and peaceful, beautiful and bright. We got back exactly at 10:00 p.m. and he thanked me for walking with him. We didn't know it at the time but that would be his last winter walk through his properties.

The tension in our home is getting thicker as the trial date approached. Byron was sleeping more hours. He went to bed around 8:00 p.m. and he was still not up at 7:30 a.m. when I left the house for work. I noticed this a few days ago and asked John if he had talked with him. I was working all day, so I didn't see much of him during the week. The attorney fees were adding up quickly. He needed another eighty thousand dollars before the trial started, twenty thousand dollars each week for four weeks. I had called Adam this week and expressed my concerns about Dilan testifying. Byron wanted him to testify because Dilan was very articulate and could speak well about Byron. Byron had helped Dilan in many ways. My fears were how the media would report the testimony. He had to go to school every day, and if all the kids knew that Byron was living in Dilan Lange's home, I didn't know what kind of retaliation he might be subject to. We had to be prepared for the worst but hope for the best. John and I would also testify to Byron's character. If the media reported a play-by-play account of every day of the trial, everyone would know that he had been living in our home, and I had only shared that with very few people. In fact, some coworkers had asked me directly where he was staying, and I had said, "With friends." It was not a lie, but I felt I needed to keep it somewhat secret for safety reasons. There had been enough threats just in the cars parading down Elm Street without having the general public knowing where he was living now. Byron did have a plan if he was acquitted. He would be packed and head out of town right away. He had a friend from his college days that had a cabin, and he was going to stay there for a month or so. The pretrial hearing was slated for March 25, so we would know more about what the prosecution was going to present.

After we returned from our routine Friday-night dinner, Byron had suggested we watch a movie. Feeling a bit tired, I agreed to a short one (meaning less than two hours), so he selected a couple, but I had never heard of either, even admitting himself that one was weird with dry humor. His first pick was Bamboozled, *the dry-humor movie, but starred Jada Pinkett-Smith and Damon Wayans, a film by Spike Lee. The other was* Topsy Turvy, *a Gilbert and Sullivan movie that had won two Academy awards in 1999 for best costume design and best makeup. Since neither of them appealed to me, I decided to pick one out tonight, so I chose* Night Shift. *I hadn't seen it in 20 years and knew it was an easy, light-humored story, so he agreed. But first, he wanted to watch a cartoon, like they used to do in the big theaters. He chose a Daffy Duck cartoon in Norwegian with Finnish subtitles. He admitted that you don't even need the words to understand the cartoon. It lasted about 20 minutes, and frankly, he is right, but I still like to hear words I can understand right away.*

Twice now Meshbesher had asked for the complete video of Thanksgiving Day and twice now it had been sent with the missing video of the intruders entering Byron's property. They knew it existed because it was mentioned at the grand jury hearing. Byron knew it existed because of the equipment he used. Law enforcement or the prosecution had completely blocked out or omitted the bits of video where it showed the burglars entering his property. The video stopped at 11:45 p.m. on Thursday and then began again at 9:30 a.m. on

Friday. Around 10:30 a.m. the video showed two people approaching Byron's property and walking over his blacktopped driveway and running back through the trees on the day after Thanksgiving. So it was as he thought: there were more burglars coming on Thanksgiving! If law enforcement would give Meshbesher the complete original video, these people could be identified. Byron's camera equipment would be able to enlarge the picture to see a face. With the copies, the resolution was six times less than the original. The prosecution team seemed to not be forthcoming with the evidence. The copies of the video presented to Meshbesher also did not show the numerous law enforcement cars going in and out on Friday afternoon. Officer Scherping was shown going in but never coming out. The video seemed to possibly be tampered with. Todd Kosovich, an assistant prosecutor, admitted to going into Byron's home to check out the crime scene, but the video did not show him entering or leaving. To date, this video had never been seen. Nothing would be turned over in original form to the defense until all appeals were exhausted.

CHAPTER 11
THE TRIAL: JURY SELECTION

Note: This section may seem lengthy to read, but it's important to note how many potential jurors were related to the Brady and Kifer families. Also notable are those who are friends of law enforcement.

On March 25, 2014, the pretrial hearing was scheduled for 1:00 p.m. As I arrived on the steps of the courthouse, there was a cameraman at the top of the stairs. No doubt that he was waiting for Byron to appear, but by this time, John and Byron were already in a small conference room waiting for his attorney. Byron was going over his list of all the members of the Haile and Nick Memorial fund and the list of their friends as I had printed them from Facebook, and he entered them into his long, prepared list. When jury selection occurred, he could have a quick look for any potential juror that was appearing for selection who might want to get on the final panel to automatically vote him guilty. Byron spent hours compiling this list from the Facebook information. Both Adam and Steve were running behind today as we discovered when they arrived about a half hour late. The prosecution delivered a package of work for them at five o'clock the afternoon before, so they were up late preparing for the day. Meshbesher announced that he would ask for a dismissal of the case due to the fact they had not been provided all the evidence they had asked for. As we proceeded to the courtroom, everyone was waiting. We filed in the back row behind the family members as Meshbesher asked for a case dismissal and cited the statute number along with the three dates he had asked for evidence. Chase Fortier's name was brought up in court as there apparently were photos of a rifle he received that belonged to Byron and had buried it on someone else's property. Nick Brady's shoe was important as per the information they received late yesterday, and Meshbesher was now demanding that it be turned over. The assistant prosecutor answered this incompliance to the judge and pointed out that Mr. Meshbesher could visit their office at any time and look at any of the evidence he chose. He could also go to the Morrison County sheriff's office and look at any photographs he chose. The judge was mainly concerned about jury selection and how long each attorney needed to present their case so he could tell potential jurors how long the trial would take. They finally settled on a week each with a week for jury selection and closing arguments. The event lasted about an hour.

As we walked out of the courtroom, the *Channel 5 Eyewitness* news reporter and cameraman were ready to get a picture and statement from Byron. As he exited the courthouse, a woman reporter pushed a microphone in his face and asked him if the law enforcement had done their job, he might not be in this mess and the kids would still be alive. He turned to answer her and said, "Please talk to my attorney." With that she followed John outside for comment, and John told her that Byron shouldn't have ever been charged. As she asked why, he closed the door on her.

A few days after the hearing, the list of names of witnesses for the prosecution came out. Cody Kasper was to join Nick and Haile on Thanksgiving as the lookout while Nick gained entry to Byron's home for yet another burglary. Cody received an invitation that day to go snowboarding with a friend, Logan, so he was not there on that fatal day. Logan had also told John that Nick had told him if Byron ever caught him stealing and he had to go to jail, he would kill Byron. John happened to be at Logan's place of work when he mentioned this along with the fact that Nick always carried a knife around his waist and wore this bullet-proof vest. Byron had mentioned that Luberts had asked him (after observing the bodies in the basement) if he saw anything on the boy's waist. Deputies had about forty-five minutes alone in his home while he sat in a sheriff's car until he was transferred to jail. When Byron received the jury pool listing with over 130 names, we went right to work to determine whom we knew on the list, who would be good and fair, and who would not. I had printed copies of the names of the Facebook friends of the teen burglars, and Byron put them in an alphabetical table along with the fans of the memorial fund. He asked me to check out some of the jury pool. The first six names I checked on Facebook were either related to Nick and Haile or were their Facebook friends. I was astonished! This couldn't be just a coincidence. When I told him that, we determined that the jury selection pool was definitely tainted. We met in Meshbesher's office one day just to go over the list. It took several hours to go through each person one by one. It was decided that during selection, Byron would indicate to his attorney if that potential juror was on his list of Facebook friends, they would decline that person.

As the trial began on April 14, the potential jurors awaited questioning while Orput and Meshbesher hammered out motions. Judge Anderson asked Meshbesher about the subpoena for Jesse Kriesel and also excluding Chad Museus from the bench during trial. The judge questioned how many burglaries did the state have evidence of other than the October 27 burglary. Judge Anderson also presided over the Kriesel plea and so was fully aware there was a June 2012 incident (burglary of Mr. Smith) alleged and admitted to. Orput chimed in that he was aware of only one prior burglary of the Smith residence, which was the October incident, and had no evidence of any other. (This was absolutely not true as Byron had reported the other incidences when he was burglarized in October.)

Meshbesher explained that there was evidence of four previous burglaries, but that Smith did not recognize that immediately, but he had reported them and presented a list of what had been taken and when. Meshbesher stated that they had subpoenaed Cody Kasper to corroborate prior burglaries. Cody Kasper participated in those burglaries as a lookout for Nick Brady and he actually watched Nick Brady commit the burglaries. Judge Anderson admitted being fully aware of September burglaries and two in October as he participated in their plea hearings. The court transcripts indicate that Judge Anderson remembered that Cody Kasper had admitted that he and Nick Brady had taken a chainsaw and some copper wire in the Smith garage during the first part of October but right after his (Cody's) birthday, which was the tenth, but before, the plea was about the seventeenth of October was what he admitted to.

Meshbesher also brought in an additional motion for Dr. Alsdurf to explain anxiety and fear. Judge Anderson stated that the court had not excluded him or included him at this point.

As the first potential jurors, twenty-two of them, entered the courtroom, Judge Anderson explained that the defendant was presumed innocent and the state had to prove guilt. Byron was introduced to the first group of potential jurors as the judge explained that he did not have to introduce evidence, ask questions, or prove his innocence. To ensure a fair trial by jury, it was necessary for the attorneys and the judge to ask questions that might seem offensive, but this was a serious matter and the court was merely seeking information to select a fair and impartial jury. The group was sworn in to tell the truth and one remained for questioning to start. Ten were excused until 1:00 p.m. The defense can refuse fifteen jurors without reason; the state has nine refusals. The first prospective juror admitted she had read about the case but not really kept up with it. She lived on a dairy farm near Hillman with her husband and young children (ages seven and six) and had never been burglarized and her family owned guns for hunting only. The first potential juror was accepted by both parties, Lisa L. She was informed she was selected, given instructions, and ordered to come back next week for the beginning of the trial.

The second potential juror, Desiree A. entered. This juror knew Chad Museus, from the disappearance of her father who had been missing for five years from Cass County. There had been no resolution in her father's case yet. She lived in Motley, and Judge Anderson heard her divorce case two years ago. She also had a permit to carry a weapon but did not practice or own guns, just took the training for it. She had brothers and sisters that also had permits and carry pistols for defense. She was an early childhood educator and, since the school year was coming to an end, had time for jury duty. She had never been burglarized. She was also accepted for duty after a few minutes of questioning.

The third prospective juror, Ms. Marshik, was a candidate who knew Haile Kifer and admitted she could not be fair. She stated she was a stepcousin to both Nick and Haile and had also donated to a memorial fund for them. This information was on her questionnaire, and so without an interview of the court, she was dismissed.

The next prospective juror was Maxine H. She admitted being charged with arson in 2001 in Becker County but had civil rights restored. She was candid about taking medications for certain health conditions and indicated they helped her concentrate after the judge asked her if they hampered her ability to concentrate. She had lived in Morrison County for two years and was close to her sister in the county, who owned guns and had a permit. Her sister was in Iraq and nephew served in Afghanistan. Both parties accepted her as the third juror. Meshbesher turned around and stated that she would be his wild card.

I noticed during this proceeding that Todd Kosovich, a Morrison County prosecutor, was sending hand gestures to Orput at this time. They were number signals with his hands, showing numbers 1, 2, 3, 4, etc., for each of the prospective jurors as they were answering questions. Although it seemed as if he was trying to conceal these gestures somewhat, he wasn't very good at it.

The next prospect was a funeral director who had embalmed the bodies of Nick and Haile. He was immediately excused as the court treated that position very similar to an investigating officer.

The next candidate was Wesley H., who was a retired computer consultant/programmer with a son-in-law who was a Brooklyn Center policeman. He told the court he was a strong Christian and believed in following the law of the land. He also obtained a permit to carry within the past year. He obtained it because of break-ins in his lake community twelve miles west of Mille Lacs. He had spoken on the phone with Deputy Luberts before about the break-ins within his community but didn't know him personally. He had grandkids ages seventeen and twenty, whom he indicated were not "pillars of the youth community." He was concerned about them needing counseling as his son and their mother had split. He went on to express the concern of his neighbors being broken into, but ultimately the perpetrator was caught. Orput asked him one question about having any problem rendering a guilty verdict, to which he answered, "No, if you have proven it beyond a reasonable doubt." This fourth juror was approved, and he was given instructions as well.

The next prospective juror was Sarah H., an admitted Jehovah's Witness who had taught Bible studies at the Morrison County Jail. She also stated that Brian-Paul Crowder, a possible defense witness, had cut her hair before, and she had done painting for his mother. She was a deer hunter but used her dad's guns, who owned ten to fifteen. She and her husband own a professional cleaning service. Meshbesher asked about her questionnaire, and after a pause in the proceedings, she was dismissed. The next one was Roger W., who worked in computer-activated design, drafting, and programming. He was also a master sergeant in the Air Force (twenty years) responsible for missile repair and became a supervisor holding high positions. He had heard about the case via television news and also the local bars. He also had a permit to carry, a .38 Ruger. He explained he was a victim of a holdup in Las Vegas in 1979 when he won three hundred dollars in the casino and a gentleman with a gun asked him for it in the dark parking lot. He surrendered the money. He stated he was an NRA member as it was a requirement for the Sportsman's Club for target shooting. He was single and had no children but was an avid reader of science fiction, Shakespeare, Milton, and Voltaire. He was passed by both parties and accepted for duty as the fifth selection.

The next prospective juror was Laura S., who worked with residents that were mentally ill. She had read some of the articles on the case in the Morrison County Record and used guns as a deer hunter. She was born in Cambridge and had lived in Morrison County for three years. She owned one gun, which was kept locked. She was asked if she wanted to be on the jury, and she stated, "Yes." But after questioning by both counsel, she was dismissed as a juror.

The next one, Jennifer H., was dismissed after questioning on knowing one of the Morrison County sergeants and stating her husband was a high school biology teacher. Melissa T. was next and questioned about her sister-in-law, who was familiar with Nick and Haile. She was dismissed. Next was Dawn R., who had heard about the case but didn't watch news. She was a personal care assistant for a month in Little Falls but was now unemployed living in Little Falls Cottages. She was born on the Red Lake Reservation when her mom moved her to Duluth and had lived in Morrison County two years. She hadn't been back to the reservation due to the amount of crimes, so family would come to see her and her two young children here. She was approved for duty as the sixth juror.

The next prospective juror was the son of a lady that pled guilty to third-degree murder in Morrison County about two years ago when she sold a fentanyl patch to a young man who ingested it and died of an overdose. Orput used one of his strikes, and he was not questioned.

The next person to enter the courtroom was Peter C. a sheet metal worker currently working in the Bismarck area. He stated that it might be difficult with his employment to serve, but nonetheless he stated he could be fair, but he was dismissed. That was the conclusion of day 1 of Byron's trial and jury selection.

Day 2 started with bringing in fifteen more potential jurors. They were sworn in, given instructions by the judge, and let half of them go until 1:00 p.m. that afternoon. The next juror had a sister-in-law who was murdered in Anoka in 2004. A twenty-one-year-old man broke into her home and shot her while she slept. The man fled as her husband chased him, a manhunt ensued, and he was eventually caught. She indicated this would not affect her to give an impartial decision in this case. She also was neighbors with a former sheriff in Morrison County as another potential juror had been as well. There was again a brief pause in the proceedings and then this juror was excused.

Carlos S. was next to be questioned. His son's girlfriend was a cousin to Haile Kifer. Although he had never met Haile, the girlfriend was in his house in tears talking about details of the shooting. She indicated drugs were involved, so he heard this from her and not the newspapers. He indicated that in his country, guns were shot in the air and people run away. (He served a year in the Romanian Army.) He candidly stated he was not the right person to be a juror in this case. He was excused. Next up was Michael W. The judge asked him about his questionnaire indicating members of police were social friends in the Pierz area and in Long Prairie. He indicated he had already formed an opinion that what Mr. Smith did was wrong and he maybe could change his mind, but he wasn't sure he could. He was excused also.

Prospective juror Jarrett Y. entered next. He had been in the army from 1975–77 as a combat engineer and was currently working at Royal Farms. He indicated that his garage had been broken into in the middle of the night with rifles stolen along with other items. He reported this, but nothing was ever solved. He also admitted to knowing Haile Kifer's mother, Jenny. He grew up and went to grade school with Jenny's dad. When asked how he felt about hearing a case about Jenny's daughter, he stated, "That one is hard to answer. I don't know." He admitted to seeing Jenny's parents three or four times a year. In the end, he stated it would be difficult for him to be open-minded about the case, and he was dismissed. Next juror candidate was Amanda Ramirez-Olson, who mentored children with behavioral health issues and took care of vulnerable adults with mental health issues. On her questionnaire, she listed that she was acquainted with the victim's sister as they knew each other growing up. She did also state she had concerns that Smith didn't call the police right away and thought that was important. She also had lost a child seven years ago from a choking incident when he was just one year old. She was also a good friend of Lewis Wilczek, who had been murdered in Morrison County several years ago. She stated that she knew a lot of people who went to the funerals of Haile and Nick and admitted being on the jury would put her in an awkward spot. She admitted that she did not want to be on this jury and was excused.

Next potential juror, Douglas R., who had been laid off from Larson Boats since 2008. He had never handled a gun, didn't hunt, and lost his wife about a year ago. He admitted truthfully that he didn't really want to be on the jury but was selected as the seventh one.

For the potential eighth juror, a man who was a former Minneapolis police officer was questioned. He worked four years in homicide and five years in forgery and fraud division. He also stated in his questionnaire that his son-in-law was related to the victims. However, the only contact he had was at his daughter's wedding. Prospective juror Dennis H. admitted that it would be uncomfortable facing his son-in-law's relatives if a not-guilty verdict was rendered. He saw the father of Nick Brady two to three times a year. He also attended the same church as Deputy Scherping. After Meshbesher questioned his work in Minneapolis at length, this juror was excused. They took a recess for lunch and were back into the courtroom in about an hour. Before beginning the proceedings, Meshbesher told the judge that he had heard about a recording from a WCCO radio show from a grand juror named Mary who said things that occurred during the grand jury proceedings. She talked about what others said, how they interpreted evidence, and Meshbesher wanted that information to go on record. Orput had not heard it, and his associate, Wartner stated that he didn't see the relevancy of the recording at this time in regards to this case. Meshbesher was concerned if the jurors selected yesterday had listened to this radio show as he hadn't asked them about it as he hadn't known it then. The judge decided to listen to the tape at 8:30 a.m. this morning with both counsel.

The next prospective juror entered, Keith E., who worked on a turkey farm. The judge did ask him if he had listened to the WCCO radio show yesterday, and he had not. He used guns for hunting deer, goose, duck, coyote, etc. He admitted to meeting Haile's brother as he was of the same age group as the victims. He stated he wanted justice for the family (of Haile). He lived at home just outside Swanville with his parents. He was excused from service. At this point, there was a mix-up with two potential jurors, Evelyn M. and Sheryl M. The biographical information was for Sheryl, but Evelyn was present for questioning. Both attorneys would be given Evelyn's questionnaire, and they would question her later that day. They moved to the next potential juror, who was Paul S., a former E-4 Navy and electronics technician. He had admitted that his car had been burglarized long ago with tools and a tire taken. He had a permit to carry and did target shooting occasionally on his farm. He owned seven handguns. He also elaborated on how convicted criminals were let out of jail too early. After a pause in proceedings, he was excused. (Just on a sidenote, Paul S. was an original member of a support group brought together for Byron by Beverly Nouis of Little Falls. He truly believed that Byron was defending self and home, and he had stated publicly that he would not have voted guilty.)

The next juror was Douglas V., a Gold'n Plump supply analyst with three young children, ages one to five. He just started working there only two months ago. He owned two guns for deer hunting and had worked at Theilen Meats in high school and then went to college in Duluth for business. He had a good friend who was a cop in Lino Lakes. After a few more questions on family, he was selected as the eighth juror.

The next prospect was Evelyn M., who had a hobby of hunting rattlesnakes. She was a gun owner and had been in farming all her life and enjoyed the challenge of hunting snakes. She and her husband caught as many as ninety-six in one day in North Dakota. She had not followed the case closely as not much of a newspaper reader. She indicated that a cousin living near the cities had taken in a homeless person and that individual killed her cousin, son, and brother-in-law that night. Meshbesher questioned her about her granddaughter, Kayla, who is seventeen years old and if she had talked about this case with her, and she had not. She was selected as the ninth juror.

Next up was Katherine M. who had been a juror in the past on a sexual abuse case. She lived on the Mississippi River south of Mr. Smith's home on the same side. On her questionnaire, she indicated that she and her husband were petitioning to the DNR to open the channel after the Highway 10 bypass when they changed the river flow. Smith did not want this done, so they were at odds over the issue, which happened twenty to thirty years ago. She had no personal confrontation with him. She also knew Deputy Scherping rather well through the Continuing Education Center. She admitted that she would give more credibility to the law enforcement profession due to their training. She also noted that Kim Brady was a student at the CEC, where she taught at the alternative high school, but she didn't have much contact with her when she worked there. She had been retired for four years. She was excused as a juror.

Prospective juror Michelle W. entered the room after the judge indicated they needed to pick up the inventories. Michelle was employed at Nisswa Marine just two weeks ago. She had previously worked for Crestliner and Larson Boats in customer service and warranty. She did have to testify as a young child in defense of her dad on an assault charge, which left her feeling that her words were twisted, but that was a long time ago. She also stated she had a cousin that killed his wife after coming back from Vietnam. They had lived near the cities. She did indicate that she thought Smith used excessive force. She also admitted working with Haile's mother and father in the boat business. She felt at this time she was in favor of the children. After extensive questioning on past incidences of violent crimes with people she was close too, she was excused as a juror.

Next was Pamela J., a postal worker for eight years. She had served on a jury once before regarding a car theft. Her children are twenty and twenty-two. Her son and husband both owned and used guns—rifles and shotguns. She wanted to be on the jury as her last experience was interesting and educational. After a few short questions, she was accepted as the next juror, the tenth. The second day of selection had come to a close around 4:30 p.m. with four more selections needed to complete the jury.

Again, on Wednesday morning, the judge instructed another group of potential jurors and retired them to the jury room and began with the first one, Judy J. Judy stated in her questionnaire that her son went to school with Nick Brady at Pillager High School, but they were not friends and he did not convey anything about him. She wrote in her questionnaire that she felt Mr. Smith crossed the line of self-protection. She elaborated that because a student went to her son's school, she took an interest in the story and read media sources. She felt that it could have been stopped at a certain point and law enforcement should have been called. She went on to admit that she didn't know if she could be fair and impartial. She was excused.

Julie L. was next. She was working at Red's Auto & Bait in Pierz. She had been there for six years and was also a supervisor. She had ten-year-old twins and lived in Lastrup with her husband, who was a truck driver. After a few questions about her personal feelings on guns, she was excused.

Kristopher B. came in next. He was a mechanic at Eagle Construction and prior to that worked at Northwood Turf and Power in Baxter. He was in the US Army from 1990 to 1994 in the Persian Gulf. He had recently been a leader in Cub Scouts and moved up to Boy Scouts. A couple of years ago, he had a back window in his minivan shot out just sitting in the driveway. It was reported, but nothing solved. He also stated he knew a police officer, Rick Heurung, whom he went to school with and played softball. He had also worked with some of the deputies: Shawn Larsen and Dave Scherping. He went to school with Scherping and also worked with him years ago. He was a dad to four young children, whose wife works in St. Cloud at the hospital. Meshbesher asked him at length about his service in Kuwait and Iraq. He witnessed injured soldiers and some who were killed. He stated it to be somewhat frightening, but it was a long time ago. When his van window was shot out, he stated Dave Scherping was the deputy he worked with, and he considers him a friend. He then admitted that he (Byron) did it a little wrong—he went too far. But he could understand it to that point. At the end, he stated that he did not want to be on the jury due to the financial strains it would place on his family. He stated that he would serve anyway as it was his duty. He was accepted for duty and given instructions to not listen to or read any media about the case. He was the eleventh one selected.

The next potential juror to take the stand was Margit L. Margit was the wife of the other funeral director in Little Falls. She first went on to explain a break-in in their garage in which a chainsaw was taken a couple of years ago. She also admitted to knowing Brian Middendorf, but they were not friends. She was also in contact with Brian-Paul Crowder, a potential witness in this case, and knew him as the manager of Oakland Cemetery, so contacted him when they have a funeral. The judge explained that Margit was in his son's high school class and she admitted being in the judge's home. She also has a nine-month-old son with Goldenhar syndrome and was scheduled for all-day testing at the University of Minnesota in the next couple of weeks. Both her and her husband would be going. She explained that it might be easier for her to hear about deceased teens due to the funeral work. She had seen deceased teens before. She admitted that she felt Mr. Smith should have contacted the police sooner, but her husband felt that Mr. Smith was in self-defense and the kids shouldn't have been in his house. Her husband owned about fifteen to twenty guns, but she did not use guns. Meshbesher asked her if she had spoken with anyone about this case other than her husband, and she said she did with a friend. She stated that she told him she thought Smith was guilty at the time but now would never say he was guilty. Orput asked her one question about a TV show, and she was excused.

The next potential one was Tina O., who had yet to be sworn in. Tina worked at Trident Seafoods in Motley in the distribution center. She stated she was a cousin of Deputy Hasten Warnberg of the Morrison County Sheriff's Department. She was also a friend of Rick Heurung, a Little Falls police officer. She had read a little of the case and heard about it on the radio and TV. She didn't own any guns and admitted that she wanted to be on the jury as she was curious to find out more. She was excused from duty after a few other short questions.

Thomas M. was next. He also worked at Eagle Construction and knew Kris B. He indicated he had friends in law enforcement at the St. Paul Police Department, but they were mainly his brother's friends. He had read a little about the case, and his only concern was the waiting period and other than that hadn't formed a concrete opinion. He had a motorcycle stolen once in about 2007, filed a police report, but it was never found. He also had an incident with an intruder in his home, which he took a baseball bat to his legs and then found out it was a friend of his girlfriend but was charged with disorderly conduct because a sheriff baited him with a comment about "swung for the fences," and he was charged at a higher degree at first. He stated this incident would not prevent him from being impartial. His wife worked at Camp Ripley in logistics, where she ran the medical warehouse. He also stated that his children were friends of the deceased. His daughter was in figure skating with Haile, and they, as parents, watched them practice. It was about a week after it happened, and everyone was talking about it. His daughter was upset, sad, and angry. She thought Mr. Smith was in the wrong. Thomas responded to his daughter about never breaking into anyone's house. He did have a permit to carry a concealed weapon. He was excused from duty after a few other questions.

A lunch recess was taken for about an hour, and then Thomas S. entered the courtroom for questioning. He worked in St. Augusta for Zip's Diesel and had been a diesel mechanic for thirteen years and was a deer hunter, owning a couple of guns. Thomas was married and had two small children, ages three and five. He was on a Stearns County jury in 2008 for resisting arrest charge, had lived in St. Cloud for ten years, and moved back to Morrison County two years ago. He had been a victim of car vandalism several years ago and also his employer had a break-in behind his business with scrap metal stolen. His mother was part of the Swanville First Response team. He was forthcoming in his views about not forming an opinion about what he heard in the news as he said he understood what happened. With no financial hardships to his service acknowledged, Thomas was accepted as the twelfth juror.

Gerald F. was next, whose wife used to teach with the judge's wife before she retired, but the judge and Gerald never knew each other. Gerald was a hunting and fishing goods distributor and a daily reader of the *Minneapolis Tribune*. He professed to have an open mind about the case and had never used guns himself. He did mention a Second Amendment right, but also there "should, maybe, be some limitations." He holds a BA in mass communications and political science from St. Cloud State. He grew up in Taylors Falls on a dairy farm and had two children living in the Minneapolis area. He was the news director at WJJY Radio in Brainerd from 1981 to 1984. He stated he covered trials as part of his job there. When asked about his thoughts on what he has read in the news, he stated that if there were intruders in someone's house, you would think there would be a 911 call right away. Meshbesher then questioned if that was going to bother and would he be able to look at the facts. He stated, "Well, it has got to be a factor." Gerald was selected as the thirteenth.

Prospective juror Kaycja G. entered the courtroom, who worked at Morey's in Motley but was now employed at Buffalo Wild Wings for one month and was taking classes online for nursing. She was originally from Montana and had shot elk, antelope, and was a current deer hunter. She also hunted grouse, waterfowl, geese, pheasants, pigeons, and doves. She had guns that were passed down to her and also owned a pistol. She admitted to pleading guilty to check forgery when she was about nineteen years old. Kaycja also stated she had been sexually assaulted at age eighteen by an unknown assailant but never pressed charges by her own choice. While living in Montana, she was also involved in a situation where she took a ride with a person going to Salt Lake City to pick up a car. The car had hidden drugs in it, which the FBI was watching, and the vehicle was pulled over with her in it. She had no knowledge of the drugs but was asked to testify in that proceeding. As far as this case, she claimed very little knowledge and was accepted as the last juror, fourteenth.

After the fourteen members of the jury had been selected through that Wednesday, the attorneys agreed to meet with the judge the next morning to go over the final proceedings.

All jurors, when asked if they could be swayed to another's opinion, answered that they would stand up for their own opinion.

On Thursday morning, April 17, 2014, the judge met with both the prosecution attorneys along with the defense attorneys for Mr. Smith. Orput presented a memo to ask the court that Dr. Alsdurf, a psychologist, who would speak about fear, be omitted from testifying. He stated that a jury knew fear and his testimony would be unnecessary. Since both the judge and Meshbesher had not had an opportunity to review the memo, a decision would be addressed later. Wartner asked if the mothers of the victims could be allowed in the courtroom even though they would be witnesses. Meshbesher was not in favor of that due to the fact he would be asking them questions of substance. The judge stated he would rule on that later.

Meshbesher then asked the court to use the original audio only pursuant to the Rules of Evidence, which required the original. His team did an analysis of the audio recording, and the marker list was a manipulation of the audio and was not a proper duplicate. There were fifty-five instances that were counted where the agent changed or eliminated and omitted and enhanced what she thought she heard. It was interesting because she compressed the time so you could listen to it quicker, getting rid of dead space. The original recording lasted six and a half hours. The Rules of Evidence talk about duplicates being unfair to admit when there is an original present. Meshbesher also went on to say that there was speech and sounds that the agent said she identified that were incorrect according to her report versus her transcript testimony. Even one of those corrections was identified by the court and what you heard didn't match up with what she thought it said. For example, on marker 34 at a certain time, there was a female voice that said, "I'm sorry." She didn't say, "I'm not sure." The agent didn't put a question mark. She put a definitive statement, and even the court disagreed with that statement. The female voice did not say, "I'm sorry." The jury could decide for themselves what they think the evidence showed, so it needed to be the original, not someone else's interpretation, especially when it was not accurate. The prosecutor offered another condensed version lasting about forty-five minutes, but still wanted to include the transcript with markers. The judge would make his decision known on Monday.

The next issue Orput brought up was in regard to Jesse Kriesel and Cody Kasper, the fact that they were both convicted and one other juvenile involved. Items were recovered that belonged to the defendant and Sergeant Luberts was prepared to testify that items were recovered from a June burglary and an October burglary and then, of course, the October 27 burglary. Meshbesher added that one of the objections to this was that Kasper gave a statement to the BCA agents about his involvement in the burglaries with Nick Brady, what was taken, what he saw in Nick Brady's home, and a conversation he said he had with Kim Brady in which he told the police that he told Kim Brady that the police were searching his house and then she told Cody Kasper that she got rid of all the guns and stolen merchandise from Nick's bedroom so that if they came, they would not find anything. She knew they could come to her after Thanksgiving when they notified her of Nick's death as they asked for permission to search the house and she said no at that time. Meshbesher wanted to be able to ask those questions not just of the officer but to those involved. In particular, Cody Kasper, who gave three statements to police but kept changing things a bit about his involvement. The jury needed to see the whole picture here. One of the guns stolen from Smith was found in a swamp area and hidden so police could not find it. This tells the story about the fear created by circumstances that Smith was put under. Even though Smith didn't know Nick Brady or Haile Kifer, he just saw two people and did what he did when he saw those two people. The judge stated that where the guns were was not relevant because Mr. Smith didn't know. An argument from Orput was initiated, and he stated that Meshbesher had gone to extraordinary lengths both in court and out of court to make every attempt to vilify the victims so that if they were sufficiently vilified, the jury wouldn't care and they would disregard the evidence. And the state objected to that.

The Prosecution

Day 5 of the trial began on April 21, 2014, with Judge Anderson clearing the courtroom. Meshbesher asked the court to reconsider the closing: "This is a public facility. Mr. Smith is on trial in a public courtroom, and I ask to allow any of the public to be allowed to be present, including media, if they choose. To not allow that would infringe upon the freedom of the public to be present as well as free press. He has the right to a public trial."

Judge Anderson said, "Well, the court is going to deny that because for the reasons it will announce in the ruling. And the pretrial ruling of the court was that the defense had given notice that it intended to offer testimony from Jesse Kriesel and Cody Kasper about their involvement in prior burglaries which, of course, involved Nick Brady as well as a coperpetrator. And the court has ruled the defendant will not disclose the names of Kriesel, Kasper, or Brady involved in prior burglaries before November 22, 2012. Disclosure can be made of the relevant facts of prior burglaries, including that they occurred, the form of entry into defendant's property, if known and items taken. The limitation is in effect because all of the information before the court at this point, including the audiotape that was at the scene, as well as Mr. Smith's statements to Deputy Luberts about November 16th, when he asked Smith who the perpetrators might be, but none of the names were Kriesel, Kasper, or Brady. So the court finds that the defendant did not know the identity of those who had broken into his home on prior occasions, and therefore it would be prejudicial. And the court is not going to allow that evidence to come in at this point. So the ruling is until further order of the court that permission cannot be provided to the jury. And for that reason, the court is not allowing the press in for this ruling because otherwise it could be printed and indeed cause risk of the jury hearing about it. Meshbesher then asked if Cody Kasper could be called and questioned about his direct involvement. The judge answered that the critical burglary on October 27th, Kasper fueled, arguably, the defendant's fear when it was a forced break-in and firearms taken, which had not been recovered by the time the November burglary occurred. Cody Kasper will not be testifying because the relevant information about the break-in, entry, etc., is chronicled by the Morrison County Sheriff." With that ruling, the jury was brought back in and administered the final oath and instructions.

Brent Wartner began with opening statements for the prosecution. He started at 1:30 p.m., "Deputy Scherping and Sergeant Luberts responded to a call to the Byron Smith residence. He told them that someone had broken into his home through the bedroom and he showed the broken window. Smith led Deputy Scherping downstairs into the basement. He explained that on this day, twenty-four hours earlier, two people had broken into his house, they came downstairs, and he shot and killed them. He told both officers that he first placed the male into a tarp and dragged him away from the stairs and also dragged the female next to the male. He explained that he didn't want to bother anyone on Thanksgiving. The officers see the bodies and place Smith under arrest. Smith tells Luberts that he believes the female to be Ashley Williams, a neighbor who he suspected of stealing from him previously. Because she lives nearby, she could see him drive passed her home anytime he left his property. Wartner also states that Mr. Smith left at about 11:30 a.m., walked back home, sat down to read, and about 12:30 he heard the door to his house rattle. He saw a shadow through the window and then heard a window break. He hears an intruder upstairs directly coming downstairs, sees his feet, legs, and then shoots the male three times." Wartner describes him shooting another intruder after Smith hears more footsteps enter the home about eleven minutes later.

Meshbesher began his opening remarks with, "This case is a tragedy. Make no mistake about it. There are two people dead. I will not attempt to deemphasize or downplay that reality." Meshbesher informed the court that Byron was raised in Little Falls. He graduated at the top of his class. He lives in the home his father built. Mr. Smith attended the University of Minnesota, then the Air Force. He worked on radar and computers for flight navigation systems for B52 bombers at the height of the Vietnam War. Mr. Smith received a Combat Air Medal for flying more than twenty-five combat missions. He received other medals and ribbons, but you won't see them because they were stolen from his home in one of the burglaries. After the Air Force, he went back to college at Cal Poly in San Luis Obispo, earning a degree in 1991. He applied at the US State Department and was tasked with secret service-related issues to protect personnel, including diplomats. He returned back home in 2009 and cared for his mother until her death. He never dreamed that he would return to Little Falls and feel less safe than he did in places he worked all over the world. Mr. Smith has also been involved in the Boy Scouts for the last forty years. He was a scoutmaster at US Embassies in Moscow and Berlin. He was also commissioner in the Boy Scouts in Arlington, Virginia, and then involved in Honor Scouts upon his return to Little Falls. The prosecutor did not say any of this. He would have you believe he is a recluse, living on the fringe, a lone bachelor with malice in his heart. He is a decent, hardworking, intelligent, upstanding veteran of the military. He is not the man painted by the prosecution a few minutes ago." Meshbesher went on to explain the start of the burglaries after he had hired teens to do yard work. "The first known burglary was when $3,000 was stolen. Smith did not realize it until August (2012) and did not report because of the delay in discovering it missing. A second occurred with $900 in cash taken along with Smith's father's heirloom Rolex, which was given to him by the French government from his service in WWII. A gold necklace was also taken worth several thousand dollars. It didn't end there. It kept going. On October 27, another violent forcible home invasion occurred, and he called the sheriff's department. Deputy Jamie Luberts responded. The deputy left without securing a door panel, which Byron noticed had a shoe print. Deputy Luberts, on October 29, two days after the shoe print was left at Mr. Smith's, acknowledged that it could be a shoe print and took a photo of it. Mr. Smith then made a list of items he knew had been taken. The list is important: a Remington Model 50 semiautomatic shotgun, a Ruger mini-14 rifle, stainless steel .223-caliber with five-shot cartridge, a Nikon camera, a special lens for that camera, Bullion value gold coins, an envelope of cash ($1,200), a gold men's ring, and nine military medals and ribbons he received during his Vietnam conflict. He began to wear a holster with a gun around his home. Sleep was becoming difficult. He was afraid day and night. On November 16, 2012, Deputy Luberts came by to follow up on the burglary. There were no leads (and Luberts left after only a few minutes). On November 22, Thanksgiving Day, Smith stayed home with plans to clean his garage before winter. He moved his Chevy S10 pick up to a cul-de-sac away from his house, in front of a home where two Minnesota State Patrolmen lived. He walked back to his home and went to read before cleaning. He had a .22 on his waist, which he had been wearing for the past few weeks. He set an audio recorder because he wanted there to be evidence in case he was ever physically harmed during a burglary. But the state has no evidence that Mr. Smith was not audio recording all the time—that it is not unique to November 22, and they can't prove that. As Mr. Smith is sitting in his basement in his favorite reading chair surrounded by all types of books, he hears a door rattling, sees a shadow through a window. He was frozen in his own chair. There is a rattle on the same door that had been forcibly kicked in on October 27. He had no idea how many people were out there or whether they were armed or not. Next, someone tries the doors on the deck. [A recording of glass breaking is played for the jury.] He hears footsteps upstairs and then hears them descend the stairway leading directly to him. He did not run upstairs to kill this person. The person, Nick Brady, came down to him. He saw his shoes, his knee, and he did not wait to find out if this person is armed as it might have cost him his life. He was concerned with protecting his own life. Mr. Smith shoots three times with only three seconds between the second and third shots. A short time after this, Smith hears more falling glass and more footsteps. There are more people in the house, and he doesn't know if they are armed. A thousand unknowns. How many people are there? A second person descends wearing a black hoodie, a sweatshirt concealing the face, black gloves, and a bag large enough for weapons. He sees the hip and fired his rifle, and it jammed. The person falls down the stairs, and he shoots with a .22. Now Mr. Smith is in his own home on Thanksgiving when two strangers in hoodies descend into his home. That kind of burglary carries up to twenty years in prison." Objection by Wartner claiming it was outside the scope of this case. The judge sustained, and Meshbesher continued to explain that Nick Brady and Haile Kifer both committed that offense on November 22. Mr. Smith had a legal right under the laws of this state to use deadly force in the defense of himself and home. He also explained, The judge will provide you with instructions before you deliberate. The prosecutor has made a lot out of the fact that Mr. Smith did not immediately phone police after the shootings, and the prosecutor will have you convict Smith partly on that evidence. This is consistent with Mr. Smith's fear. It is true, he did not immediately phone police, but the fact is he did eventually. The facts show he was not engaged in activity. Instead, he was crouched in his basement, clutching a weapon for fear more people were either in or near his house wanting to kill him. After enough time passed to deal with that fear, he took action he felt necessary. Mr. Smith voluntarily spoke with officers on the scene and at length at the sheriff's office. He had nothing to hide. He acted lawfully when he defended himself and his home against unknown burglars on November 22nd.

The state called its first witness, Deputy David Scherping. Scherping was called to the scene along with Sergeant Luberts. He stated Byron came out with his hands up and wanted to tell him something. He showed the broken window and then took them downstairs and showed him the chair he had been sitting in when the window broke, and then he shot somebody as they came down the stairs. He then said he put the bodies in a room just adjacent and then opened the door and showed two bodies, which appeared to be teenagers. He stated he put the bodies there because he thought the female's father would be stopping to look for her. "We then handcuffed him and searched for safety. He had bullets in his pockets. We escorted him out and placed him in the squad car." On cross-examination, Meshbesher illuminated the fact that Byron was forthright in showing both Jeremy Luberts and Deputy Scherping everything that happened and appeared to be open and honest in his explanations. Scherping explained that Luberts froze the scene at that point. Meshbesher also questioned Scherping on a photo of a water bottle and explained there was no lunch bag as was stated in other testimony. He also drilled down the fact that the incident reports read by next shift deputies included Mr. Smith reporting other burglaries on November 16 to Jamie Luberts and Scherping had previously testified to only one burglary. Orput objected a few times during this for lack of foundation.

The next witness was Kim Brady. She identified her son, Nick, in a picture and verified that he was a student at Pillager High School at the time of his death. Meshbesher did not cross-examine. The next witness was Jenny Kifer. She was also shown a picture and verified that it was her daughter, Haile, and she was a student at Little Falls High School. Meshbesher had no questions for her either.

The next witness was Sergeant Jeremy Luberts from the Morrison County Sheriff's Department. His job with the sheriff's department was to investigate the felony-level crimes. He stated that Scherping had received a call from William Anderson as there was another burglary at the Byron Smith home. He was off duty but changed into his uniform, and Deputy Scherping and Deputy Rick Mattison followed him to the Smith home in separate squad cars. Orput then questioned him on the burglaries previous to this date. Luberts admitted knowing that there had been another burglary in June of 2012 and October 17, 2012. Luberts explained that Byron came out of his home with his hands in the air, asked if he was Byron Smith (Jeremy Luberts had never met him before), and Byron invited him in the house. Byron showed the officers the broken glass and then said he had to show them something downstairs. Byron then showed them the chair he had been sitting in when he heard the glass break. He expressed concern about the shoes underneath the chair and the repaired door where a panel was broken previously to gain entry. Byron then detailed how he heard the doorknobs rattle, glass breaking, and footsteps upstairs. He then shot a person descending, and at that time he could see it was a male, and he shot him until he was dead. He then placed the body on a nearby tarp and into his workshop area and sat back down in his chair. Luberts told that Byron stated he reloaded his gun because he was scared and nervous at this point. Byron then heard other footsteps and then saw feet coming down the stairs and fired at the hip area. That person fell, and he knew then it was a female. Byron explained that when he tried to shoot again, the gun jammed, and it seemed then as if the female smirked or laughed at him, which was when he reached for his waist, where he had the .22-caliber revolver and shot her in the chest. He then placed her next to the male. He noticed she was gasping for breath, and while he couldn't stand to see animals or people suffer, he described to Luberts that he gave her "a good, clean finishing shot." Luberts stated that Mr. Smith seemed nervous when he was telling about the events. He then opened the door of the workshop area, and a younger male and female were observed lying on the floor appearing to be deceased. Luberts stated that he could see blood on the female's stomach and noted that there were no shoes on the male. He lifted the tarp to see that the male party had a gunshot wound to the head. Smith indicated he did not know the male party but suspected the female was a neighbor, Ashley Williams. Luberts then explained he was placing Byron under arrest, and Scherping put handcuffs on him. Byron also told him the guns he used were placed back in his closet upstairs. At that point, Luberts had Deputy Mattison come and walk Mr. Smith out to one of the squad cards. Luberts then contacted Sheriff Michel Wetzel to inform him and had dispatch contact the BCA to have them respond to the scene. Luberts then began to photograph the outside of the residence and inside. Sheriff Wetzel arrived on the scene. Luberts went back to the sheriff's department to interview Mr. Smith. He did one interview at about 3:00 p.m. and a second interview at 12:58 a.m. The transcripts of the interviews were entered as exhibits. During the interview, Byron explained why and where he parked his truck on Thanksgiving. Luberts did a search of the truck with nothing significant found. Another vehicle, a red Mitsubishi Eclipse, was found to be parked on Smith Avenue, which came back to an owner of Jason Brady, but the car was driven by Nick Brady. A search warrant was issued to search that vehicle as well.

At that point, Meshbesher started his cross-examination of Jeremy Luberts. Meshbesher brought out the point that Byron had met law enforcement at the door with his hands up to show that he had nothing in his hands and it was safe to approach. (Luberts had stated earlier that it was like he was giving himself up.) Meshbesher then brought out the fact that Luberts had testified to the grand jury in April of 2013 about being aware of only one burglary (October 27, 2012) when in fact Byron had told him about the other burglaries on the scene and had also reported them to his brother (Jamie Luberts) on November 16, 2012. Meshbesher was making it clear that the evidence given to the grand jury was not accurate and, in fact, untruthful at times. Meshbesher also emphasized that Mr. Smith had complied willingly with every request asked of him: a DNA sample, his clothing, all interviews without an attorney, where his guns were placed back in the closet (because he didn't want officers nervous having them in sight), and why he parked his truck at a state patrolman's residence. Mr. Smith could have remained silent throughout the process, but he fully cooperated. That was the end of day 5 of this trial.

Day 6 began with testimony from Karla Bearce, a state trooper who lived on Oak Lane in Little Falls where Mr. Smith parked his truck. She stated her family left around 11:00 a.m. on Thanksgiving, and when they returned around 4:00 p.m., they noted a strange truck parked in front of their home and called in the plate. Upon cross-examination by Adam Johnson for the defense, she stated that they often left their patrol cars outside the garage. Johnson asked then if neighbors would know their profession then, to which she stated yes. Since she was not working that day, her squad car was parked there all day along with her husband's car, who was also a state patrolman. Both had been parked there all day on Thanksgiving. (Note: Byron Smith was aware that they lived there and had made statements to law enforcement that he parked his truck there to prevent it from being vandalized while he cleaned his garage that day.)

The next witness was Senior Agent Chad Museus with the Bureau of Criminal Apprehension (BCA). The BCA assists local law enforcement in investigations. They had a crime scene team made up of a forensic scientist leader, another forensic scientist, and a special agent who did photography. After being contacted, he met with Jeremy Luberts and then-sheriff Wetzel and proceeded to the Smith residence. It was around 6:00 p.m., and he assisted the team in removing the bodies of Haile Kifer and Nick Brady. He contacted the Ramsey County medical examiner, and then he stated he called 911 from a landline phone in the same room where the two bodies lay. He wanted to make sure the phone worked. After removal, he went to the home of Jay and Jenny Kifer and informed Mr. Kifer that his daughter was found dead. He waited for Jenny Kifer to come home and later made notification to Jason Brady, who had arrived at the Kifer residence that his son was also dead. He then traveled to the Ramsey County Medical Examiner's office to view the autopsies the next day. He stated that he needed to provide the scene and case information to Dr. Mills, the forensic pathologist. He then later provided her with the audio found in Smith's home. He later returned to the Smith home on November 29 to conduct a follow-up search. Since Smith had an audio, he thought him to be more tech savvy than the normal citizen so wanted to go back and gather more electronic media. Sergeant Luberts obtained another search warrant, and they went back and took hard drives, storage media for cameras, along with thumb drives. He stated he also obtained records for Smith's landline phone. He observed on Thursday morning, November 22, there were three unanswered calls to the Smith house from FedEx. There were three other calls in the evening, where Byron called his brother, Bruce, and a return call from Bruce to Byron that appeared to be unanswered, but a third call from Byron back to Bruce. The deceased cell phones were also checked. He wanted to see if there was a connection between Smith and Brady or Kifer. Records show an early morning call between Brady and Kifer and then again at 12:49, 12:51, and 12:52 that Brady missed from Kifer.

At this point, a recess was given while counsel met in chambers. Meshbesher wanted permission to ask Museus about texts and calls between Brady and Cody Kasper and the content of those text messages as was discovered on Cody Kasper's phone during this investigation. Meshbesher explained that this witness had told the grand jury in April of 2013 that his review of text messages did not yield any information about Smith's house, but in fact that was not true. "The analysis shows that Cody Kasper and Nick Brady had a plan, and I believe I should ask about that." Orput argued, "We are trying a murder, not two burglaries," so nothing before November 22 should be admitted as the judge had ruled at the beginning because Smith did not know who was committing the burglaries. Orput also stated, "On the audio, you can hear a cell phone ringing as Brady is laying dead." (Note: the cell phone ringing statement is only drama from Orput. Since Smith didn't have cell phone use for the last couple of months, he actually had a device that deactivated cell phones from working in his home, so Brady's phone ringing is impossible.) Meshbesher went on to argue with the judge, who even stated he was aware in Cody's plea that a text between Cody Kasper and Brady existed and they were discussing going to "Bryans" on October 26, and then the next day Byron Smith was burglarized. The judge stated, "This doesn't get us anywhere because Cody is not involved on November 22," and if Haile was available and Cody wasn't, he might have called Kriesel and said, "Hey, I need a lookout." This was something that Smith did not know. The fact that planning had occurred did not make any difference according to Judge Anderson. So Meshbesher's request to question about texts would not be admissible. At this time, Wartner also asked the judge to renew an objection regarding the use of grand jury transcript under cross-examination. He declared Meshbesher's questions improper impeachment (of witnesses). Since there were multiple witnesses coming up that gave grand jury testimony, he needed to give them the opportunity to answer the question before he impeached them. Meshbesher argued that it was sworn testimony asked of them word for word. The judge told Meshbesher that he needed to ask them and they first have to testify inconsistently before he would seek impeachment.

Upon cross-examination of Museus, Meshbesher began asking about cell phone messages between Rachel Brady and Haile Kifer. Orput objected right away, and the judge sustained. Meshbesher kept asking about his grand jury testimony, and Orput kept objecting, and the judge kept sustaining. Meshbesher went on to ask about the witness's statements about Smith's internet use. His grand jury testimony indicated he stated that Smith had browsed the internet on eBay on the evening of the twenty-second. Museus then stated that he found out later, after he had given testimony, based on a report by Agent Donny Cheung that they were off on dates. He admitted to being mistaken in his grand jury testimony. Defense then asked about the execution of a search warrant on November 23 and the time they entered. Witness stated he didn't recall the time they seized evidence from the home. He also stated he didn't have an opinion on if the breaking of a two-paned window into a home was a violent act. Meshbesher continued to demonstrate exhibits (photos) of damage to doors and doorframes and agreed that Smith had not sought out Brady but that Brady had broken into the home. Photographs were shown of the layout of the home, and if Smith had attempted to leave his position from any chair in his living area of the basement, he would have been seen by someone from the outside. He was then questioned about Smith's cell phone, which was not found in the residence so if Smith had attempted to use a phone upstairs or anywhere, he would have exposed himself to whatever was beyond the picture window. Museus stated he didn't recall exactly which door had been previously broken (to gain entry in October burglary), but he knew from the video that Brady had attempted for about twelve minutes to gain entry through doors. (All had been locked and dead bolted by Smith to avoid further burglaries.)

Meshbesher then questioned him about Deputy Mattison identifying the bodies because he had dealt with both of them previously. Museus couldn't recall his conversation with Mattison. He then asked about Brady's clothing and his wearing of a camouflage jacket and a T-shirt that said Taylor Gang or Die. Kifer also had a bag with her containing a marijuana smoking device. This item was not taken into evidence or chemically analyzed, and Museus stated he did not know what happened to it. The BCA also did not seize the phone that he claimed to have called 911 from to see if it worked. (Byron stated that phone in this workshop was outdated and had not worked for a long time. His only working phone is in the kitchen. When I had been in his home when the phone has rung, I had only heard one phone—the one in the kitchen.)

Museus later retrieved phone records from CenturyLink for the landline at Smith's home. The 911 call he claimed to make was not indicated in the records.

Meshbesher then asked about the content of Nick Brady's car. The judge indicated that any search of the contents of the car after November 22 was irrelevant and would not be admitted, so the witness was not made to answer the question. (The contents of the car were prescription drugs taken from another home on the south end of Little Falls, a Louisville Slugger collectible bat, foreign coins, sex toys, gold watch, and other personal items of Kifer's and Brady's.)

When the jury retired for noon lunch that day, Meshbesher asked for a mistrial based on his limitations asking about text messages between Kasper, Brady, and Kifer, which were key to this case. He stated it was tantamount to misconduct and asked for a mistrial. He also asked for another motion for mistrial as Orput referenced in front of media that he could "try this case in front of twelve NRA members and win because Smith is guilty." The judge answered that there had been comments since this trial started. Meshbesher said, "Whoa, whoa, whoa, whoa. The prosecutor is making a statement to media regarding the National Rifle Association and is saying 'No problem.'" Judge stated that he actually had seen that news clip, but the jury had not if they were abiding by the rules. The judge denied both reasons for a mistrial stating that moving forward, no comments should be given to the press other than facts. Meshbesher pressed the fact to the judge that his client couldn't get a fair trial based on Orput's comment as "it was aired on every station in the state. Everyone saw it, including you, the judge. There is no way to get a fair trial based on that." The judge stated again that no juror heard that comment. The mistrial was denied.

After lunch, Orput cross-examined Museus with only one reference to the fact it was eleven minutes, not twelve, that Nick Brady took before entering the home. Museus stated he "wanted to be accurate for the jury." (Possibly because he had been inaccurate before.)

Meshbesher recrossed asking why the marijuana pipe in Haile's purse had not been analyzed for cocaine or heroin or that it was even inventoried. He, again, didn't recall inventorying the purse. Meshbesher then asked about analyzing report data that indicated whether Smith had been warned that Kifer and Brady might be planning to burglarize on November 22. Meshbesher approached the witness to show him an investigative supplemental report dated December 4, 2012. It was one of his own reports, to which Meshbesher asks, "Is there any reference to anyone providing information that Mr. Smith knew that burglary was going to come on November 22, 2012, in this report?" The answer was no.

The next witness was Nathaniel Pearlson, a forensic scientist employed by the BCA in the forensic science laboratory for twenty-two years. Nathaniel was the team leader ultimately responsible for all aspects of processing a scene for forensic evidence. He had put together a Powerpoint slide presentation of photographs taken at the Smith home on November 23 and 24. He first processed the scene at 6:43 p.m. on the twenty-third and finished the next day. First concerns were securing the video system before it started to overwrite and then removing the bodies. Upon arrival he first noticed and photographed tool marks on the exterior face of the door and a crack in the doorjamb. He explained his team moved more quickly than normal due to getting bodies removed and securing video. At first notice in the workshop area, the body of Kifer with her purse was laying on top of Brady, who was mostly wrapped in a camouflage tarp. They bagged the hands to preserve any potential evidence and then placed the bodies in bags. Brady's cell phone was found in his right front pocket and also took a cell phone from Haile Kifer. In the room was surveillance equipment, which was collected by Agent Bill Bennett. When they arrived, the lights were off in the basement, and three fixtures did not have light bulbs, but there were six bulbs on the floor. Also photographed was the chair among bookshelves with a jug of water and some snack bars. Also was a digital audio recorder on the top shelf of the bookshelf. Viewing the south room at the base of the stairs was a door with a portion missing that had been patched with a piece of wood. One bullet was recovered from the floor, a crater-type mark in the cinderblock wall was photographed toward the foot of the stairs, and a second one in the block wall. They tested positive for presence of lead. There was some ammunition found on the table along with four .22 long rifle caliber cartridges and six .223 Remington caliber cartridges. What appeared to be bloodstains on the wall were photographed and samples taken. A rug that appeared to be covering bloodstains and a towel was removed along with carpet pieces appearing to have bloodstains. Also collected was a whole tent in a bag with stains on the exterior of the bag. There was also a pair of Nike tennis shoes underneath a chair. There were a pair of blue pants on the floor folded and after presumptive testing was positive for blood. Proceeding into the next area of the house was a shotgun with a live shot shell in the chamber. Pearlson retracted the bolt as the safety was on, but the shell remained in the chamber. He observed that the extractor was missing from the bolt. There was a fiberglass rod leaning against the wall, so he used that to pop out the shell. There was also a box for a Ruger rifle, which was located upstairs. Going upstairs to the bedroom with the broken window, where a fair amount of glass was on the desktop. Other rooms on the upper level indicated no forensic evidence for collection. In the laundry room closet, however, were found a holstered nine-shot revolver observing nine live cartridges. The revolver was also collected as evidence. Another rifle leaning against the north wall of the closet, a mini-14, was located and observed with two live rounds in the magazine. As he tried to retract the bolt to clear the chamber, it felt harder than expected, but once the rounds cleared, it felt easier. Also collected were three boxes of ammunition similar to what was in the basement. The clothing of both Kifer and Brady were examined and presented for distance contact bullet holes. Nothing was indicated on Brady's clothing. On Kifer's hooded sweatshirt, there were two holes in the hood that revealed a distance between contact and one foot and the other between contact and six inches.

The judge recessed court for the day to produce equipment for the next part of Pearlson's testimony. The judge would have the photographs set up so the press could look at and study in more detail between 3:30 and 4:30.

Before the jury was allowed in, the judge asked the attorneys to come in. His question was, "Does the state agree Nick Brady was committing a felony at the time that he was shot?" Orput stated, "Yes, sir." The judge then asked if the state agreed that Haile Kifer was committing a felony at the time she was shot. Orput stated that it was debatable because she went in to find Nick. He wasn't going to quibble about a trespass or a burglary, so conceded. Nathan Pearlson was then cross-examined by Meshbesher. He asked the time he entered the Smith home (6:30 p.m. the twenty-third) and if other officers were there before he was and they were. He admitted to executing a search warrant by Sergeant Jeremy Luberts. Meshbesher asked him about not testing the metal pipe that was leaning against the window broken to gain entry. Pearlson stated his team decided not to admit it into evidence or test it for DNA. Meshbesher also laid foundation that the DVR system in Pearlson's report was taken into custody and the location of that equipment was in a room two rooms and two doors down from Smith's reading chair. Pearlson stated that Special Agent Bennett took parts of the DVR into custody. He also answered questions about Kifer's hoodie, which was pulled tight to partially cover her face. She was also observed wearing a dark glove on one hand. He looked in her purse and observed a glass pipe, but it was never tested or entered into as evidence. He observed Brady as wearing silver-colored gloves on both hands, a camouflage jacket, and also a T-shirt that said Taylor Gang or die. When they came back the next day, the team had seized a total of thirty-six items from the home. Meshbesher pointed out the fact that they found shell casings on the floor and there was no indication that Smith had attempted to pick them up to dispose of them. Pearlson stated that they did not find any shell casings concealed or in the garbage. When asked about the six light bulbs, he admitted that he did not know when they were removed—if it was before or after the shooting as there was no evidence to show when. Pearlson began to testify about his conclusions in his report, and in the middle of Pearlson's testimony, Meshbesher asked for a recess to discuss Pearlson's file regarding gunshot distance conclusions on Haile Kifer that the defense attorneys had never seen or read. Adam Johnson, coattorney for the defense, motioned for a mistrial because the defense was just learning of an extensive file containing notes, computerized data, and photographs of testing that Pearlson conducted and the conclusions he drew from that testing. Adam stated that the defense was not in a position to just look at a large file and continue the examination of the witness. There was too much there and this issue was too important. The state responded that they had been back and forth over this issue and provided counsel multiple opportunities to come and view everything in the file. Even a break from trial would not be sufficient because they would have to collaborate with experts. The judge reminded the state that it was state's obligation to produce when asked by the defense and that nothing was ridiculous as this was an important matter we were dealing with. Typically, the state also would not have every item that an evaluator or forensic scientist might have utilized to achieve the written report. The judge denied the motion for a mistrial but allowed some additional time, but the defense stated that time won't help because they were not experts, so with that, Pearlson was brought back into court to continue cross-examination. Meshbesher asked for a break for copies to be made. The witness stated it was about one hundred pages but also that the prosecution was not given his notes either. Meshbesher stated to the court that since it was placing the burden on the defense that it was our obligation to find things we didn't know exist, the court had just described a Sixth Amendment violation of ineffective assistance of counsel. Whether there was a reversible error because of Brady, prosecutorial misconduct, or ineffective assistance didn't matter. Mr. Smith was not getting a fair trial. "And what you just described, Your Honor, with all due respect, is ineffective assistance, and you created a record of reversible error that it is my obligation, and I will concede we didn't go there. We didn't see those notes, and we don't know what they mean. We have asked for rough notes, and it is the state's obligation to provide that, and we are now finding out for the first time there is all these rough notes, and to place that burden on us is wrong. Mr. Smith is not getting a fair trial. If there is anything exculpatory in there and he is found guilty, this is a petition for postconviction relief or reversible error. It is that simple. Exculpatory evidence is huge. It doesn't get bigger than that."

The judge had reviewed Pearlson's report dated May 28, 2013, and it was consistent with the testimony that he gave that the holes on the left side of the hooded sweatshirt, one was estimated distance of 0–6 inches and one was 0–12 inches. That disclosure was made. While the supporting notes in the file might not have been made available in the file, opportunity or notification was given to defense that they could speak to Mr. Pearlson specifically. The court denied the motion for mistrial but would certainly make the eighty pages of the report available and mark it as an exhibit. Meshbesher was allowed a twenty-minute break to review the notes with Pearlson. As court resumed, he asked Pearlson about not being able to determine muzzle-to-target distance of holes in Brady's clothing but could in Kifer's hooded sweatshirt. Under redirect, Pearlson was asked about photographing a chalkboard in the basement because "it was potentially interesting." They didn't know what it meant, but maybe could find out later. (This chalkboard was used by Byron for his own calculations, which had been written months before this event.)

The next witness was Jason Worlie, an investigative sergeant with the Morrison County Sheriff's Office. He was assigned to do the nonforensic search warrant at the Smith residence. He along with other officers retrieved an audio recorder in a bookshelf, a .22 rifle placed in a shower stall, another audio recorder without batteries in the shop area, and a video recorder. There were two loaded guns and ammunition also turned over to the BCA to Special Agent Bennett.

Meshbesher asked Worlie if he noticed a phone in the shop area while he searched. He stated he didn't notice any phones or phone jacks.

Special Agent William Bennett was then called to the stand. His duties were part of the crime scene team and cell phone investigations. He assisted Sergeant Worlie. As part of his search, he stated he found a digital recorder that was sticking out on the top bookshelf. It was still on so thought it might be of investigative interest. In the back storeroom was a shotgun and then a similar recorder in the workroom area with a lot of computer devices as well with a DVR surveillance camera-type system that was operational in that storeroom. The DVR was recording off four cameras on the outside of the residence. When he searched the upstairs, he noticed a cell phone jammer or interrupter on the kitchen counter. The device would jam both types of cell signals (CDMA and GSM technology). It's of high-end quality. When he tried to make a call from his cell phone, it was inoperable. The device was not seized or tested to see if it worked outside the home. He also stated he did not test the phone in the basement to see if it worked.

After a lunch recess, Special Agent Janet Nelson was called to the stand. Agent Nelson acted as a liaison between law enforcement and the Crime Scene Team processing all the digital evidence recorded at the scene for investigation and court purposes. She did assist the other agents in the execution of a search warrant at the Smith residence. Numerous items were seized on November 29: a laptop, a home-built computer, desktop computer, a couple of hard drives, two or three external hard drives, storage drives, numerous thumb drives, compact flash cards, SD cards, and mini SD cards. When inspected, most contained day-to-day photos. From the video surveillance camera with four separate monitors, she created a timeline starting at 11:25 a.m. when Smith entered his vehicle and backed out and left the driveway. At 11:45 a.m., he returns to his residence. At 12:33, you would see Brady running up the stairs and coming back down. He was looking in the windows. He spotted the camera in the woodpile. He held his hand over his face on Camera 3 and goes back and turns the camera in the woodpile, leaving it upside down. At 12:37 he is walking around in front of the house.

You could see Haile Kifer in the trees. At 12:39 was the last we see of him on the camera. At 12:51, you'd see Haile Kifer run across the driveway in the front yard. She walked on the upper deck on the river side carrying a large red purse. She appeared to be on her cell phone. At 12:53, she was walking off camera, and that was the last we see of either of them.

Agent Nelson examined two Zoom Handy recorders. One in the shop had a lot of sharp rapid reports and a voice-over a PA system and the batteries were dead. The other, identical recorder was located on the top of the bookcase. It contained what sounded like a Scout meeting, and the rest was a very long recording, six hours, twenty-four minutes. She transferred the media card to her computer and created markers, increasing or decreasing volume as needed. The sounds she heard were thumps, glass breaking, footsteps, heavy breathing, shots being fired, screams, male voices talking then a female voice, more shots, another male voice, and a lot of rustling around that sounded like dragging. She heard a male voice talking to himself. From the audio files that contained speaking or sounds of activity, she selected clips from the six hours and twenty-four minutes. The prosecutor provided to the jury the condensed transcript that Agent Nelson compiled, and then they were instructed to listen to the audio, and if the jury believed the findings that she made were not correct, they should disregard and rely upon what they heard.

Upon cross-examination, Adam Johnson asked Agent Nelson about observing a telephone in the basement. She stated she didn't recall any phones. She did recall testifying before the grand jury on April 24, 2013. He showed her a copy of her testimony, in which she was advised by other agents that there was not a telephone in the basement, but didn't recall who told her that. The video surveillance cameras were in question when Adam asked Agent Nelson who was in the trees around 10:00 a.m. on Thanksgiving Day. She agreed it was a person, but no identification was officially made. As Smith left in his truck at 11:25 a.m. and returned on foot at 11:45, you could see Smith on the south side of the house, which was an open area and could be seen clearly from the highway, which was the same location Brady came from, approximately forty-five minutes after Smith was standing behind his house. She agreed when Kifer and Brady approached the house, they were dressed to conceal themselves, and there could have been a gun in her purse as it was large enough. Based on the video, one could determine Smith was active around 8:00 a.m. as he was out in his yard doing things. He didn't wake up and move his truck. He was fixing the deck and other things. She was then asked about her marker list. Adam asked her about marker 128 as she quoted a person using the name Chris. When she listened later, it sounded like Bruce, but all that was heard was the *s* sound. She admitted to having difficulty hearing the whispered voices. She explained when she increased the volume of the whispers, it also increased background noises. She also kept out sounds of heavy breathing, which Adam described as an attribute of a person's emotional state, and she kept out a number of them. She agreed according to the video that Smith was not in the shop room (where video monitor was located) but sitting in the chair as there were sounds of chair movement after glass breaking. Again, she did not recall a phone in the basement, and with Orput's objection, Adam Johnson clearly wanted to address the credibility of Agent Museus (who claimed to see a phone, but none was ever seized). She also testified that the sound of the unscrewing of light bulbs had been heard on the audio five hours after the shootings. (Orput had led the grand jury to believe that light bulbs were taken out before as part of his premeditation theory.) The light bulb sounds were in the original transcript, but not the one presented to the jury at the time. She stated that she had not included some of the sounds, including the light bulbs, and stated the attorneys might have selected certain markers to highlight. By attorneys, she meant the prosecutor, who had put it together for the grand jury. She testified that she put the list together at someone's direction: the prosecution.

Court was adjourned that day at 3:57 p.m. There are two more witnesses for the prosecution.

The Defense

On day 8 of the trial, before the start, the defense team asked for a mistrial based on the fact they had eighty pages of notes from Pearlson's testimony that they did not know existed. Adam Johnson had an opportunity to review last evening, but explained that they needed to ask their own expert before they could ask Pearlson back to the stand for more questions. The judge denied the motion, and the defense then asked for a continuance based on not being allowed to be clear on Kifer's two holes in her sleeve. The judge temporarily denied a continuance as the medical examiner's testimony was forthcoming and clarity could be coming from that testimony. He stated that he was going to wait until the state's case in chief was finished and then would consider the continuance motion.

The court had one issue before the jury was brought in. He had fashioned a new defense of dwelling instruction in which there are three elements or conditions that have to be met for the defense of dwelling to be considered fair and reasonable. The first issue was whether the action was done to prevent commission of a felony. The court proposed this: In this case, the parties stipulated that Nicolas Brady and Haile Kifer were committing or intending to commit felony burglary in defendant's dwelling. There was still the issue of gravity, his perception of gravity was reasonable, and if his election to use deadly force was reasonable in light of the circumstances perceived. With that said, they brought the jury in and the trial started at 9:40 a.m. that morning.

The next witness was William Anderson. Mr. Wartner began to question him about talking with Byron Smith on Thanksgiving morning. He testified that Ashley Williams had driven by in her vehicle several times and was asked what Mr. Smith said, to which he stated that he did not recall. Mr. Wartner then asked Anderson to look at his transcript of his interview with Sergeant Worlie and asked again what Smith said, to which Anderson responded that he did not recall.

The next witness was Brent Matzke, a forensic scientist with the BCA in the DNA profiling laboratory division and a member of the crime investigation team. He testified that he had tested trousers that belonged to Smith and there was evidence of Kifer's DNA on the pants. Meshbesher cross-examined and asked if he had made notes of the clothing and guns he had tested, and he replied that he had volumes of notes regarding tests he had done, which was never given to his defense team and prosecution is required to provide it. As when Pearlson was on the stand revealing he had eighty pages of notes, which was never provided to the defense, Meshbesher was truly frustrated, while Orput claimed the defense could have gone on their own to view it. After some arguing, the judge required the notes be copied and made available to the defense. He did not hold the prosecution in violation for not providing the documents.

The next witness for the state was Dr. Kelly Mills, the principal assistant medical examiner at the Ramsey County Medical Examiner's Office. She did an autopsy of Nick Brady, which showed numerous gunshot wound defects to the head, abrasions on his nose, abdomen abrasions, an exit wound to the palm of the right hand, entrance wound on left thumb, wound to back left shoulder region, and an exit wound to the right side of the back and on the back of his right hand. His body came to her in a sealed bag, fully clothed and also in a tarp. He was wearing a T-shirt and a camouflage jacket. His hands were bagged. After taking the bags off, he had gloves on both hands. She could see gunpowder stippling on his hands and gunshot wounds to the gloves and hands. His first wound was to the back of his hand exiting through bones and soft tissue. Next wound was to temple region of head on right side through the skull and into brain where she recovered a bullet. She described a grazing wound to left thumb, entry wound to left side of abdomen, damaging the liver and going through chest wall. There were lengthy questions and answers from Dr. Mills on the trajectory of bullets, and each entry and exit was shown with a projector slide show with details of ammunition colors and soot presence. For the sequence of shots, she looked at the BCA testing of clothes and listened to the audio for voice patterns as most immediately to the brain, he would not have been vocalizing anymore, so that's what she was listening for. The one to the brain would have been the last gun shot.

She then performed an autopsy on Haile Kifer. A Powerpoint presentation with photos was also prepared. Ms. Kifer also came in a bag, fully clothed, wearing a sweatshirt, jeans, with her hands bagged. There was a bit of blood on her face and hip. She was wearing a glove on her left hand. She had a grazed wound on her right thumb. There was some black material surrounding a gunshot wound defect to the right jaw and neck region. There was a gunshot wound by her left eye, which one slide showed, and then the next slide went to a view of her face showing that the bullet went through her face to the bony ridge of the eye, socket, and internal bony structure of her face. She recovered a small bullet fragment from this gunshot. Another shot behind her left ear was shown. She examined the hood of the black sweatshirt but stated it was hard to detect soot on gray or black but learned it was positive for residue according to the BCA and evidence of close-range firing. Wartner then asked her about the condition of the sweatshirt, whether it was dry or not. She answered that it was bloody and wet. She described the fatal shot that went through the soft tissue of the neck, the left tonsil, went into the skull, and damaged the brain stem. The next slide was the bullet fragment taken from the fatal shot and then another slide of Kifer from the right side, seeing soot around her neck. More descriptions given and slides shown of another gunshot wound in the abdomen, going through the liver and the right side of the diaphragm. She identified two different types of ammunition and a total of six gunshot wounds. Ms. Kifer tested positive for dextromethorphan and a marijuana metabolite.

During the lunch recess, the judge ruled on the mistrial and denied it based on the fact that notes were then supplied to the defense and Minnesota Rule 9.01 was complied. The judge felt after Dr. Mills's testimony, it was evident that the question of two bullets to the hooded sweatshirt had been answered and noted it was close-range firing. Meshbesher then asked the judge "if Dr. Alsdurf could testify to the anxiety and fear, the psychological psychiatric terminology, and how it affects human beings when they are in an extreme situation in terms of memory and loss. Dr. Alsdurf can assist the jury in understanding in this case as no one has experienced the fear when your window is shattered and someone is coming into your home in a burglary situation." Orput's argument was all those feelings would be universal. Without a decision, Meshbesher then began his cross-examination of Dr. Mills. His questions were informative of the firing position of Mr. Smith as Brady descended the stairs and one of the gunshots sustained by Brady was at the highest point of him descending and the range of the gun was more than thirty inches away. Dr. Mills noted that the first two gunshots would not have left him unconscious, and he would have been able to move. He would have still had the ability to stand. Meshbesher asked if he would have had a firearm in his left hand, would he have been able to use it, to which she replied, "Theoretically possible, yes." She could not rule out that he could have been reaching into his belt based on the line between the graze of his thumb to the entrance to left abdomen. The shot to his head was not contact but from a distance. Based on the first two gunshots he received, she testified that he could still have been moving around in a threatening or violent way. She explained the word *homicide* simply means one human being killed by another and is not synonymous with murder. On Haile Kifer, she changed her initial report from five gunshot wounds to six after listening to the audio recording and hearing six shots. She agreed that after two shots, she would still be able to have use of her legs and arms. Three other shots were fired in quick succession and then a final one a minute and a half later. Meshbesher made a point that after the gunshot wound number 2, she would have been deceased, but breathing sounds could still have been heard from the body, as Mr. Smith testified to law enforcement that he heard sounds coming from her body. Dr. Mills also testified to observing numerous cut marks on Haile Kifer's arms, a total of sixty-six in different stages of healing. There were thirteen on the front of her right forearm, seven on the back of right forearm, thirty-two on the front of her left forearm, and fourteen on the back. She testified that these wounds would have been inflicted by Ms. Kifer herself. She also testified that the amount of dextromethorphan in Kifer's body was one thousand three hundred nanograms per milliliter, which would have caused intoxication. In chronic abusers, the reactions of this drug could be hallucinations or dissociation. She described dissociation as an out-of-body experience and could also cause alterations in consciousness, changing perceptions or a feeling of floating. He questioned her on Brady's toxicology report as dextromethorphan was not on the drug panel list submitted for him. She stated that was not on the list they tested for.

After Mills's testimony, Nathaniel Pearlson was again called to the stand. He was questioned again about Museus using a landline phone at the Smith residence. It wasn't in any of his notes or references during the processing of a crime scene. He stated that he didn't note it because it didn't directly pertain to his duties for processing the crime scene. Meshbesher asked him to take a look at his one hundred pages of notes, and if there was any reference to that observation, please let it be known. The reference wasn't there. His notes also included an assumption about the distance of the two defects in the sleeve of Kifer's hoodie.

With that testimony, the state had no more witnesses. Before the defense started their case, Meshbesher made a motion for judgment of acquittal and dismiss the state's case. Orput asked the judge to deny the motion, and the judge did.

Meshbesher wanted to call Sheriff Wetzel to the witness stand with a shotgun that was found that had been taken from the Smith residence on October 27 and reported as stolen. The judge stated there would be no shotgun allowed in court, but Meshbesher went on record stating that was taken from the Smith home and it was relevant for the jury to see and that the sheriff went with another person in his squad car and found it and it was connected back to the Smith burglary of the twenty-seventh. Meshbesher explained that the fear factor went back to the size and type of guns that were stolen. Meshbesher wanted to be able to show the jury that the gun was stolen and recovered, and he knew it had been stolen, and this was what Smith was afraid of, that they would come to his house with that gun and shoot him in his own house. It went directly to the state of mind and his fear on November 22. Meshbesher wanted to demonstrate where the fear comes from and not from a photograph. Fear was an important component to this case. It was the heart of this case. Orput argued that the whole point that it was completely irrelevant and invites rampant speculation. Meshbesher replied to say that the gun was "irrelevant" was ridiculous. The judge declared that the gun was not coming in. He stated that one wouldn't break into a house with a shotgun, but they would bring in a nice, clean .223 that has the firepower to kill fifteen or twenty people in Colorado or Massachusetts. Meshbesher replied, "It goes to his state of mind and not yours."

The first defense witness was Jamie Luberts, a deputy with the Morrison County Sheriff's Department. He arrived at the Smith home on October 27 at about 6:53 p.m., in which Mr. Smith had informed him that he had been the victim of a burglary and that someone had kicked out a panel on a basement level door. Someone had also unlocked the dead bolt inside the door. He testified that he did not take any fingerprints on the interior of the door, the handle of the door, or on the dead bolt. Luberts explained that there was evidence that persons who broke in had been in several rooms of the house both downstairs and upstairs. He did try to obtain a fingerprint from dust on a nightstand in Mr. Smith's bedroom but wasn't sure if the BCA had run it through the database. The bedroom appeared to be the main target of the burglary. He was then asked if there was a reason he didn't take the door panel that was kicked in into evidence, and he stated he took a photo of it. Meshbesher also questioned him as to why he didn't write a report on the visit with Mr. Smith on November 16 for follow-up to October 27 burglary until November 24, which was two days after Thanksgiving. Luberts testified that another supplemental report was made on December 1 after Smith was charged. He stated that he was asked to make a follow-up summary report by someone in the sheriff's office. He was then asked after twenty days (after October 27 burglary) had there been any advances made in the investigation with no suspects. There had been nothing. Mr. Smith also stated that he had been suffering from burglaries more than once before October 27. Smith had given Luberts paperwork entitled "Request for Investigation and Documentation," which he dated October 29 and indicated his property adjacent to his Elm Street property had also been vandalized. When asked if he investigated, he stated that he had not. Mr. Smith had also given Luberts a list of property stolen from several different burglaries, including shotguns with receipts from those purchases. When asked if he examined the receipts Mr. Smith had given him or if he had recovered any of the stolen items or even went to pawnshops in St. Cloud, his response was no.

The next witness was Sheriff Michel Wetzel. Meshbesher questioned him on receiving information on a stolen gun from Smith's house. On November 29, he learned the identity of the person who had information about the gun. He traveled to Bellevue Township with the person in the squad car. The stolen item was a 12-gauge semiautomatic shotgun, Remington Model 350. He stated that he drove .7 miles north of 103rd street on 140th Avenue in a swampy, secluded area. The gun was located covered in grass and snow.

(Side note: The informant was a relative of Sheriff Wetzel, Chase Fortier. He was sixteen years old at the time and had received the gun from Jesse Kreisel, who had stolen it from the Smith home along with Cody Kasper. Chase was never charged with any crime.)

Meshbesher's next witness was Glenn Negan, a firearms expert. Orput argued that this was a waste of time and added nothing to the case. He wanted to speak about the effects deadly encounters have on a person's ability to hear, the auditory and visual blockings that take place and describe his experience in dealing with high-stress encounters. Also, he will inform the role adrenaline plays and that a deadly-force situation is unique. Glenn was a retired officer from the Willmar Police Department with thirty-four years of experience and trained civilians in handling of firearms. As much as Meshbesher argued the case to present this witness, the judge denied that his testimony would not aid the jury. Judge Anderson stated that a jury would look at all the facts and decide if his action was reasonable under the circumstances. The defendant might not have realized how many shots he fired, but it wasn't relevant because the ultimate number of shots was determined by the medical examiner and the audiotape. Meshbesher argued that Smith might not have been aware of the number, and it would go to intent, whether someone shoots six, ten times, or two, because they didn't realize when they were so stressed and adrenaline was so high. Orput argued that he "just wanted to try this homicide case for what it is, Your Honor." Meshbesher stated, "No, what Orput wants to do is convict him, period. He wants to win this case. He doesn't want to try it, and he is not seeking justice. And I have a client to defend." The judge again denied this defense witness. A three-hour recess had to be taken before the next witness arrived.

Mr. Negan, the judge, and the attorneys gathered in chambers. The witness was allowed there to testify that he was a firearms instructor, training both civilians and police officers. He stated, "When anyone, including police officers, are in high-stress situations, they suffered from the effects of critical-incident stress, which would be tunnel vision, auditory deprivation, and slow-motion referral. The brain is processing so much information and so fast to help survival it gives the perception that things are happening in slow motion when in fact it is in real time. Mr. Negan was asked by the judge what his testimony could do for a jury." He stated that he would point out some of the psychological feelings that he might be feeling when that happened by talking about how it affects everyone, how he is feeling and his reactions. Another factor is auditory deprivation. Inability to hear helps lead to the fear factor. This happens where multiple people are shot many times. There have been incidences where three officers were present and fired nine rounds and nobody knew how many were fired. It is a common occurrence that people don't comprehend. The judge went on to say that he was certain Wetzel was called because of the Gordon Wheeler shooting, in which he was shot numerous times by law enforcement, and in the course of a very brief period, he was killed. In the end, the judge declared the firearms expert's testimony would not assist the jury.

The next defense witness was Brian-Paul Crowder, a member of the Little Falls City Council for the past seven years. Brian-Paul knew Byron's parents, Ted and Ida, as Ida had been a client at his hair salon. Byron's parents had deeds at the Oakland Cemetery where Brian-Paul was the caretaker and did bookkeeping and journal entries, so Byron had called him early in November since his parents had deceased and wanted the deeds transferred into his name. The Saturday before Thanksgiving, Brian-Paul and his mother went to the Smith home upon an open invitation from Byron to stop by anytime. On that Saturday, they were in the neighborhood and decided to stop in. When Brian-Paul rang the doorbell, there was no answer. He went back to his car, and his mother told him to knock as the doorbell might not be working. Byron did answer the door then. When he came to the door, he seemed very afraid, but then when Brian-Paul introduced himself, his demeanor seemed to change to relief. When he couldn't locate the paperwork for the deeds, he offered to give a tour of his property, which included an adjacent home he had just purchased. He spoke about the trees he had cleared, hiring help to clean debris, and then stated how worried he was that he had been broken into so many times. Brian-Paul stated that they, too, had concerns because of those issues, and when authorities were called, nothing had ever been done. Brian-Paul again described how upset, worried, and concerned Byron presented. When Brian-Paul learned of the shootings a week later, he called Sheriff Wetzel and told him about his visit with Byron and then later gave a statement to Sgt. Jason Worlie.

The next witness was Bill Anderson, a neighbor of Byron who had also taken care of his mother, Ida, helping her with lawn mowing and grocery shopping. He explained that Byron had knocked on his door early on Sunday, October 28, 2012, wanting to talk. He seemed very frightened and very reluctant but then started describing all the break-ins that had occurred over the last few months. On the day after Thanksgiving, Bill and his wife went to Brainerd in the morning, and when they returned, he had noticed that Byron had called. At 12:30 p.m. Bill returned the call, which Byron had asked him to find a lawyer to talk with. Since it was the day after Thanksgiving, Bill called several offices with no answer. He finally received a call back from Greg Larson, a local attorney, and then informed Byron who had then asked him to call the sheriff's office to send the investigator in charge of his burglary case to his home. Byron had told Bill that he solved the burglaries. Upon cross-examination, Wartner asked him about his neighbor, Ashley Williams, as he had seen Ashley wearing an Air Force jacket on her way to the bus several years ago. Bill had told Byron that he was suspicious of Ashley and that she might be watching his house. The Air Force jacket had been stolen in the early nineties. The Williams' home was located just as one approached the driveway to the Smith home, so entry and exit was easily seen.

The next witness for the defense was Bill's wife, Georgia Anderson. She had talked about helping Ida, Byron's mom, with shopping, getting mail, and doctor's appointments. At one time they suspected someone had been taking her mail, and Ida had also called the police about a break-in to the shop on the property. The morning Byron came to the Anderson home, October 28, Georgia stated that he didn't even look like himself. He was scared, frightened, and looked like he had no sleep.

The next witness was Ross Rolshoven, an investigator with Great Plains Claims for thirty-five years working with law firms, the city of Grand Forks Police Department and sheriff's department as well as Fargo Police Department and Cass County Sheriff's Department. He was a member of the National Association of Legal Investigators, which has high standards and is by invitation only. He was a licensed private investigator in North Dakota and Minnesota. Ross was hired by Meshbesher to assist with this case. He first inspected the scene on December 6, 2012, with other visits made on February 7, 2013, and March 20, 2013. He had taken photographs of the other break-ins to Smith's adjacent property. A window to a three-stall garage had been broken, a door kicked in, and a ground floor window to the house was kicked in to obtain entry along with a basement walk-in door that was kicked in. He explained that where Nick Brady's car was parked on Riverwood and Smith Avenue, there was another gravel driveway, an easement road, that ran parallel along the paved driveway through pine trees where detection would be less visible. Smith installed a chain across the road to keep car traffic from going down. Inside the home, he had marked his initial *R* in the dust on the bookcases to prove they had not been moved as the prosecutor had once inferred to Smith's reading area as a deer stand and this had been set up as part of his pre meditation plan. Ross described where Smith had installed new locks and hooks to keep the door closed because burglars had broken doorknobs. He did establish that the shoe print from the door panel that was kicked in on October 27 was a match to the shoe (worn by Nick Brady) found at the scene. This witness's testimony ended abruptly with objection by prosecution as defense was trying to establish who had previously broken in. The judge had already ruled that to be irrelevant, so the witness was not allowed to answer any questions about shoes and what that might show. Meshbesher's statements in trying to adhere to the judge's ruling explained that Smith had set the shoes to the side showing his state of mind when he saw this person walking down the stairs. Many exhibits offered by the defense from this witness were excluded, determined as irrelevant.

On Monday, April 28, 2012, Mr. Rolshoven was back on the stand after the weekend recess. He described for the jury that when one descended Smith's basement stairs only his feet and shin would be visible and one would not be able to detect if they were carrying a gun or weapon until they reached the bottom of the stairs. He took another picture of the pink purse that Haile Kifer was carrying upon entry. It was large enough to hold weapons. The only item in the purse was a glass, ceramic drug pipe. He showed a photograph of the back of Byron's head that revealed an injury he had sustained to the back of his head. A police report indicated it was two to three inches, but clearly this photo showed it was longer than that. Byron had fallen down in his stairway carrying some heavy objects prior to the Thanksgiving Day incident. As part of his investigation, he also checked Byron's background. He was in the Air Force for four years during Vietnam and was honorably discharged in April of 1972. He underwent a very intensive forty-eight-week training involving radar computers for bombing and navigation systems on B-52 airplanes that were dropping bombs on North Vietnam at the time. He received a total of nine medals for his service. When asked about the location of the medals, the judge only allowed if inventory shows where they were. (They were listed on a police report of stolen property in the burglaries.) The next witness was Bruce Smith, Byron's brother. He was a year and a half older than Byron. When asked about his brother's honesty, he commented on Byron's work with the Eagle Scouts and assisting three generations of scouts. Bruce commented that he and his family were highly regarded in the community. Upon cross-examination, the only question was if Bruce had known anyone to act out of character. He replied no, and that was the end of his testimony.

The next witness was Dilan Lange, John and Kathy's son and neighbor and friend to Byron. He was sixteen years old and currently attended Little Falls High School. He informed the jury that Byron had been living in his home since after the shootings. When Dilan explained that Byron helped with his homework, the prosecution objected. Dilan answered that Byron was a very honest person. Upon cross-examination, Orput asked Dilan, "It was well-known around here that you don't mess with that guy. Isn't that true?" Meshbesher objected as the question that was talked about was honesty and according to the rules set forth by the court. It was one of few questions allowed. Discussion was held at the bench, out of hearing of jury. Meshbesher stated, "If the defense objects to questions outside his reputation for honesty in the community, it rises to the level of prosecutorial misconduct, and I would ask for a mistrial." Orput stated that he had a right to cross-examine on reputation, and the judge agreed. Meshbesher again argued that if questions get outside honesty, it was prosecutorial misconduct and a reversible error. He would motion for mistrial. Orput again asked Dilan the same question about "you don't mess with that guy." Meshbesher again objected and asked for a mistrial. The judge agreed that it was a leading question but allowed on cross. Meshbesher stated it is absolutely inappropriate. Again, Orput was allowed to ask the same question with another objection from Meshbesher and another ask for a mistrial. Orput stated that if Meshbesher wanted a sanction, he invited the sanction and was tired of intimidation of this counsel. The objection was finally sustained, so Orput asked Dilan if his band was kicked out of Smith's garage, to which Dilan answered, "No, we left." Orput stated that he told people he kicked you out. Meshbesher again objected as it didn't have anything to do with honesty. The judge overruled, and Meshbesher redirected. Dilan explained that his band had a new drummer, and they left of their own accord because the drummer lived farther away and they didn't want to constantly move the drum equipment.

The next witness was Dilan's mom, Kathy Lange, and also the author of this book. Again, a question was asked about Byron's honesty in the community and with a short yes answer that she observed nothing but honesty as he had shown while living with them. That was the end of the defense witness portion of this trial.

Byron was asked if he would testify in his own behalf, and he waived the right to testify. This portion concluded by 10:45 a.m., and the jury was instructed to be back at 1:00 p.m. with further instructions.

During this time the judge and both attorneys addressed the self-defense instruction, whereby three conditions had to be met since this happened inside the home and he had no duty to retreat. The judge gave instructions to the jury when they returned at 1:00 p.m. He noted that no more evidence would be presented and they would discuss among themselves and then each decide on individual judgment. He went on to tell them that they are the sole judges of a witness, the believability and the weight, as there are no hard or fast rules to guide. Also, the defendant had the right not to testify. The State must prove beyond a reasonable doubt that he was guilty. In this case, the defendant had been charged with multiple offenses, four charges, and each would be considered separately. These were as follows: Count 1, first-degree murder of Nicholas Brady with premeditation and with intent to cause the death of a human. First, the death of Nicolas Brady must be proven. Second, the defendant caused the death of Nick Brady. Third, the defendant acted with intent to kill Nicholas Brady. In order to have intent, the defendant must have acted with the purpose of causing death and the act would have that result. Fourth, the defendant acted with premeditation meaning he planned and prepared for the act. It was not necessary that premeditation exist for any specific length of time. However, an unconsidered or rash impulse, even though it included an intent to kill, was not premediated. Fifth, the defendant's act took place on November 22, 2012, in Morrison County. If all these elements would have been proven beyond a reasonable doubt, the defendant was guilty in the first degree. If any element would not be proven, the defendant was not guilty. The same was read for Haile Kifer for count 2. Count 3 for second-degree murder included intent to cause death but without premeditation.

The self-defense instruction stated that no crime is committed when a person takes a life, even intentionally, if the action was taken in preventing one's own death or great bodily harm. The killing must be done in belief that it was necessary to avert death or great bodily injury; second, the judgment of the defendant as to the gravity of the peril to which he was exposed must have been reasonable under the circumstances; and third, the election to defend oneself must have been such as a reasonable person would have made in light of the danger perceived.

Next was the explanation of defense of dwelling. No crime is committed when a person takes the life of another in preventing the commission of a felony in the defendant's place of abode. First, the action was done to prevent the commission of a felony in the dwelling. Both parties have stipulated that Nick Brady and Haile Kifer were committing a felony in defendant's dwelling. Second, the defendant's judgment as to the gravity of the situation was reasonable under the circumstances. Third, the defendant's election to defend his dwelling was such as a reasonable person would have made in light of the danger perceived. All three conditions must be met.

The members were given the form to complete and to be signed by the foreperson. They were instructed to come back the following morning for closing arguments and plan to start deliberations.

On April 29, 2014, closing arguments began. Orput began by telling the jury that Byron's plan started with moving his truck, stopping by to chat with his neighbor, and activating a recorder. He had snack bars and extra ammunition as he sat down to read and wait until they came. Orput stressed premeditation and his comments on the audio about wanting Nick dead after he shot him as he was descending the stairs and Haile saying "I'm sorry." Most of his arguments were taken from the audio and his interrogation from Luberts detailing the shootings themselves. He waited for another accomplice because both he and Bill had discussed that the neighbors might be part of all the burglaries. Orput called this a coincidence that two teenagers came by at the same time the defendant was "setting a trap" for the neighbor. Since he left his house at 11:30 a.m. and both shootings were done by 1:00 p.m. After his arguments, which consisted of audio statements, Meshbesher asked for a bench discussion. Both attorneys had agreed not to object during closing arguments, but Orput had referred to Haile Kifer saying "I'm sorry." This statement was omitted from the marker list as unclear and for Orput to disregard the court's ruling was no less than misconduct. He again asked for a mistrial. Orput's response was that he had heard the "I'm sorry" and had just asked them if they heard it. The judge stated that he listened six times and did not hear "I'm sorry." While the mistrial was not granted, a cautionary instruction needed to be given indicating that there was no indication that she said "I'm sorry." Orput commenting about it was in defiance of the court order, it was improper, and he disagreed with cautionary instruction. If the court was issuing a caution instruction, it should be specific to Orput's closing comment on that that was not true and disregard what he said. Orput's argument was that others (on his team) heard it. The court did not hear the words so it could be argumentative. A mistrial was denied. Before the defense's closing remarks, the alternates were elected traditionally: Kaycja and Gerald were the alternates as they were the last in the selection.

Meshbesher began his closing arguments with detailing Nick Brady's violent act of breaking a window to enter a home he did not belong in. "Both he and Haile Kifer had hoods over their faces and gloves on their hands. Now the reasonable inference is that she heard the three gunshots and thought Nick had shot the homeowner. Maybe because of her intoxicated state or out-of-body experience, as testified to, she chose to crawl through the window too. If they hadn't made those choices, they would be alive today. But they were not murdered. This case is about taking responsibility for how this even occurred. We have to quit blaming the victim. Byron Smith is a victim. He was scared. He was confused. He is the victim of burglary. The state played only a part of the audio recording. When Meshbesher asked the witness who did the audio recording about hearing the unscrewing of light bulbs, she stated she heard it about four and a half hours after the shootings, not before. Why was it left out? Because the prosecutor told her to. The deputy forgot the door panel that was kicked in, and Byron Smith brought it to him the following Monday. He waited quite some time for the deputy to come back in the office and gave it to him. They took some photos of it. Now, Byron sees these shoes of this person walking down the stairway and thinks it's the same type of shoe that kicked in the door panel and the prints might match. He puts the shoes aside (for the police). He thinks, 'You are the police. You investigate, but I am going to try to help you.' The state tries to say, 'The steel rod might have been placed there by Smith.' But when the officer is asked if the rod was ever checked for fingerprints, palm prints, DNA, or hair follicles, the answer is no. These are standard tests done today. Why wasn't this done? To say Smith planted it there is just talk. The sheriff's department has access to BCA and a scientific laboratory and nothing happened. But we want to convict anyway because they are two young kids. The problem is, Smith didn't know that. They came into his home with hoods over their faces. They decided not to just walk around upstairs and steal there, but decided to go downstairs. He was confronted with a situation—do or die, because guns had been stolen before. The burglaries started out small but then became more violent. He was afraid to live in his own home. He was not only fearful of burglary and violence but fear of being assaulted and killed. So on Thanksgiving, it's a holiday, no one is in a hurry, so he just wants to clean the garage, relax, and read. When he hears glass break, he freezes, doesn't move, hoping they will go away. The state wants the jury to believe that he wants them to come downstairs so he can shoot them. In Minnesota when somebody comes into your home, you have the right to use deadly force and you don't have to figure out what they are doing there. He didn't pursue them. They pursued him. Mr. Smith had the right under the laws to use deadly force in defense of his home at 14319 Elm Street in Little Falls, Minnesota. Mr. Smith had all the windows and doors locked and dead bolted. Even though there is a recording and it is not pretty, you cannot convict out of feelings and reacting to emotion is not the right way to convict."

The jury was given final deliberation instructions by the judge and exited the courtroom at 12:00 noon. At 1:14 p.m., the jury had a question: "If a person is guilty of first-degree murder, are they automatically guilty of second-degree murder?" At 3:34 p.m. the judge entered the courtroom, and a verdict had been delivered. Byron Smith was found guilty on all counts of both first- and second-degree murder. The court proceeded immediately to sentencing. The sentence for first degree is life without parole, but the prosecutor, for the sake of families, wanted consecutive sentencing for second degree too. Restitution was discussed and would be kept open for thirty days so they could get a list together. Impact statements were also requested to be read. Laurie Skipper, the sister of Jay Kifer and aunt of Haile, displayed her emotional feelings in the loss of her niece, having two empty seats at holiday tables and the mental stress and anguish that Mr. Smith caused the entire family.

Kimberly Brady, mother of Nick Brady, spoke about her son, whose smile lit up a room, and how he would be missed by all. Bonnie Schaeffel also spoke about Nick being an extremely special young man who never left the room without saying, "I love you, Grandma." She referred to Byron as a sour, angry, old recluse who felt he was above the law.

After those statements were done, the judge asked Byron for a statement of his own, of which he declined. The judge declined to impose two life sentences. They would be concurrent sentences: one life sentence for Nicholas Brady and one life sentence for Haile Kifer. Byron was remanded to custody that day. Meshbesher retrieved the fifty-thousand-dollar cash bail bond to use for appeals, and court was adjourned at 3:57 p.m., April 29, 2014.

CHAPTER 12
AFTERTHOUGHTS

Since, John, Dilan, and I were on the witness list, we were not allowed in the courtroom during trial. Byron was given only six passes for family and friends, while the Kifer and Brady families were given twenty-five to thirty each day. The number was set by the judge. I was scheduled to testify on a Friday, but it didn't occur, so I sat in a conference room outside the courtroom all day long. The following Monday I still didn't get to the witness stand, and Ross was extremely disappointed in the fact he was only allowed to give 15 percent of his investigative testimony before the jury. According to Byron's attorney, Judge Anderson was putting stringent restrictions about what evidence was relevant. I was beginning to really worry. Brian-Paul Crowder had testified as the first defense witness. He had seen Byron a week before and had noticed his fearful mood. During the courtroom break, we went to Perkins for lunch, but Byron did not go as it would be too difficult to get past all the media outside. He chose to wait in one of the conference rooms instead of being seen in public. I brought him back a piece of pie and took it to him. He was sitting there alone, napping. He quickly ate the pie. He was right about the media. It was difficult for him, and he didn't like that they waited for him to come through and the cameras flashed. About fifteen to twenty members of the media were standing in the lobby outside the hallway of the courtroom every day, all day. As we made small talk before the trial resumed, he seemed very calm. One of the courtroom officials opened the door and told Byron it was time for him to enter the courtroom, so I left the room and stood outside. A lady sitting on the bench waiting for court gave me the coldest stare as I stood there waiting. I assumed she was a family member of the burglars given the cold stare on her face toward me and Byron. She worried me because she seemed to be purposefully sitting, carefully watching Byron as he sat in that room, like a stalker.

On Tuesday morning, Meshbesher told me I needed to have Dilan at the courthouse by 10:00 a.m. I knew today would be our testimony and had warned Dilan that I would need to get him out of school for a bit, but I didn't realize it was going to be this quick. Ross was still finishing his testimony, and I thought he had a couple of hours to finish. It happened quicker due to what he was allowed to reveal about his investigation. John quickly went to the school for Dilan while Bruce testified then I would be next. Meshbesher told me that I would only be testifying to Byron's honesty. None of us had been prepped. John would not be testifying because Meshbesher changed his mind about needing his testimony, so John could enter the courtroom. Everything seemed to be happening very quickly, but later we learned the judge was allowing only certain questions for the defense. It all seemed odd. My testimony was extremely short. I answered only a few questions and was just getting warmed up and was told I was done. I would be the last witness for the defense.

When the words *guilty* were repeatedly uttered by the clerk, I was quite shocked. He was found guilty on two counts of murder in both the first and second degree. I was stunned and in total disbelief. On April 29, 2014, the verdict came in after eight days of trial and only a few hours of deliberation. After the verdict was read and Orput muttered out the words *restitution*, I couldn't listen to anymore and left the courtroom. I sat outside on a bench in tears wondering what just happened. It seemed so wrong. The parents and families that raised these two burglars were celebrating by cheering, clapping, and smiling. This celebration was wrong on so many levels. Their kids had been killed in the commission of a crime. The bottom line was that if Haile and Nick would have been with their families instead of burglarizing, they would be alive today. They entered where they didn't belong. They caused this event and risked their lives for it. Byron was minding his own business in quiet retirement. He had all the doors locked to prevent entry and prevent a confrontation. The jury thought Byron planned this, but it made no sense. What sixty-four-year-old man living alone wanted a confrontation with burglars he suspected were younger and stronger than he was? Not only that, they had stolen his guns. I couldn't imagine how Byron felt after the verdict was read. It would have been a hundred times more the sadness and anguish that I was feeling. John tried to comfort me, but there was no comfort in this day. I could hear someone from the media say, "Kathy, how do you feel?" I ignored them, trying to compose myself from within. For the past sixteen months, we had been by his side, helping to keep him positive, helping him feel safe again, and now it was over. He hadn't asked for this. The burglaries had drove him to such fear that he felt unsafe in his own home. He felt helpless with nowhere to turn. Unfortunately, we live in a society today that needs to place blame on someone else when an accident occurs. Let's place the blame on Byron because he should have saved them. He should have saved two people breaking into his home, coming down his stairs with black hoodies. Let's disregard his incomprehensible fear for the last several months because, according to this prosecutor, we all know what fear is. Well, I for one can't imagine not feeling safe in my own home for months. Plus, returning home and finding it has been ransacked with every drawer overturned and picked over. He was sentenced to life in prison without parole. Maybe I thought that when Dilan and I testified, it would help. The jury would hear the good things about him. We were the last witnesses for him, but our limited testimony was worthless. Orput's bully-like questioning of Dilan while on the witness stand was no different from the teenagers that bullied Byron with consistent stealing. John was so upset with his questioning that he flew out of the courtroom after Dilan took the stand. He couldn't believe how Orput was treating our son. He was objecting to everything that Dilan said that was good about Byron. My friend Mary Kay was in the audience for support and she told me that Orput was very mean and she thought the jury noticed. Dilan kept his cool, I am told. I wasn't allowed in the courtroom because I was next to testify. We were only allowed to talk about his honesty. I could tell Meshbesher was losing faith every day as another trial day concluded. The judge wouldn't allow testimony from his psychologist or the firearms expert and only a small portion of Ross's investigation. As far as we were concerned, along with many others, the trial had been totally unfair. Ross had been worried right from the start that things were not going in Byron's favor. He said he had never seen anything like it. The judge favored every move the prosecution presented. Meshbesher had filed several motions for a mistrial. They were denied every time. We didn't realize at the time, but he has setting the path for an appeal in case the jury convicted him, and that's exactly what happened.

Jack Ertelt came from North Dakota to support Byron too. There were other supporters attending every day for Byron too. Many of the supporters of the burglars were dressed like they just got out of bed. During the closing arguments, one of the family members, a young girl with lime-green sweatpants, messy hair, pulled into a ponytail, glasses sliding down her face, was sobbing through closing arguments. John went up to Jeremy Luberts on a break and asked to have her removed for the disruption. He promptly replied, "John, I can't do that." I looked at him and boldly stated that, "There's not much you law enforcement do anymore, is there?" He returned with, "That was very inappropriate." I looked back and told him that in this circumstance, it was very appropriate. If Jamie Luberts had done any investigation at all, Kifer and Brady could have been apprehended. The previous night, Brady had run out of gas on the south end of town, and a sheriff's deputy stopped to help him. If this deputy would have been a little suspicious of his activity and checked into it, this tragedy might not have ever occurred. The deputy even told us that he had Nick Brady in the back of his car the night before Thanksgiving but assisted him with getting more gas.

Brian Middendorf, the county prosecutor, told the media that all involved would be prosecuted to the full extent of the law, but on November 29, 2012, Sheriff Wetzel himself went to a location where one of Byron's guns had been placed. Sergeant Strack from the Little Falls Police department had indicated to Sheriff Wetzel that a gun on Byron's list of stolen property had come into the possession of Chase Fortier, a relative of the sheriff. The sheriff was told by Chase that he had received the gun from Jesse Kriesel. Jesse, of course, insisted that he had no idea the weapon was stolen. Chase Fortier told Wetzel that he traded his bike for the 12-gauge shotgun. In Sheriff Wetzel's incident report from December 4, 2014, he stated that Sergeant Strack from the Little Falls Police Department indicated to him that he believed Fortier came into possession of the shotgun after he traded a space heater to Jesse Kriesel for the shotgun. Fortier told Wetzel that he had retained possession of the gun in mid-October and had kept it until Cody Kasper approached him in school and told him that the shotgun had been stolen from the Smith residence and Fortier should get rid of it. Fortier also told Wetzel that after Kasper told him the gun had been stolen, he also spoke with Jesse Kriesel. Fortier stated that he was upset that Kriesel would have traded him a stolen gun and asked him what he thought they should do about it. According to Fortier, Kriesel told him, "Don't tell anything to the cops about it, and I won't either." Chase Fortier agreed to show Wetzel where the gun was located. Once there, they both exited the car, and Fortier walked directly into the swamp and pointed into the grass where the weapon was laying. There was some snow present on the weapon, but no rust, so it did not appear as if the weapon had been there for a long period of time. The above information was taken directly from ICR 12007272 (Morrison County Sheriff's Office). Chase Fortier was fifteen years old at this time. To date, he had not been prosecuted for possession of a firearm or possession of stolen property. The students at Little Falls High School at the time were rumored to have been waiting to see if Chase Fortier would ever be punished by Sheriff Wetzel. They realized that maybe if you know or were related to the sheriff, you would not be punished.

The red car belonging to Nick Brady (1998 Red Mitsubishi XPH-777), address 27367 Lost Lake Pass, Randall, Minnesota 56345, contained the following items when seized: red box containing jewelry; two-dollar bill in plastic sleeve; weapon (not firearm or knife); six prescription pill bottles with pills labeled for another homeowner who was burglarized; Kodak digital camera; black Calvin Klein bag containing sex toys (big black dildo, anal beads); hand crank flashlight; Truper brand hedge clippers with Tony written on handle; Minnesota driver's license application for Haile Kifer; a public school schedule for Nick Brady found in a backpack in back seat; miscellaneous collectible coins found loose in the center console, including foreign coins; (ceramic) container, Nick, with miscellaneous foreign bills and collectible coins from Saudi Arabia, Nicaragua, and Costa Rica found in the back seat; and a gold in color Pulsar brand watch found in the center console. None of this evidence was presented or allowed at trial. Law enforcement testified in front of a grand jury (April 23–24, 2013) that they did not know of any previous crimes committed by the pair. The evidence of a phone call made by Kim Brady to Cody Kasper telling him that she got rid of some things out of Nick's room was not admitted either. The fact that law enforcement wanted to search his room but was refused and was not admitted into evidence in the grand jury testimony or the trial. Kimberly Brady knew from Cody that law enforcement had searched his home and would be back to search her home for stolen property. Meshbesher wanted to bring forth charges of obstruction of justice, but the judge wouldn't allow the testimony and evidence at trial.

Minnesota Statute 609.065, Justifiable Taking of Life, states, "The intentional taking of the life of another is not authorized by section 609.06, except when necessary in resisting or preventing an offense which the actor reasonably believes exposes the actor or another to great bodily harm or death, or preventing the commission of a felony in the actor's place of abode." It is beyond dispute that at the time Byron used deadly force against Brady and Kifer he was preventing the commission of a felony in his dwelling. Brady had broken a window and forcibly entered an occupied dwelling by climbing through that window. Kifer followed minutes later. The belief that Byron was preventing a burglary of his home was obvious. Byron was confronted by two hooded strangers descending the stairs of his home. His home had been previously burglarized, during which firearms were stolen. If a person cannot lawfully defend his home in this situation, when can one do it? Twelve out of sixteen grand jurors had to vote to indict him on first-degree murder charges, and they did. One of the grand jurors was heard on WCCO Radio's John Williams show right before the trial started (April of 2014.) She told the listening audience that she sat on the grand jury and that she was told that he purposefully moved his vehicle to set the trap for the burglars to come that day. She was truly convinced by the prosecutor that Byron did this. In reality, would a sixty-four-year-old man want to be confronted by bold criminals who were suspected to be younger and stronger than him and had previously stolen his guns? Criminals who also had previously violently kicked in a dead bolted door to gain entry. Also, if a trap was supposedly set, there had to be a contact person who would inform the criminals that it was time to enter. Did law enforcement ever investigate that because no person was ever discovered to be the watcher? The jury then believed that it was just a coincidence that Nick and Haile came on his property within forty-five minutes after Byron was back home. Someone would have had to have seen and reported it. One could not see from Riverwood Drive if Byron's vehicle was there or not. The driveway was too long, and unless you specifically drove up to the Smith home, you could not view his garage doors from the street. So when Byron drove from his home on Thanksgiving Day, a single phone call should have come from one of only about twenty homes that he passed. Was that ever investigated? Let's think about how Byron Smith could have known that at some random time, on any random day, a watcher would be observing his driving and would be certain to be seen so burglars would be sure it was safe to go in as they knew he wasn't present.

Unfortunately, Byron's attorney was not allowed to present the defense that he wanted. The jury believed the prosecution's theory of a trap. Law enforcement was happy in their victory. Not only were they hugging and shaking hands with criminal parents (Brady's) but were smiling victoriously for kids who were criminals themselves.

The prosecutor's fabricated story of a trap was exactly that. When I first heard this trap story and he was going to use that as his main platform to convict, I actually thought it was a joke, so did Byron. Byron was consistent in that he knew maybe the burglars, the home attackers, or whatever name you want to give them would return, so he prepared to defend himself. He actually revealed proof of not setting this trap while he was interviewed in the Morrison County Jail by Jeremy Luberts. It was exhibit B in court documents. The date was November 24, 2012, and the time was 12:58. Luberts was conducting a follow-up interview with Byron. He began with asking him routine questions like has he talked with an attorney and if he was okay speaking to law enforcement. He asked about the four cameras he installed and if there were any set up inside the house. Byron revealed the security codes for the cameras that were set up outside (none inside) and gave some instructions on how to operate them. Luberts continued to ask him about his cell phone, and Byron stated that it was a prepaid minutes phone and that he hasn't had use of it for a couple of months because he hadn't been able to shop for more minutes. Luberts still asked for the phone number, and Byron freely gave him the number. Then Luberts asked him about his vehicles:

Luberts: Okay, um, how many vehicles do you own Byron?
Smith: Ah, that's a complicated question because I don't use all of them. Ah, see, I have a silver Chevy S-10 pickup, and I have a Cayenne. Those are the two vehicles I keep in the garage. Ah, I only use the Cayenne for road trips, ah, it's not a grocery car, it's a heavy car. I inherited a maroon Oldsmobile Cutlass, '90–'94 I think, from my mom, and currently I'm just keeping it because it only has sixteen thousand miles and is extremely good condition. I have a, I also have a '69 Chevy Nova that was running, but a tree fell on it and restoration is on hold for lack of time.
Luberts: Okay. How, um, to clarify with ya, how many pickup trucks do you own?
Smith: One.
Luberts: One, and what kind of pickup truck is that?
Smith: A silver Chevy S-10, '95.
Luberts: Okay, where is that pickup currently parked at?
Smith: It's parked in a cul-de-sac north of ah, my other property, which is the adjacent property to the north.
Luberts: Um, this other property, ah, do you remember what road, or where the truck is parked that

you said? Do you remember what road that is? You know the name of the road?

Smith: No, I don't.

Luberts: Okay, how far from your, your, ah, residence that you live at is it parked?

Smith: Three-minute walk.

Luberts: About a three-minute walk, okay, so are we talking, like, ah, how many blocks do you think? How many blocks away?

Smith: One.

Luberts: One block, okay, so fairly close. Ah, why do you have that vehicle parked over there?

Smith: I needed to clean out the garage, and I wanted it out of the way for a while.

Luberts: Okay.

Smith: It's, ah, time of the year to clean out the garage before it gets too cold to do it.

Luberts: Okay, and you said, ah, that where you have the, where you had the truck parked, um, is in in front of some property that you own there?

Smith: No, no, it's, ah, out of the way, out of sight. I didn't want it vandalized.

Luberts: Okay, when did you park that truck there?

Smith: Ah, let's see, I was starting cleanup, that would have been, ah, Thursday morning.

Luberts: So Thursday morning you said you parked it there?

Smith: Um, oh, no, that would have been the trigger for them coming to see me. That would have been the trigger. That's why they came. They thought I had gone away.

Luberts: Okay.

Smith: They saw me drive the truck and didn't see me come back because I walked back and that's why they came.

Smith went on to tell Luberts that the correct time he left his home should be on the videotape. He revealed that he had an injury to his head about a week ago when he fell down the stairs carrying boxes, so they talked about some blood drips, and then Byron again stated to Luberts, "I now realize why they came while I was there… because they thought I was gone. I moved the truck out of vandalism range, and so they assumed I was gone."

Luberts then concludes this twenty-one-minute interrogation interview at 01:19 hours. If this interview had been videotaped, one would have clearly seen the look on Byron's face when he realized why the burglars came on Thanksgiving Day as they (or someone who was watching) had seen him leave his home. What are the odds of Nick Brady just driving by Elm Street at the same time Byron was leaving his property? Not likely, and it was not possible from Elm Street to see if his cars were parked outside noting whether he would be home or not. They either had to have been tipped off that he had left or just took the chance he wouldn't be home on Thanksgiving, if you believe in that many coincidences.

Up until that point, Byron Smith was in the county jail unaware that the burglars were good friends of Cody Kasper and why they had come on a holiday when everyone should be with family.

The days that followed the verdict were hard. We went back home where Byron's jeans lay on the bed as he had left for the courthouse in a hurry. His papers were scattered on the dresser as if he would be returning to straighten them later. Dilan was angry and kept pestering me about leaving Little Falls for good. He even looked over my shoulder while he demanded that I apply for jobs in another state. He was serious about wanting to leave Little Falls. He did not want to graduate from Little Falls High School. He says that it was full of bad kids. The kids in school seemed happy because the "killer" was sent to prison. Byron was Dilan's friend, and he knew him very differently from what the kids in school thought about him. He kept saying that he didn't deserve this and that Little Falls was full of bad people. Law enforcement was bad, judges were bad, and attorneys were disrespectful and mean. It was hard for me to focus on anything except worrying about how this affected my son. The last day of the trial, I had quickly rushed Byron home after thirty reporters had followed him as cameras were flashing from right inside my car. Bruce followed us in his car, and I made the three of us a quick lunch. After lunch, Byron sat down to read, and Bruce went back to the family home. After a couple of hours, Meshbesher called Byron and ordered him to come back to the courthouse. I decided to make a grocery run for a nice dinner that evening. I had two overnight guests, along with Bruce and Byron, so I needed to prepare dinner. I had suggested a ham to Byron because it was flexible. We didn't know how long the jury would deliberate, so it was a good choice. He also suggested I buy Swiss cheese to make with the ham for sandwiches. I spent about a half hour at the store choosing the right cheese for him as he suggested. I was called to come back to the courthouse as soon as I got back. A verdict was in already. We were told this was a bad sign. John had gone downtown to eat with some friends, along with Jack and Sebastian, Jack's son. As I look back on my last lunch with Byron and Bruce, two brothers sharing conversation, I can't help but think that I never, in a million years, thought he would not be back for that ham dinner.

A few days later, I went into our extra bedroom where he had stayed since December 18, 2012. He had a suitcase near the bed neatly packed with all he needed for a two-week vacation. His phone charger and umbrella were sitting on top and his shoes neatly placed alongside. It was clearly apparent that he was not anticipating a guilty verdict. None of us were. We just all thought that the bad guys could never win. He was a retiree minding his own business, just wanting a quiet life back in his hometown, and misguided teenagers changed all that. A few days after the trial, I went to the court administrator's office. On public display were tables filled with pictures of the case which included his reading chair and many other exhibits. It seemed as if the prosecution hadn't demonized him enough, so they had to give it another attempt.

Bruce had left on the Saturday after the verdict. He was ready to get back to California. He had been working in Nigeria for months right before the trial, had gone to Pennsylvania to see his grandchildren, and then came to Minnesota for his brother's trial. As I walked down the pine tree driveway to Byron's home that Saturday,

I felt overwhelmingly sad. It was a beautiful Saturday morning. The sun was bright, and the birds were singing. The Mississippi River was quietly flowing only feet from his home. Spring was in full bloom. I couldn't help but feel overcome with this sadness that Byron wasn't here to enjoy this peaceful property, his home. A property he had lived with his parents and a home he helped build and grew up in. Two careless teens caused all this. While the prosecutors and sheriff's department were applauding and hugging the parents that raised these kids, Byron was being sent to prison for life. His home on the river would never again be the same. There was no more laughter to be had here, no more good times with family and friends. We would miss our friend walking down to our home every New Year's Eve with a bottle of champagne to celebrate. I went in to say goodbye to Bruce, who was packed and ready to leave. There was still food in the fridge, clothes in the closet, and everything neatly in place, like someone was coming home soon. We exchanged pleasant conversation before his ride to the airport. We avoided any conversation about Byron for now. I sat there in the Smith living room overlooking the river and took in the beautiful scenery thinking how everything changed that Thanksgiving Day.

Dilan stayed home from school the next day and I stayed home from work. I was glad I had taken the extra day because it was hard to concentrate. When I told Dilan I was going to be gone for about a half hour, his look told me not to stay very long. He was attempting homework, but I knew he was having difficulty concentrating on it. We drifted through the next couple of days, and then a couple of *Dateline* producers came over to encourage us to be interviewed. I had previously declined their invitation to participate in their show, but they said that they were interested in Byron's side, and if we didn't tell it, it would never be heard. I refused again after another ask from them. I wanted no part of being on a show with the parents of those kids who had ruined Byron's life. If those misguided teens would have been home on Thanksgiving, they would still be alive, and our friend would not be going to prison! I eventually caved and agreed for our family to participate in the *Dateline* episode. I decided that I didn't want it to be all about the kids. We decided that we could present his side of the story and maybe someone would listen because the trial certainly didn't expose his side. They were sending NBC's Kate Snow to interview with no prepared questions because they wanted it to be natural.

On that Tuesday morning after the verdict, about six vehicles drove into our yard, complete with camera vans and cameramen from Chicago and Minneapolis. *Dateline* contracted with a camera crew from Minneapolis and Chicago. They came in, assessed the lighting in our home, and decided upon a spot to shoot and then started to move all the furniture. It took two hours to rearrange my home. A makeup artist was sent to do our makeup. Dilan went first. The makeup artist was Bonnie, and she had done the makeup for the Republican Convention last fall and had also done makeup for Hillary Clinton and Paul McCartney. She seemed very kind. Kate Snow arrived around 10:00 a.m. She had flown into Little Falls last evening and was working in her hotel room while the camera crew set up. She looked thinner in person than on TV, dressed beautifully casual in a bright-blue top and black, slimming pants with black wedge shoes. Bonnie touched up her makeup and used a straightener on her hair. We talked about how we loved the *Big Bang Theory* and how she thought it was the most ridiculous show ever. I had mentioned to her Byron's similar comment to the *Big Bang*'s "fly in Penny's mouth" episode. We started taping, and then the questions flew. She asked about the town of Little Falls, how we knew Byron, the kind of person he was, if he talked about the shooting with us, and if I ever, for a minute, thought he was guilty of premeditated murder. I replied, "Absolutely not, never." One of her last questions was if we had heard from him. Ironically, a letter had been sitting in our mailbox all morning, but we never went to check on the mail that day. I wish I could have responded differently to that question. It would have made the ending more complete. After about an hour of questions, she interviewed Dilan. Dilan was very articulate and definite in his answers. She asked him how it was at school for him and how the kids reacted to the verdict. He answered each one very eloquently and positively. Byron would have been proud of Dilan's profile of him as a caring member of the community. It was nice to see

Dilan enjoy himself with the producers and Kate. He posted a selfie with him and Kate on Facebook, and she obliged with many pictures. After taping, the camera crew started asking us more questions about Byron. They added that they sometimes didn't really pay attention to the story someone is telling, but confessed to listening to our every word. They had interviewed both attorneys right before us and they had skepticism about some aspects of the story. But after listening to our side, they were convinced that Byron was an innocent man that was not given a fair trial. That evening two of the producers took us to a nice dinner at one of our local restaurants. We showed them the letter from Byron and were glad to hear he was doing okay. The accommodations at the St. Cloud prison were "better than okay." They continued to ask about him over dinner and they both seemed genuinely drawn to their work. The Byron Smith Story entitled "12 Minutes on Elm Street" aired on May 16, 2014, at 7:00 p.m. on NBC's *Dateline*. They didn't get the story quite right, though. They didn't talk about the fact they had robbed someone else the evening before Thanksgiving. They didn't mention the fact his sister, Rachel Brady, had pawned off some things Nick had stolen. They didn't talk about Nick's mother, Kimberly, obstructing justice by removing items from her son's room. There were hours of taping that turned into only a few minutes. Dilan was upset that they had only aired a small portion of what he said and the good things we said about Byron were not aired. He was upset because the one thing he said that he hoped wasn't aired, was the very statement that they selected to include. I told him he told the truth and he should hold his head high. The statement was about Nick's reputation is school as a bully. One of his friends had even stated that they were not surprised that he was killed in the commission of a crime.

There were two other TV shows that my family participated in just to give a voice to Byron Smith and make sure he was represented. Unfortunately, both of those came up even shorter than the *Dateline* episode. The ID channel aired a story called "Hear No Evil," which featured the BCA as top-notch investigators, not even mentioning the assumptions and untruths that were told by them in court proceedings. The ID channel contracted the recording work to a group from London, England. There were three young men who came into our home that day and taped interviews with us for hours. It was interesting to hear them comment on our side of the story as they had no idea what really happened to Byron as none of it came out in court and they only knew what the general media reported. We were informed that they would hand off the interviews to the producers and the show would be aired according to what the producers wanted to reveal. No indication was made of who could have possibly been the watcher or any investigation into that. The show led into a scene where neighbor Bill Anderson was shown with Byron (both actors) where they were both in Byron's basement and Byron was tossing a book on the floor in frustration after the October twenty-seventh burglary. Such a scene never happened in real life. When I saw it, I asked Byron specifically about this on one of my visits to him in prison. He stated that he was so upset after he called 911 that after law enforcement left, he sat alone in his home with a bottle of alcohol. Bill Anderson must have misled the producers of such an incident because Byron said it never happened like that. The third TV show was *Crime Watch Daily* with Chris Hansen. This was an even worse attempt at depicting actual events with false information and misleading comments.

A letter from Byron arrived several days after the verdict. I had written him right away to reassure him that we were here to support him in any way he needed. His four-page letter had a list of things he needed done and some special requests. He had given specific instructions where keys were stored and to be put away. I noticed when I went over to his home that things seemed orderly and there was no indication that a shooting had taken place there just seventeen months ago. There were clean rugs at the end of the staircase and the numbers for the bullet holes were no longer on the cement wall. I went about the task of locating keys, a magazine he needed, and the suit he wore to court every day was to be cleaned at his request. I noticed the purple velvet plants in the kitchen that he was separating into different pots. I decided to take them and care for them. I knew how much they had meant to him after surviving that motorcycle ride. They had held up well the past week without water, so they were still healthy looking. He had promised me one for my office, so I took it there.

Byron also wanted me to order two books for him: *A Stranger in a Strange Land* by Heinlein and an English-Spanish dictionary published by the University of Chicago. I assumed there must be a number of Hispanics in prison with whom he wanted to communicate and how appropriate that he be a stranger in the strange land of prison. He also instructed me to go to a legal documents website and find a financial power of attorney so I could pay his bills and continue to keep his homes maintained. He would also need to buy his clothing and necessities within the prison system so money would need to be sent to him there.

The concept of his life ending in a prison sentence was such a far reach for a man who dedicated himself in work for his country. Byron Smith was a unique man who had worked all over the world, a man who had visited many places in the world, a man who knew every river in the world and who knew the cities that each river ran through. He was a veteran who defended his country in the Vietnam war and earned the Combat Air Medal for twenty-five plus missions, the Air Force Personal Commendation Medal for "distinctive meritorious achievement and service," the Air Force Outstanding Unit Award for marked distinction in difficult or hazardous conditions, the Vietnam Gallantry Cross medal from the Vietnamese government for valor and heroism, the Air Force Good Conduct Medal, the National Defense Service Medal, the Vietnam Service award with bronze star for support of ground troops, the Air Force Longevity Award, and the Vietnam Campaign Medal for direct combat support. He defended his country but was not allowed to defend himself and his family home.

On the last day of his freedom, I could still see him in our living room reading, quietly by himself, seemingly to escape from the events that have just surrounded his life. That life was in the hands of a jury at that moment in time. Yet a huge question still remains: Who was watching Byron's home to report that he had driven away? Who was watching Elm Street that Thanksgiving Day?

CHAPTER 13
THE AFTERMATH

We visited him at the prison in St. Cloud soon after we were approved as visitors to the Minnesota Correctional Facility, which was a process that took several weeks. He looked well and was working in the library at the St. Cloud site. He would be transferred to Stillwater shortly after that. He talked in length about an appeal and how the other prisoners thought that of all the prisoners there, he was the one that least likely belonged there. After all, they told him, "Who goes back and repeatedly commits burglary at the same house?" Even the burglars in prison said that was something you just didn't do. With the majority of the prison population under age thirty and uneducated, there were few opportunities for him to have any productive conversations or friendships.

Dilan chose not to attend Little Falls High School as a senior, but instead attended St. Cloud State University to finish high school in their postsecondary program. He did, however, choose to attend the graduation ceremonies with the rest of his classmates.

Thanksgiving 2014 came and went without Byron at our table. I was finally given possession of Byron's Nikon 800 camera, which was stolen on October 27, 2012. After asking the county attorney and working with the police department and the sheriff's department, they finally gave up possession of some of the stolen items. Sergeant Strack had called me to tell me he had possession of Byron's expensive camera. An informant had told him the location and he retrieved it in a plastic garbage bag outside near the riverbank. The camera card was still inside, which surprised me. And for another surprise, there were 111 pictures on the card! I loaded a CD with all pictures and took it to the county attorney as new evidence so they could prosecute as a felony. The county attorney needed a report from the sheriff's department, but after two months of asking, the report still had not reached his desk. To date, nothing has been done with it.

The Brady parents have had tattoos in memory of Nick. Nick's dad has a tattoo of a dodging ram. Is this befitting of a child rumored to be a bully? On November 18, 2014, an order was filed against Byron in Morrison County to issue restitution to the Brady and Kifer families. The families subsequently submitted affidavits to the court documenting out-of-pocket expenses resulting from the crime and requested restitution in the amount of $20,242.76 (Brady) and for $21,859.70 to the Kifer family. Here's the breakdown of those expenses:

Nick Brady	
$9,311.50	Funeral
$150.00	Cemetery plot
$10,049.46	Headstone (estimate)
$54.00	Memory ads
$449.00	Miscellaneous expenses
<u>$228.80</u>	Mileage to and from court hearings
$20,242.76	Total

Haile Kifer	
$8,921.50	Funeral
$725.68	Memorial cards
$595.00	Funeral flowers
$150.00	Cemetery plot
$9,400.16	Headstone (estimate)
$13.20	Mileage to and from court hearings
$942.20	Lost wages, father
<u>$1,111.68</u>	Lost wages, mother
$21,859.70	Total

On June 3, 2014, Byron's attorney filed notice challenging the restitution awarded to both families. On August 21, 2014, five days before the restitution hearing, he filed an affidavit setting forth the challenges to restitution. In that affidavit, it was noted that Nicholas Brady had burglarized his home on several occasions in 2012 prior to the November 22, 2012 shooting and claimed a loss of $53,359.00, of which $7,374.43 was recouped through insurance. At the hearing on August 24, Byron's attorney introduced evidence establishing that Nick Brady burglarized the Smith home on at least three occasions in 2012—in July, September, and October 27, 2012. Questioned by defense counsel, Cody Kasper testified that he was one of Brady's best friends and that he stood lookout for Brady on each of the prior burglaries. Kasper recounted some of the various items that were taken from the Smith residence (including cash); however, with the exception of a white Acura (purchased for $1,800 from cash stolen at the Smith residence) and a Honda four-wheeler, Kasper was unable to state whether any of the stolen items were at Brady's home or in his possession at the time of his death. On the issue of a memorial fund, both Brady's father and Kifer's mother testified that they had not received any money from the fund for funeral expenses. Restitution for the headstones were denied as they were not expenses that had been incurred yet. (It should be noted here that Kifer's grandfather was buried next to her with a small headstone valued at approximately $3,000.00. Yet they were asking for a $10,000.00 headstone.) In the end, the judge reduced the amount of restitution by omitting the headstone expenses and subtracting $615.50 each from the memorial fund. It totaled $9,577.80 for Brady and $11,844.04 for the Kifer family. Jenny and Jerry Kifer filed a judgment against Byron on September 12, 2016, for $20,773.97. This was in the public court records. Jason and Kimberly Jo Brady filed on October 25, 2017, in the amount of $19,246.98. As of June 7, 2019, Haile Kifer has a beautifully engraved front and back headstone. Nick Brady's plot still remained empty of a headstone as of that time.

Shortly after the trial, an ad appeared in the Morrison County Record for anyone interested in supporting Byron should call a listed phone number. There was no name given in the ad, but the number listed was that of Beverly Nouis. Beverly was a well-known resident and business owner in Little Falls. She is very passionate about her feelings after the conclusion of Byron's trial, especially when she learned that he would have to pay for the funerals of those who were stealing from him. She wanted to form an organized support group to assist him and his case and also let him know he had support of some community members. A time and date was set for the first meeting at the library with around twenty people present. There was a good representation from all areas of the county, even from Crow Wing County. Guest speakers were brought in to educate on the law and how judges are appointed and elected. Officers were elected and formal organization as a nonprofit was established for Citizens for Justice. Money was raised to have Atty. Kathleen Zellner, a private attorney in Chicago who has a notable reputation for winning appeals, review Byron's case, and offer suggestions. The group has a website: www.byronsmithcoalition.org. Beverly has tried at times to show her support by installing flower beds and signs Bring Byron Home on the west side of town on her son's property, but someone always destroyed them, but she continues to be an advocate for justice for Byron.

When Byron was transferred to the Bayport facility near Stillwater, he had asked me to send him the list of potential jurors. After his trial, I knew one of the jurors through a friend. I had heard that Evelyn M. was forthcoming in her belief that she believed the prosecution's theory that Byron had set the trap for the perpetrators on that Thanksgiving Day. I felt compelled to call her and explain why this was not true. Hesitating, I dialed her number. I wasn't sure if she would even speak with me. She answered right away, and I explained who I was, that I had testified at his trial, and she did remember. What she revealed was quite amazing to me. She asked me how he was doing in prison and hoped he was coping well. She had been frustrated with the trial process as all jurors felt they wanted to know more, and every time it seemed as if they would learn more, they were dismissed from the courtroom, and when they returned, the discussion and witnesses had all changed. She directly asked me if Byron was a Vietnam vet as the jury was not sure. I assured her he was and could send her proof if she would like it. She also revealed that she was not happy about serving on this jury as it was emotionally draining and upsetting. I spoke with her compassionately for about a half hour as she repeatedly expressed concern for his welfare. She said in the end she was the only holdout for a "not guilty" vote. There were two others who thought the same, but in the end the others convinced them that they should vote "guilty."

Another juror, Wes Hatlestad, explained the jury's decision in an article in Morrison County Record dated May 4, 2014, written by Terry Lehrke. He stated that the recording was the key in his conviction, which was played the very first day and set the tone for the trial. At that point, he said the jury hadn't heard "an awful lot of testimony regarding indications of premeditation or anything like that." He said the jurors spent the first part of their deliberation reviewing the substance of the self-defense and defense of dwelling laws. "We unanimously ended up determining that all of the provisions of those two laws—at least one of the provisions had not been met. It had to be the act any rational human being would have taken. We all pretty much felt that this had to be planned and prepared, for one thing with the car having been parked in the driveway in the morning and then moved four blocks so he could clean the garage. That's pretty silly." (Unfortunately, it was not silly at all, but very true. If one really reviews his last police interview, he did not move his truck to purposefully entice burglars to come over that day. He moved it because he was afraid of vandalism. Again, common sense is that an older man would not want this confrontation from younger persons with guns!)

As Byron examined every detail of the pool of 131 candidates, he came to the conclusion that the list had to be deliberately hand-selected in spite of a Minnesota statute that requires random selection. The following analysis is the discovery that came to his conclusion that the jury selected for his trial could not possibly have been random. The following detail and analysis provided here was written by Byron Smith.

Fair Cross Section

The *Minnesota Jury Defense Manual* (MJDM) states in section IIIA, article I, section 6 of the Minnesota Constitution mirrors the (US) Sixth Amendment. The Sixth Amendment requires an impartial jury, which the Supreme Court reads, "To require that a jury be drawn from a fair cross section of the community." Also, while state constitutions may also contain fair cross-section provisions, they cannot negate the "impartial" requirement of the U.S. Constitution (MJDM, p. 12).

The US Supreme Court has held that to establish a fair cross-section violation, a defendant must show the following: (1) That the group(s) alleged to be excluded (or excessive) are "distinctive" group(s) in the community, (2) that the representation of this group (Juror Profile List of 131 candidates) in from which juries are selected is not fair and reasonable in relations to the number of such persons in the community (county), and (3) that this under (or over) representation is due to systematic exclusion of the group in the jury selection process (Duron v. Missouri, 439 U.S. 357, 364 [1979]). Representativeness is achieved when the percentages of cognizable (meaning known or perceived) group members on the source lists are reasonably proportionate to their corresponding percentages in the population (Principles for Juries and Jury Trials, ABA at 54 [August 05]). Then this must also be true of the Morrison County source list of twenty-three thousand names (voter eligibility) and thus also true of the 131 prospective jurors randomly drawn from it, if truly random. Notes: (1) Distinctive implies that individual members of the group may be accurately identified: twenty-one- and twenty-two-year-olds are, but young people are not, and farmers owning and earning their livelihood from land are, but people who do outdoor work are not. (2) In Minnesota's 2016 Jury Source List, data details, race and gender are analyzed to the nearest 0.1 percent; thus, variations of less than 0.1 percent are not significant. Then 1.0% variation is probably significant, 10 percent is absolutely significant, and multiples more than that are certainly not "fair and reasonable" and thus illegal. (3) Systematic exclusion is not required to be proved by method of accomplishment. Statistical proof is sufficient. It is also implied that systematic overinclusion is also prohibited. Results are sufficient proof, if those results are sufficiently nonrepresentative to be statistically unbelievable, that is, 10 percent or more. At the end of this analysis, a nonrepresentative method of selection is proposed that appears to be both easy to accomplish and likely to identify the perpetrators of a nonrandom and therefore illegal selection. In MJDM, Dec 2009, Section IIIA, the Minnesota Supreme Court has also stated that, in its opinion, the key part of a Sixth Amendment challenge is a showing that "over a significant period of time, panel after panel, month after month—the group of eligible jurors in question has been significantly under-represented on the panels and that this results from "systematic exclusion" *State v. Williams*, 525 N.W.2d, 538, 543 (Minn. 1994). Element 3 is the most critical (in MJDM) because it is the only point at which the underlying jury source list itself can be attacked.

The juror source list is a state generated list and is not under attack from *Minnesota v. Smith*. Neither is the county-specific juror source list of about 23,000 potential jurors. What is being called into question is the specific juror profile list of April 14, 2014, with 131 names. With the challenge that only this particular list was hand-selected to influence the verdict only on this particular high-profile case, the Minnesota Supreme Court ruling about a "significant period of time" falls away. One specific willful denial of justice does not need to be repeated in order to be unjust or to require correction.

Representation and Randomness

"Juror source pool should be assembled so as to insure representativeness and inclusiveness." Courts should use random selection procedures throughout the juror selection process." (ABA Principles for Juries and Jury Trials, pp. 51–53). These two statements are drawn together in *US v. Hanson*, 618 F.2d 1261, 1054, and 1268 (8th Cir. 1980), where the federal district court stated, "The procedures in the (Federal Jury) Act, despite its imperfections, achieve the goal of the Sixth Amendment through random selection from voter lists, defendants are assured of a jury pool randomly from a fair cross-section of the community." In MJDM IV AZ, it states, "Federal and state constitutional and statutory law requires that the jury pools from which jurors are summoned reflect a fair cross-section of the community, specifically, its racial, ethnic and gender demographics." But specifically "does not mean exclusively." In a trial that contested a property owner against nonproperty owners, and that also contested a retiree against teenagers, and that also contested a single homeowner against multiple violent attackers, there will certainly be demographic characteristics more relevant than race or ethnicity. For further specific examples of other demographic characteristics, Minn. R. Gen. Pract. 809 provides that "a citizen shall not be excluded from jury duty for race, color, creed…age, occupations, or economic status." And in MJDM, IV.D.1.(d).(3), prospective jurors are required to "provide(ing)… age…occupation…address…occupation of spouse and age(s) of any children." Factors relevant to *Minnesota v. Smith* are examined in the following sections. Because the April 14, 2014, juror profile list was presented in alphabetical order, the possible nonrandomness of other characteristics was not obvious before or during the trial. It has now become obvious that these lists are never given more than a cursory examination for valid sourcing.

Jury Group Numbers

The first resequencing of the juror profile list reorganized the 131 names by group numbers as shown in the upper right of each candidate's profile block. The highest group number is 350, so 350 out of 23,000 suggest that the entire county list is divided into groups of about 70 eligible jurors per group. The group number list is shown in figure A. The sequence from 001 to 350 is displayed in sequential vertical columns. Because column length is arbitrary, there are no valid horizontal relationships. To provide more information, each group with a juror candidate is marked with a two-letter code indicating the city of residence of that candidate. There are several anomalies that appear to be nonrandom. The large clusters of jurors beginning at 21, 57, 141, 188, 221, and 227 look unlikely to be random. Together with the long blank stretches at 128, 243, and 260, true randomness is much less likely to exist. Also notice clusters of identical spacings at 004, 275, and 306. Even though these anomalies are not sufficient for legal proof, they are much more than enough to raise suspicions of nonrandom selection. For more detailed analysis, the group number results are then split out by city. First in figure B, is the city of Pierz (PZ). The tight clusters and long spaces of unused groups provide stronger evidence of nonrandom choices. Next is Swanville (SV) in figure C, where the clusters and large unused gap in the center strain believability. Then the Bowlus (BW) shows the opposite, all the used groups in the middle and none at the beginning or end, figure D. Even more strange, all of Bowlus lies within the Swanville gap. There is no overlap between them. Finally, the Little Falls (LF) chart in figure E shows statistically strange sequences of equally spaced gaps between groups. Imagine a person unfamiliar with mathematical randomness just simulating it when hand-pulling group folders: pull-a-folder, flip-flip, pull, flip-flip, pull, etc.

Figure A

LF (Little Falls), PZ (Pierz), HM (Hillman), SV (Swanville), HD (Holdingford), RY (Royalton), Bowlus (BW), RD (Randall), ML (Motley)

	01	31	61	91	121	151	181	211	241	271	301	331
1		LF						HM	PZ	HF		
2								LF	LF			
3			LF	LF			RY	PZ				LF
4	SV											
5								BW		ML		
6		PZ	RY	HM	LF	LF		RY			ML	LF
7	LF				RD					HM		
8			LF	SV			HM				LF	
9				LF	SV		RY			LF		LF
0	LF	ML					LF				PZ	
1		LF	HM			LF	UP	LF		LF		
2				LF		BW	LF	BW			LF	
3	ML			CU				LF		LF	HM	ML
4	RY	RD	LF			LF		PZ			CU	
5				LF				LF				
6			LF	LF			RD		RY			
7								PZ				
8	SV	RY				HM		PZ				HM
9								PZ	BW			LF
0		LF	HM			RY		RY		SV	LF	RY
1	PZ				HF	LF						
2	PZ			RD	HM			LF	BW			
3	PZ	RD		PZ	HL				CU	RD		
4	PZ	SV	HM		PZ	BW	PZ					
5			LF		BW			LF				
6	RY				ML		LF	PZ				
7	ML	LF			RD			RY			LF	
8	LF	HM		PZ		LF						
9		ML	LF							SV		
0		LF	HM	PZ	LF					SV		

Figure B
Pierz Chart

	01	31	61	91	121	151	181	211	241	271	301	331
1									PZ			
2												
3												
4								PZ				
5												
6		PZ							PZ			
7												
8												
9												
0											PZ	
1												
2												
3												
4								PZ				
5												
6												
7								PZ				
8								PZ				
9								PZ				
0												
1	PZ											
2	PZ		PZ									
3	PZ		PZ									
4	PZ			PZ		PZ						
5												
6												
7												
8			PZ									
9												
0			PZ									

Figure C
Swanville Chart

	01	31	61	91	121	151	181	211	241	271	301	331
1												
2												
3												
4	SV											
5												
6												
7												
8		SV										
9												
0												
1												
2												
3												
4												
5												
6												
7												
8	SV											
9												
0										SV		
1												
2												
3												
4												
5												
6												
7												
8												
9											SV	
0											SV SV	

Figure D
Bowlus Chart

	01	31	61	91	121	151	181	211	241	271	301	331
1												
2			BW									
3												
4												
5												
6								BW				
7												
8												
9												
0												
1												
2						BW		BW				
3												
4												
5												
6												
7												
8												
9									BW			
0												
1												
2												
3												
4						BW						
5					BW							
6												
7												
8												
9												
0												

Figure E
Little Falls Chart

	01	31	61	91	121	151	181	211	241	271	301	331
1												
2								LF				
3			LF	LF								LF
4												
5												
6					LF	LF						
7	LF											LF
8			LF								LF	
9				LF								LF
0	LF						LF			LF		
1		LF				LF		LF		LF		
2				LF			LF				LF	
3								LF		LF		
4			LF			LF						
5				LF				LF				
6			LF									
7				LF								
8												
9												LF
0		LF									LF	
1						LF						
2								LF				
3												
4				LF								
5			LF					LF				
6							LF					
7		LF									LF	
8	LF					LF						
9					LF							
0	LF	LF	LF									

Nonrandom: 9 times of 3 spacings, 6 times of 2 spacings, 1 time of 4 spacings, 1 of 1.

Age / Birth Year

Because of the group number sequence shows multiple strong indications of nonrandom selection, the list of 131 juror candidates was resequenced again, this time by the years of their births. This list is shown in figure F.

Figure F
Age Distribution of Candidates

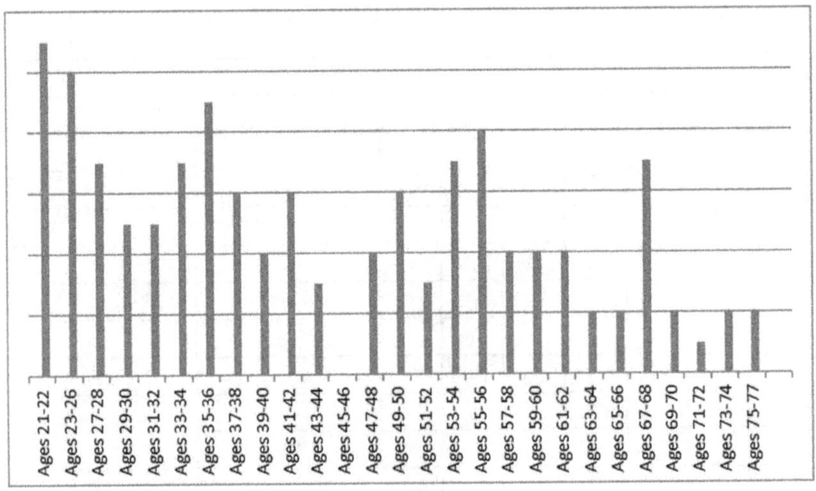

By population statistics this should be a smooth curve, relatively straight from age 20 to age 50 and then narrowing as the oldest generation passes. Baby boomers would be a slight bulge in their 60s and narrow notches are only from catastrophic disasters, such as war or plague. However, this chart is nothing at all like that normal statistical distribution. Some variation should be expected because of the moderate sample size, but certainly not the extreme dips and spikes seen here.

As the first example, consider the age 21–22 group. Because the state's master juror list is primarily drawn from voter registration, a relatively smaller group should be expected. Instead, it's the largest of any group, 20 percent more than the next largest. With approximately equal numbers of births per year, the second group 23–24 years old, should be about the same size. But it has only four members, about one-third the size of the first group. This 3 times multiple (275 percent) is ridiculous compared to the 0.1 percent variations in the state's data tables for representativeness. Is it possible that those who appear to have handpicked the juror groups also handpicked the individual juror candidates? It's obvious that 21- and 22-year-old jurors might be most likely to identify with and feel sorry for two 18-year-old attackers.

To draw more detail out of the age distribution charts, they are next split out by city. Except for Little Falls, these cities range in size from about 100 to 1,200 population and there is usually one deputy per city. In most of these city charts, large clusters of age-related potential jurors are seen at one specific age with few selections and large gaps elsewhere as shown in figures G and H. Because data on the deputies has been difficult to obtain, possible causes are speculative. The most interesting speculation is that the clusters match the ages of the deputies who live in those cities. It is very possible that the ages of the deputies who lived in that city in 2014 match the potential jurors. For example, Royalton's police chief was in his midthirties and the Randall police chief in his 50s in 2014. A statistician would be most helpful, someone who could replace guesses at "believable" by providing hard numbers on the true percentage chances. Although it's junior year math, the work of a graduate math student is more credible. We want to know whether all this is more, or less, likely than winning the lottery, twice.

Figure G
Age Distribution in Little Falls

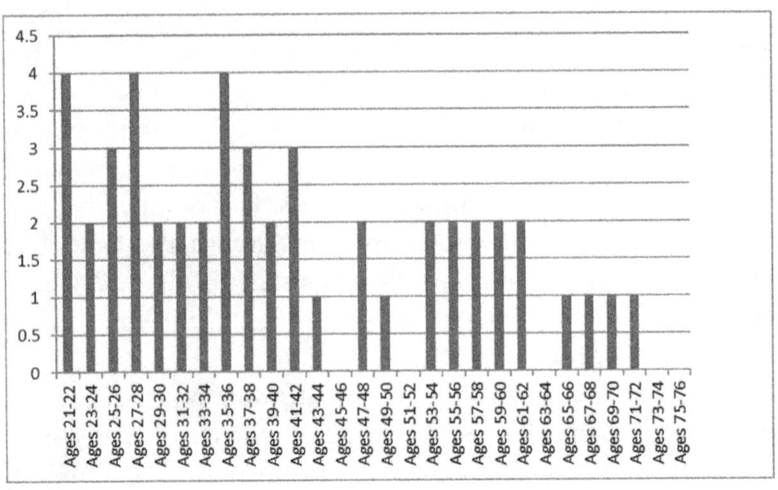

Figure H
Royalton Groups
Number of Potential Jurors

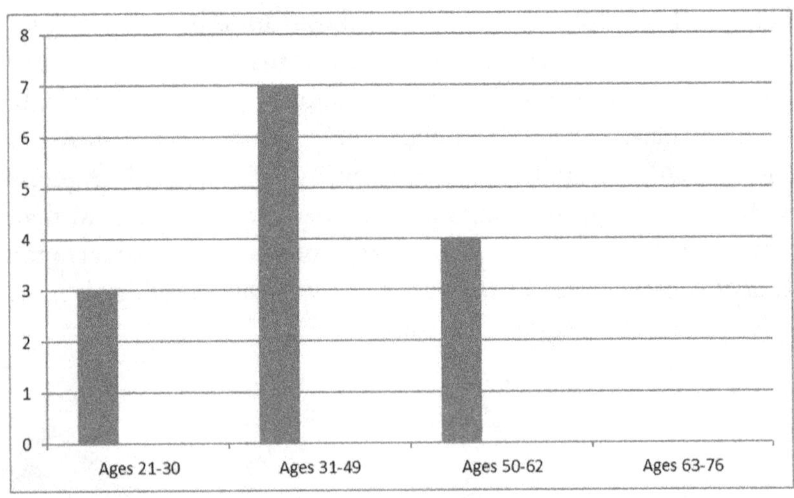

Randall Groups
Number of Potential Jurors

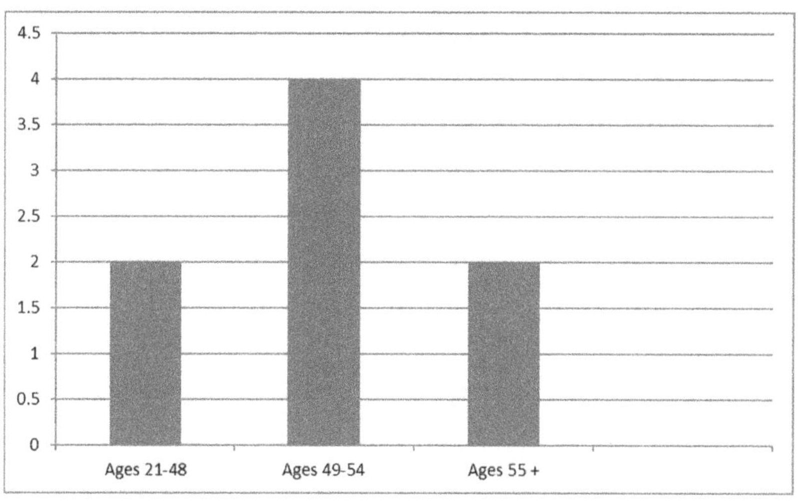

Uniform Representation

The goal of random selection is to provide uniform representation, as stated in MJDM IIIA. "State statute provides it is the policy of this state that all persons selected for jury service be selected at random from the broadest possible cross section of the population."

Between cities, Morrison County has 16 cities. In this analysis, Little Falls with an approximate population of 9,000 is excluded because of multiple obscuring influences and then the 15 smaller are compared. Uniform representation is compared between those eight cities known or believed to have resident deputy sheriffs and those without a resident deputy.

With Deputies Without Deputies

City	Population	Jurors	City	Population	Jurors
Bowlus	286	6	Buckman	289	0
Hillman	40	13	Elmdale	107	0
Motley	644	9	Flensburg	228	0
Pierz	1,452	18	Harding	119	2
Randall	631	7	Lastrup	99	0
Royalton	1,234	7	Sobieski	188	0
Swanville	335	8	Upsala	428	1
Totals	4,622	74		1,355	3

One candidate per 62 population. One candidate per 364 population.

The results show a 6 1/2 times (650 percent) nonrepresentational distribution. Harding is adjacent to Hillman. If combined, the misrepresentational proportion is 2,200 percent (State's goal, 0.1 percent).

Between Rural and City

The preliminary 2015 population and household estimates for Morrison County dated June 1, 2016, lists its 16 cities and 30 townships and their populations. If cities are assumed to be urban and the townships rural, the population ratio is 44 percent city and 56 percent rural. This is admittedly an approximation, but because the county zoning board explicitly tries to maintain that separation, it's relatively close. Juror profiles were then examined to find any jury candidates for whom either the candidate or spouse listed any occupation related to farming or agriculture. This yielded 9 out of 131 or 6.8 percent of the candidates' families as agricultural. In a county that is 56 percent rural, to have only 6.8 percent of the candidates working in agriculture could not possibly be considered representative. This is important for the primary law, the Sixth Amendment, which requires an "unbiased jury." Just as 21- and 20-year-olds would be likely to sympathize with the 18-year-old attackers, rural property owners living in relatively isolated locations such as farms would be sympathetic toward a frequently and severely victimized homeowner living in an isolated location. For a representative jury, they must not be excluded.

If these statistically invaliding tests had random effects on the jury's biases, they might simply be the results of a flawed process. But all the statistical invalidations point toward increasing the likelihood of a guilty verdict. This overarching layer of nonrandomness proves intentional manipulation of the juror candidate list.

CHAPTER 14
THE EASEMENT ROAD

In July of 2012, Byron was finally successful in acquiring the property adjacent to the family residence on Elm Street. The property included a five-thousand-plus square foot home along with approximately eleven acres of woods. It, too, was along the banks of the Mississippi, so he thought it would make a perfect vacation rental. The previous owner and he finally agreed upon a selling price and Byron's plan was to modify the property for vacationers to allow river access. Right before his trial, we observed surveyors down Elm Street and around the area, but thought it was just routine, so never questioned it. In 2013, Byron had begun talks with the property owners of another eight acres of wooded area right to the east of his rental property. There was no access at that time to electricity or city water and sewer, but he was interested in preserving the woods for the wildlife there. After Byron's trial, the land was sold to Roach Development to build townhomes. On June 23, 2015, the city of Little Falls sent out a notice of public hearing to neighborhood residents affected by the building of eight single-story fourplex residential units on Riverwood Drive. They would be clearing out most of the woods to make room for housing. This would be thirty-eight townhomes in a small section of a neighborhood known for homes that set on half an acre or more each. Most all the nearby homeowners were opposed and went to the city council vehemently expressing opposition. The Riverwood Drive area, or Belle Prairie, as it is referred to, had recently been annexed into the City. Of course, property taxes doubled as the city supplied water and sewer along the streets of Riverwood Drive. Roach Development needed a conditional use permit to allow for a planned unit development for this construction. Under current zoning, the property could be subdivided into eighteen with a duplex built on each. The developer wanted to build eight fourplex units. Their first application was denied by the city council on April 20, 2015, due to the opposition in the neighborhood. The reapplication and second attempt to build on that property was approved in July of 2015 with further pressure from Roach Development. What is significant about this property is that there is an easement to Byron's rental property that runs along the southern edge for access to this home. It is the only driveway into the property, and when the Roaches started building, they blocked the road with piles of dirt and debris while the trees were being cleared. At this same time, we were beginning to start painting inside the home to make it available for renters. As Byron sat in prison, he was kept informed of the new development and insisted that they could not block the right of passage as the easement was a legal part of his property purchase. With the easement blocked by the developers, the property could not be accessed, even by emergency vehicles. Also, they were building the fourplexes right to the edge of the easement, so traveling down the road would be a hazardous situation if small children were playing in the backyard as the backyard was actually a driveway. Byron hired an attorney who specialized in real estate to fight the situation. Even though the property he purchased in 2012 came with a legal easement, it was literally being stolen by the developers. So while the development was progressing and blocking access to a driveway, the attorneys for Roach Development answered our complaint about the blocking by offering to construct a new access on Derosier Drive. The letter stated that they would create this access only with the signature of a quit claim deed extinguishing the easement that crosses the Roach property. Byron declined this offer as he felt, once again, that he was being robbed of something that was rightfully and legally his. Also, the easement ran along next to his Elm Street property and for his ease of maintenance wanted to keep it there. He didn't want an access on a different street. The challenge was we needed access to the home to repair, paint, and do routine home maintenance to preserve its value. We were being denied a legal access to this property. I went to the city council to inform them of the blocking by Roach Development to this property. When presented the information, they all looked like a deer stung in headlights. Not one council member said a word. They did nothing. A visit to Larson Abstract, who assisted in the sale of the property to Roach, was futile. After questioning the owner on how the sale even took place, she admittedly stated, "I have to be careful what I tell you." After several attempts to drive through the dirt and construction mess to access the home, Roach Development fully blocked that driveway with large boulders and logs, so it would be physically impossible to drive a vehicle using the easement. After complaining to the Little Falls Police Department and showing them the legal right of passage, after the Roaches physically blocked the driveway, they stated it was a civil matter and had to be settled in a court. Another visit to city hall to talk with the city administrator about the problem was also futile. Since the city approved this, they should be responsible for the property owners that have previously resided there and certainly be obligated to enforce the legal rights of current property owners. The city administrator was walking from his office as I entered the building, took one look at me, and said, "I'm not talking to you." He just walked off in a hurry to get away from me. During the city council sessions, the city engineer had drawn and shown construction plans of the developer. We didn't realize until the townhomes were being built how close to the road they were. In total frustration of not having access, one Saturday morning I drove straight down the street to Judge Anderson's home. He invited me in, and I explained how the Roaches were blocking a legal entrance to a property. He was unable to offer any solution other than hiring a lawyer. With Byron Smith in prison, the Roaches and the city engineer may have assumed that it would be no problem to build over the easement. It is not only misguided teens stripping away at Byron Smith's property, but did the city of Little Falls and Roach Development do the same? To date, Roach Development has not offered any compensation to Byron Smith for the stealing of the easement and the city officially changed the address of that property from Riverwood Drive to Derosier Drive. It's still not accurate on Google maps.

CHAPTER 15
THE MINNESOTA SUPREME COURT HEARING

On September 3, 2015, a group of local, loyal supporters for Byron got into a van to hear Steve Meshbesher address the Minnesota Supreme Court to request a new trial for Byron. The main argument would be the closing of the trial by Judge Anderson on the first day the defense was to present its case. Meshbesher had requested a dismissal due to this unusual decision, but he did not prevail. Also attending the hearing were the parents of both Brady and Kifer and several media representatives, which one was Paul Blume. Paul Blume with Fox 9 had covered the case from the very start, and he and Nick's grandfather, Steve Schaeffel, were engaged in a humorous conversation as both were laughing and joking with each other as we arrived. Attorney Brent Wartner, who assisted Orput, was also present to represent the prosecution's side.

As both Meshbesher and Wartner spoke before the justices, the opportunity came for them to ask questions. Justice David Lillehaug questioned the unfair jury trial immediately. Meshbesher stated that the trial opened at 10:00 a.m. with opening statements to be heard. At 10:03 a.m., the trial was closed by Judge Anderson, who rescinded witnesses from the defense's list. There was no chamber meeting with the judge. Justice David Stras stated that he was troubled by this closure and asked what was the explanation or why not a sidebar or what was the discussion? Meshbesher stated that certain defense witnesses would not be allowed to testify. These witnesses are namely friends of Nick Brady who were involved in previous burglaries.

(Rachel Brady, Cody Kasper, Jesse Kriesel, and Chase Fortier were seated in the waiting area of the courthouse that morning as they had been previously noted as defense witnesses.) Justice Christopher Dietzen asked again about the judge. "He dropped this courtroom closure on top of everyone without any notice to anybody? How isn't this a violation of court rules governing closing hearings to the public?" Meshbesher added, "The judge stopped the proceeding on his own, even after I told him he couldn't do that."

Justice Wilhelmina Wright chimed in and asked what would the public have gleaned from being there, but it's up to democracy: the availability of same as a chambers meeting, but chambers didn't take place. She also asked Meshbesher if he had a chance to make a record of who the witnesses were and who was all involved. Meshbesher answered, "The people who were testifying would have shown Smith's fear and how he reacted when he did. The purpose of the expert witnesses, of one which is in law enforcement and a certified shooting instructor, is that he would have spoken about the hearing, tingling, and seeing sensations after such violence, and this would have explained the surprise he had when another person came in and its psychological component—critical incident stress. What would have been presented was the difference between a law enforcement officer who is trained to shoot compared to one who is not trained."

After about thirty minutes had passed, Wartner was asked by Chief Justice Lorie Skjerven how the defendant got a fair trial. He responded by saying that no expert witnesses were needed to determine reasonable use of force and firearms use. A jury already knew that. The allegedly stolen guns were not allowed in the courtroom, but a photograph was.

Justice David Stras asked Wartner what was the judge's reason that it was okay to close the trial. Wartner replied that so no press could identify the witnesses. If the jurors didn't follow their oath of abstaining from the news, there was too much risk of it being published and jurors hearing about it. The judge was just reiterating how the attorneys should conduct themselves. He stated, "This was not a courtroom closure, this was about a bench conference." It lasted about four minutes at most and didn't have any impact on the trial. Justice Stras added, "All important decisions are to be made in public view. The press viewing is part of the defendant's right to a fair trial." Justice Wilhelmina asked if a copy of the judge's ruling was given before he handed it down. Wartner responded that on April 21, 2014, there was a copy order of the closure.

Chief Justice Lorie Skjerven added that admissible expert testimony should be allowed. The reactions of victims might be outside the common understanding of the common juror.

Wartner then asked to address the issue of the headstones being excluded from the restitution order. Justice Skjerven responded, "How do we know the money will be used for headstones?" (Justice Stras was crossing his arms now with an irritated, frustrated look.)

Meshbesher also informed the court that William Anderson testified to Smith asking for a lawyer. Prosecutor Orput stated to grand jurors that he asked for a criminal defense attorney. Anderson then asked to be shown the document. Orput did not produce the document but told him to just answer the question. The state was trying to destroy the credibility of Anderson, his neighbor, with improper information to the grand jury. Judge Wilhelmina Wright then asked for an explanation of the grand jury charge. Meshbesher explained that Orput's use of "criminal defense lawyer" (wording) should not have been allowed. "While maybe not harmful, it made an implication. The same implication is made with the words 'I'm sorry' of Kifer. There was nothing on the tape to indicate that, and the prosecutor refers to it in closing argument when it does not exist. He is going for emotion and not the facts when he is asking for a guilty verdict. My client needs a new trial. The only way this can be corrected is to have a do-over."

Justice Wright asked about the impact on the verdict. Meshbesher responded, "It's critical for due process of law. The expert witnesses [preapproved by the judge and then not allowed] were needed to explain the fear and for critical incident stress. This could or may have gone to recklessness or manslaughter, five other possible things. The recorded interview would be one thing the psychologist would have explained to jurors."

When the final decision was handed down on March 9 of 2016, I was totally shocked by it. The questions asked and responses during this proceeding seemed to be clearly in favor of a new trial. The Supreme Court also reversed the lower court and awarded restitution to pay for the headstones. Justice Lillehaug wrote in his forty-three-page decision that the Morrison County Court had not made mistakes when it closed the trial nor did it violate Byron Smith's right to a complete defense by excluding certain evidence.

About a year later, I had the opportunity to ask Chief Justice Skjerven personally why the decision seemed so opposite of what the hearing perceived. She was presenting a general insight into the work of the appeals court in Brainerd on the campus of Central Lakes College at the time. When it was time for the audience to ask questions, I stood up and asked about the Smith hearing. She responded that during these hearings, the justices would have a conversation about the case and then they'd go back and study precedent and review similar cases and then come to a final determination after all had been reviewed.

CHAPTER 16
CONTINUED THEFT

In the middle of December in 2017, I received Byron's monthly bank statement from the State Department Credit Union. I noticed there was a $49,027 loan balance for a 2017 Chevrolet Silverado 1500. I immediately called his brother to see if he knew anything about the purchase of Chevy pickup to Byron's account. He knew nothing, just as I had suspected. I then called the bank, located in Washington, DC, and informed them that this was an error, and if this purchase was truly made to his account, we had to investigate identity theft. I was then given instructions by the bank as to their procedures that I needed to follow to eliminate this balance from his account. As soon as I reported the identify theft and fraudulent use of his credit to all three credit reporting agencies and the Federal Trade Commission, I was to return all reports to the bank. They also stated that I would need to get a local police report. So over my Christmas holiday, I drove down to the Little Falls Police Department and talked with Officer West. With bank account statements in hand, I proceeded to explain to him that it would be impossible for Byron Smith to purchase a new truck due to the fact that he was sitting in prison. Prisoners were not allowed access to finances, and any mail that was sent that included maps, criminal, or financial information was not given to the inmate. The inmate would receive a notice that they were sent mail of this nature, but not allowed to have it. I had sent several things to him via the US Postal Service that had been confiscated by prison officials that were not allowed for inmate's view. All letters were opened and searched except for those from his attorney. After filing an incident report with the Little Falls Police, as I walked out the door, the officer told me not to worry as this wouldn't cost Byron anything because banks have insurance to cover the fraud. I had never given this much thought and was just worried about getting this removed from his account because a payment book arrived shortly after that and the payments on this truck were over $1,000 monthly. Another clue to the fraud and identity theft was a letter that arrived from GEICO (Government Employees Insurance Company). The letter was a thank-you for insuring through GEICO and confirming automatic payments from his Navy Federal Credit Union account ending in 4644. Again, I called his bank in DC and told them of the letter. Speaking with their fraud investigator, I explained that Byron had been in the Air Force, not the Navy. Furthermore, he had no bank accounts that ended in those four numbers. It seemed obvious to me that someone now had hacked into another consumer's Navy Credit Union account to charge for this truck's insurance. The very next day, a bill came from Geico for $20, which was the balance due for a canceled policy. I decided to meet with the fraud investigator at the bank face-to-face, so the next time I was in Washington, DC, I took the opportunity to meet with her and to see if she had discovered anything. If the check on their bank was written to a car dealer, she could have possibly found out where the truck had been purchased and identify the thief. The bank was about a 20-minute taxi ride from my hotel, so I arrived in downtown Alexandria, Virginia, to the bank's address and waited in line for several minutes. I didn't have an appointment, but the investigator was available and could come down and meet with me. We had emailed back and forth many times by now, but I showed her my ID and paperwork. She informed me that a check had been written directly to Byron Smith for the purchase of a truck, and obviously the thief pocketed the money and had to show proof of insurance to the bank, thus the one-day insurance purchase. After submitting all paperwork to the bank, it took months before a credit was issued to his account. The first credit was $44,000, which I assumed was the bank's insurance carrier covering the fraud. It took until the next June, another six months, before the final $5,400 leftover balance was removed from his account. I never heard anything more about it: if the perpetrator was ever identified or even how much investigation was done on the part of his bank. I was just told by the investigator that no truck was even intended to be purchased and the thief got away with $49,027 in cash by using Byron's credit. I didn't let Byron know about this incident until after I had it all resolved. It was difficult to even tell him about more people stealing from him while he sat in prison. After all was resolved with this identify theft, on my next prison visit, I finally told him what happened. I thought he would be shocked and concerned, but he just started laughing. I explained the procedures I took and informed all the reporting agencies. Everything was complete, and I would continue to closely watch any other incidents of that nature.

CHAPTER 17
FEDERAL APPEAL

On August 6, 2018, a federal judge, the Honorable John R. Tunheim, chief judge for the United States District Court for the District of Minnesota, granted Byron the opportunity to appeal a Minnesota Supreme Court decision to uphold his conviction. The argument was that his constitutional rights were violated when the trial was closed to the public on day 5. Judge Tunheim stated that Minnesota had a disturbing trend of restricting public access to criminal trials. He also stated that some other court could resolve the issues differently and that the issues deserved further proceedings.

Smith's attorney filed his appeal to the Eighth Circuit Court of Appeals, which was heard on November 13, 2019, before Judge Steven M. Colloton, Judge Roger Wollman, and Judge Duane Benton. The following are my notes from the proceeding.

Steve Meshbesher's Fifteen Minutes

He opened at 10:45 a.m. by saying that on day 5 of the trial, Judge Anderson closed the courtroom without notice. The courtroom was packed with people and media. The judge was giving out tickets because there was full attendance. Judge Tunheim states that this didn't make sense and was confused by the decision to close. Judge Stras, who at the time was on the Minnesota Supreme Court, was noted and asked by Judge Benton if he heard this case and voted in favor of new trial. Meshbeser explained that Stras also voted to uphold district court and vote was unanimous. Meshbesher stated that the county attorney could reprosecute this case. A new trial was needed as both Sixth Amendment and First Amendment rights had been violated by the closing. The reason for closing was not administrative as witnesses that had been subpoenaed were cancelled. Specifically, two witnesses, Jesse Kriesel (who was brought out of prison) and Cody Kasper, were both involved in burglaries with Nick Brady. The judge did not want their testimony heard. The witnesses would have provided insight to Smith's fear and to self-defense. Brady and Kifer didn't have to go into the basement. They were upstairs. By closing the courtroom, the media wasn't allowed to print the names of these witnesses even though their names had been made public during each of their own hearings for being involved in prior burglaries. Meshbesher cited other Supreme Court cases where the Sixth Amendment was challenged. He also mentioned that on June 26, 2014, Justice Skerjven of the Minnesota Supreme Court stated the Minnesota Courtroom doors should remain open. And her statement was publicized after she denied the Smith appeal.

Brent Wartner, Prosecutor, Fifteen Minutes

He asked this court to affirm the district court's denial. The Minnesota Supreme Court upheld this conviction stating the closing was administrative in nature. Judge Benton asked Wartner if it was a full closure and if the nature of the closing was administrative. Wartner explained it deprived the public of two names. In *Garcia*, a North Dakota case (state, not federal), there was no public trial violation in a partial closure.

Meshbesher added in rebuttal that any public violation whether administrative in nature or not should not cancel testimony of witnesses. "That can't be right."

The proceeding for Smith was completed around 11:15 a.m. at the United States Courthouse in St. Paul, Minnesota.

The testimony of witnesses Meshbesher referred to were Cody Kasper, Jesse Kreisel, and Kimberly Brady, mother of Nick Brady. Kasper and Kreisel both had been involved in previous burglaries with Brady. All names previously were in the public record. The explanation the court gave was that their testimony was inadmissible because Smith did not know the identity of those who broke into his home before Thanksgiving. And for that reason, the court was not allowing the press in this for this ruling because otherwise it could be printed, and indeed, while the jurors hopefully would follow the admonition not to read or hear anything in the press and TV and such in the meantime while this case was pending, certainly the media would publish and print the substance of the court's pretrial ruling, and then of course, it ran the risk of getting to the jury if for some reason they didn't adhere to their oath. The order ruled that the evidence of prior bad acts by Brady or Kifer, of which Smith was not aware at the time of the shooting, would be inadmissible at trial. The order explained, "Insofar as the [evidence that Smith was the victim of prior burglaries occurring before the shooting, that forcible entry was made, and that weapons were taken and not recovered at the time of the shooting] may be received through the testimony of law enforcement agents. There will be no need to seek its admission through more prejudicial means [i.e., through the testimony of Brady's mother or of a perpetrator of the prior break-ins]." After the procedure that day, Meshbesher commented that it was very odd that Wartner had referred to a state case during a federal proceeding.

Author's Comment on Above

The fact that Smith did not know the identity of those who broke in before Thanksgiving was not exactly true. Once he saw the shoes of the male who broke in on Thanksgiving as a close match to the shoe print of the October 27 burglary, it became apparent to Smith that previous burglars who had stolen his guns had come back on Thanksgiving.

IN CLOSING

When Michel Wetzel did not seek reelection, a new sheriff, Shawn Larsen, was elected and has made positive changes. When a burglary occurs of even a small magnitude, residents can be alerted about it in the newspaper and on Facebook or hear about on the local radio station. Byron's October burglary on October 27, 2012, of approximately $50,000 was never announced publicly, as if it never happened. Sheriff Larsen has changed the office in a positive direction and is dedicated to protecting the safety of our county's citizens.

CBS Minnesota News (WCCO/AP) had written an article shortly after the shootings (November 26, 2012) and cited that Crystal Schaeffel stated that Kifer had stolen prescription drugs from her home before. Little Falls police records show Crystal Schaffel reported a theft August 28, but the department said the report was not public because the investigation named juveniles. The theft of prescription drugs is a huge issue across our nation and one that went unnoticed for years. It has increased across the United States driving the opioid epidemic to a national health emergency. When an emergency room nurse, Jane Smalley, alerted me in 2014 that our local hospital was also seeing a high volume of patients requesting opioids in the ER, my position there allowed me to successfully seek funding to address the problem locally. The first grant award came in the amount of $364,112 from the Minnesota Department of Health and Human Services. It paid for salaries of clinic staff to meet with patients using opioids to mitigate their use and reduce overall prescribing while offering other pain management options and access to treatment. The grant required community partners. I led the community task force for four years and had nominated the program for several state and national awards, which all were received. I met with our federal legislators in Washington, DC, to seek further funding for this program when grant funding would expire. I became an advocate for opioid reform. Former Congressman Rick Nolan attended and spoke at our first community forum at the Falls Ballroom upon my invitation. I met with Senator Tina Smith in Washington to talk about the success of reducing opioid use in our county. Senator Klobuchar made a special visit to Little Falls to speak with our community partners. I remember the day I greeted her as she entered the hospital and stayed over an hour to learn about what our community was doing to reduce the use of opioids. Sheriff Larsen participated in that meeting. Our state legislators, Representative Ron Kresha and Senate Majority Leader Paul Gazelka, are both awesome at working to fund the program. We are so lucky in Morrison County to have them as our elected officials. From 2015 to 2018, I had raised a total of $4.1 million together with grants and legislative funding with their support. (Unfortunately, Governor Dayton vetoed the 2018 spending budget with $2 million designated for the program, so that was not realized.)

Byron's story of multiple burglaries was included in many of the grants that were written, not just by me, but by other community entities as well. The success of the program was very important to me. I had experienced the ripple effects from seeing our neighbor forced to address a situation that involved theft, drug use, and drug traffic, which ultimately sent him to prison. It's not fair or right that a hardworking homeowner minding his own business was thrown into the world of drug seekers. I remember making a presentation to the Department of Health in St. Paul back in 2015 about our grant program and the county's overuse of opioids, and I overheard someone whispering about the drug problems in Morrison County. At that very moment, I felt shame for even living in Morrison County. But it wasn't long after that, the whole nation had discovered that almost every county had an opioid problem and the opioid epidemic was declared a public health emergency. The culmination of success came in August of 2018 when the White House's Office of National Drug Policy phoned me and wanted to include a chapter about the Morrison County Rural Opioid Program in their next publication! I was overwhelmed with pride about that accomplishment. On one trip to Washington, I had scheduled a meeting with them and our team to discuss our program's success. Several health policy advisers were included and listened and noted every single word. The experience was so productive and so enlightening it was then that I felt I had possibly made a difference in preventing another homeowner from going to prison. In this tragedy and the results that came from it, I was personally driven to make a difference in our community and address the root of this event: Drugs and Addiction. Unfortunately, Byron Smith, a law-abiding citizen without as much as a parking ticket, was caught in this cross fire.

The best compliment I ever received was when Tom West was the editor of the *Record* and I was in the local newspaper office to pick up some papers. He stated to me, "I don't know what religion you and your family are, but supporting and housing Byron Smith is the most Christian thing that I know anyone has ever done." Throughout my family's support for our friend and neighbor, I always took comfort in the fact that this is what Jesus would do. We helped our neighbor in his darkest hour. I have been asked many times by different people if I ever regretted supporting him or having him live with us. My answer was and is, "No." Clearly, there were no winners in this tragedy. Prescription drugs and illegal drugs are clearly the root of this event. Young people's lives were taken from a homeowner's fear and then the life he knew was taken and changed forever. Make no mistake about how much fear Byron Smith endured. If the audio recording had been heard in its entirety and original sequence instead of manipulation by the prosecution, that fear would have been revealed. It seems the only ones without fear paid for that with their lives. Drug abuse changes families' lives and changes the lives of all of us forever. What we all need to do is make certain a tragedy of this magnitude never happens again.

The End

EPILOGUE

Byron Smith is currently serving a life sentence without the possibility of parole at the Oak Park Heights Correctional Facility near Stillwater, Minnesota. Depending on release date of this book, he is currently waiting for a decision from the U.S. Eighth Circuit Court of Appeals to grant him a new trial.

Byron Smith had long-term residency visas in six countries, visited fifty-one countries and eighty-four foreign cities. He never felt unsafe anywhere until he came back to Little Falls, Minnesota. Byron once stated, "Home attacks are worse than terrorism. After radicals attack the subway or the streets, people can go home. When a person's home becomes unsafe, the victim is both unable to leave and unsafe to stay."

"If Nick Brady would have told me to stop, please don't shoot, I'm sorry, I would not have shot him a second time. That didn't happen. He came towards me with a face so full of anger that I had no choice but to defend myself, "stated Byron Smith.

Nick Brady could have saved himself and his cousin that day had he only showed some remorse for breaking into Byron's home.

Minnesota Statute 611A.08, Subd. 2—Injuries to Perpetrator

A perpetrator assumes the risk of loss, injury, or death resulting from violent crime.

Minnesota Statute 609.065—Justified Taking of Life

The intentional taking of the life of another is not authorized EXCEPT:

When necessary in resisting or preventing an offense which the actor reasonably believes exposes the actor or another to great bodily harm or death or preventing the commission of a felony in the actor's place of abode.

Minnesota Statute 605.749, Subd. 5—Stalking

A person who engages in stalking with respect to a single victim which the actor knows or has reason to know would cause the victim under the circumstances to feel terrorized or to fear bodily harm and which does cause this reaction on the part of the victim, is guilty of a felony and may be sentenced to imprisonment for not more than ten years or to payment of a fine of not more than $20,000, or both. For purposes of this subdivision, "stalking" means two or more acts within a five-year period.

Minnesota Judges Criminal Bench book—A Minnesota state publication for judges

Chapters 1001.03, Section II Courtroom Procedure and 1309.09 Defenses, Section IV Defense of Dwelling. A trial judge who has heard the probable cause portion of the Omnibus Hearing should not be the trier of fact (trial judge).

Byron Smith, 2013.
Byron photo from website: www.byronsmithcoalition.org

Byron as an Eagle Scout with his father.
Smith family photo.

Byron with his mom taken outside their home on the Mississippi.
Smith family photo.

During his time in the United States Air Force,
Byron earned several military decorations:

1. *Air Medal.* For air combat duty, twenty-five missions or more.
2. *Air Force Personal Commendation Medal.* For "distinctive meritorious achievement and service."
3. *Air Force Outstanding Unit Award with Oak Leaf Cluster (Two Campaigns) Ribbon.* For "marked distinction in difficult or hazardous conditions," Vietnam B-52 service.
4. *Air Force Good Conduct Medal.* For three years continuous service with efficiency ratings of excellent or higher.

5. *National Defense Service Medal.* For voluntary service during a national emergency (the Vietnam conflict).
6. *Vietnam Service Award w/ Bronze Star (Two Campaigns) Ribbon.* For direct support of ground troops.
7. *Air Force Longevity Award Ribbon.* For four years or more of service.
8. *Vietnam Gallantry Cross Medal.* From the Vietnamese government for valor or heroism.
9. *Vietnam Campaign Medal.* For direct combat support of at least six months.

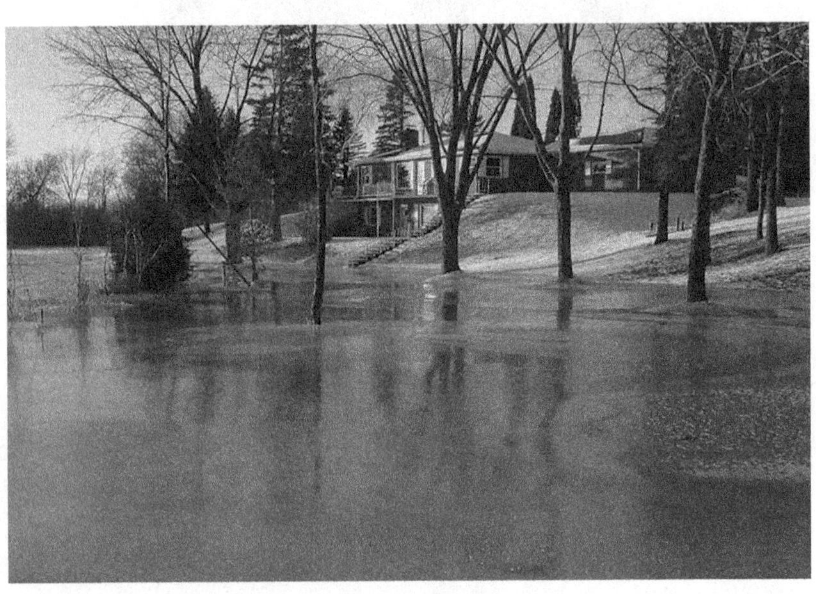

Byron's Home along the Mississippi River. This picture is taken from the southeast. (Photo by Byron Smith)

Byron Smith's Photography

A trip to Duluth, July 26, 2013.
John, Kathy, and Byron at Gooseberry Falls.
Lange family photo.

Prescription pill bottles found in Brady's car stolen the night before.
(Photo, Morrison County Sheriff.)

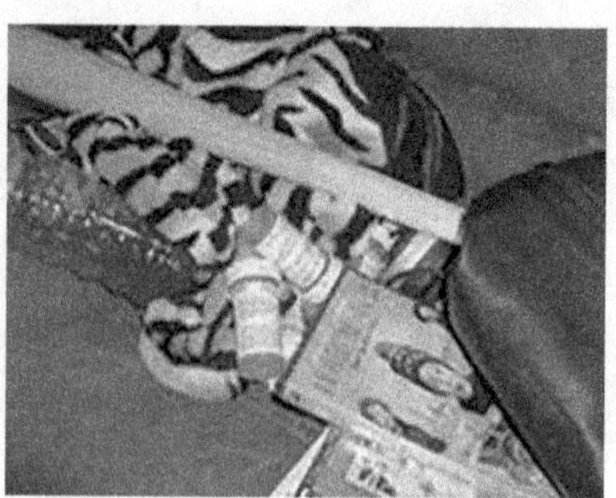

Nick Brady (Facebook profile picture).
Haile Kifer (online photo).

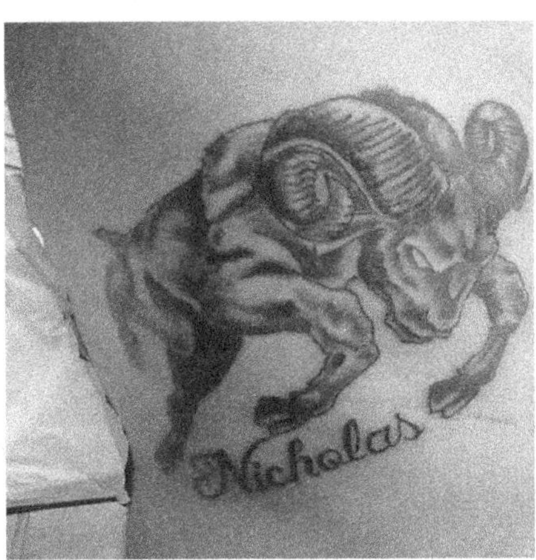

On-line photo of tattoo on Nick's father in memory of Nick. Cody Kasper pictured above which is one of the pictures retrieved from the SIM card of Byron's camera stolen by Nick and Cody Kasper (small child was cropped out).

Driving Byron back home on last day of court in the media frenzy. (Photo by Dave Schwarz, *St. Cloud Times.*)

The easement road where Roach Development before the building of townhouses that blocked entrance to Byron's property. (Lange Photo.)

Same view after trees removed and foundations set for townhomes, the edge of these homes are right along the easement.
(Lange photo.)

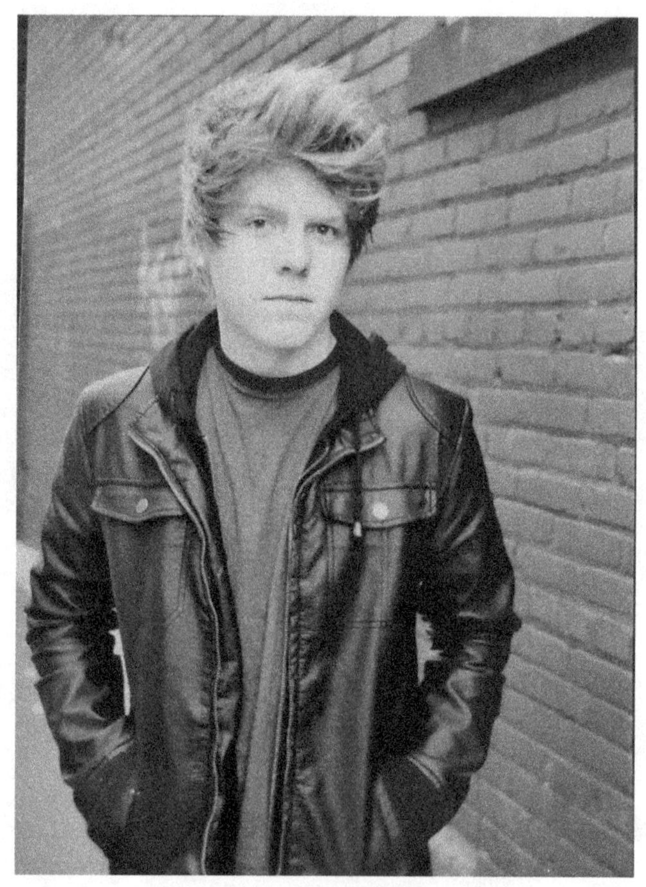

Dilan's Graduation Picture

REFERENCES

1. State of Minnesota, Seventh Judicial District, Trial Court Transcripts, File A14-0941, April 14, 2014, through April 29, 2014.
2. Grand Jury Transcript of Proceedings, State of Minnesota, Seventh Judicial District, April 23–24, 2013, Court File 49-CV-532.
3. File Transcript, State of Minnesota, Seventh Judicial District, November 18, 2014, Court File 49-CR-12-1882, State of Minnesota v. Byron David Smith.
4. Exhibit B, Morrison County Sheriff's Office, Trial Court Transcripts, File A14-0941.
5. Criminal Case Records Search Results, http://pa.courts.state.mn.us. Jason Brady, Kimberly Brady.
6. Morrison County Sheriff's Office, ICR: 12007272. 12/04/2012.
7. https://kstp.com/news/byron-smith-judge-allows-for-appeal-of-conviction-in-byron-smith-case-to-continue-/5020089/.
8. United States District Court, District of Minnesota, Case No. 17-cv-673 (JRT/TNL) Report and Recommendation, Byron Smith v. Michelle Smith, Warden, Minnesota Correctional Facility, Oak Park Heights.

ABOUT THE AUTHOR

Christina Johnson Photography

Kathy Lange lives with her family in Little Falls, Minnesota. She felt compelled to write her first book experiencing the tragic story of her neighbor's burglaries resulting in the death of teens due to the rippling effects of drug addiction. Kathy has worked in health-care fund and program development for over twenty years organizing fundraisers and writing successful grants. She has coauthored an article on the opioid epidemic in the *American Journal of Public Health*, led a community drug abuse task force, and assisted in writing of a soon-to-be released chapter on the opioid epidemic in Morrison County for the White House's Office of National Drug Control Policy.

CPSIA information can be obtained
at www.ICGtesting.com
Printed in the USA
LVHW020817140920
665910LV00002B/3